Clarifying and Furthering Existential Psychotherapy

Stefan E. Schulenberg
Editor

Clarifying and Furthering Existential Psychotherapy

Theories, Methods, and Practices

Springer

Editor
Stefan E. Schulenberg
Department of Psychology
Clinical-Disaster Research Center
The University of Mississippi
Oxford, MS
USA

ISBN 978-3-319-31085-5 ISBN 978-3-319-31086-2 (eBook)
DOI 10.1007/978-3-319-31086-2

Library of Congress Control Number: 2016942902

Printed on acid-free paper

This Springer imprint is published by Springer Nature
The registered company is Springer International Publishing AG Switzerland

All, everything that I understand, I only understand because I love.

— Leo Tolstoy

For Teacup (Laura),

A well-spring of meaning

A wondrous spirit

Kind, gentle, compassionate

Encouraging, resourceful, inspiring

An existentialist at heart

You taught me a great deal about life

I never thought I could understand so much

— Stove (Stefan)

Foreword

Existential psychotherapy is undergoing a remarkable renaissance. As this volume well attests, the field is blossoming on many fronts, from theory and research to philosophy and application, and from innovations in clinical practice to explorations of spiritual and societal well-being. As a student of this field for many years I am also gratified to see existential psychotherapy making its mark on the discipline of psychology as a whole. With a surfeit of new books, videos, and training institutions emerging both from within mainstream professional organizations, such as the American Psychological Association and the academic publishing industry, as well as outside those arenas, it is clear that the impact of existential psychotherapy is broadening.

Inspired by the *first* World Congress of Existential Psychotherapy in May 2015, this book represents rich samples of the thinking and practice of some 650 individuals from a diversity of nations who participated in that momentous event. In this vein, it is also noteworthy that there is a fresh breeze of multiculturalism within existential ranks, and a clarion call for an enlarged appreciation of what it means to be human and not just as individuals from particular regions but as participants in the world! My sense is that if they were alive today, our forebears, such as Ludwig Binswanger, Otto Rank, Rollo May, would be zealously celebrating this rejuvenation of existential perspectives. They would acknowledge the vigorous efforts already underway and urge even greater efforts to bridge-build with the world. This book is a testament to that energy and hope. My profound congratulations to the editor of this volume, Stefan Schulenberg, for pursuing this trailblazing volume, and to the diverse contributors who grace its pages.

April 2015

Kirk Schneider, Ph.D.
Adjunct Faculty, Saybrook University
and
Teachers College Columbia University
Vice President, The Existential-Humanistic Institute

Contents

Editor and Contributors

About the Editor

Stefan E. Schulenberg (Ph.D., Clinical Psychology-Clinical/Disaster Specialty Track, University of South Dakota, 2001) is a licensed psychologist in the state of Mississippi, a professor in the University of Mississippi's Psychology Department, and a logotherapy diplomate. Dr. Schulenberg is the director of the University of Mississippi's Clinical-Disaster Research Center (UM-CDRC), an integrated research, teaching, and training center with emphases in disaster mental health and positive psychology.

Dr. Schulenberg's research interests include disaster mental health, perceived meaning, purpose in life, positive psychology, and psychological assessment. He served as a mental health consultant on a National Science Foundation Research Grant issued in response to Hurricane Katrina and conducted evaluation research funded by the Mississippi Department of Mental Health relating to the effects of the Gulf oil spill (*Deepwater Horizon* oil spill). He conducts workshops and provides training on disaster preparedness, psychological first aid, disaster response, meaning and purpose in life, resilience, and posttraumatic growth.

Dr. Schulenberg is a disaster mental health volunteer and supervisor in the American Red Cross and has worked with various other volunteer organizations, such as Mississippi's Disaster Response Network, United Way, and the American Foundation for Suicide Prevention. He teaches the graduate cognitive assessment course for the University of Mississippi's doctoral program in clinical psychology, where he has also developed seminars in disaster mental health and positive psychology. At the undergraduate level, Dr. Schulenberg teaches courses in disaster mental health, positive psychology, psychology and law, and abnormal psychology, as well as sections of the Honors Freshman Seminar for the University of Mississippi's Sally McDonnell Barksdale Honors College.

Contributors

Lucia Berdondini Department of Counselling, University of Strathclyde, Glasgow, UK

Heatherlyn P. Cleare-Hoffman University of Colorado at Colorado Springs, Colorado Springs, CO, USA

Mick Cooper Department of Psychology, University of Roehampton, London, UK

Edgar A. Correia Lisbon, Portugal; Department of Counselling, University of Strathclyde, Glasgow, UK

Todd DuBose Department of Clinical Psychology, The Chicago School of Professional Psychology, Chicago, IL, USA

Ivonne Andrea Flórez University of Mississippi, University, MS, USA

Louis Hoffman Department of Humanistic and Clinical Psychology, Saybrook University, Oakland, CA, USA

Dmitry A. Leontiev National Research University Higher School of Economics, Moscow, Russia

Efren Martinez Ortiz Society for the Advancement of Meaning-Centered Psychotherapy, Bogotá, Colombia

Shawn Rubin The Humanitarian Alliance, Washington, DC, USA

Kirk J. Schneider Saybrook University, Oakland, CA, USA; Columbia University, New York, NY, USA; Existential-Humanistic Institute, San Francisco, CA, USA

Stefan E. Schulenberg Psychology Department, Clinical-Disaster Research Center (CDRC), The University of Mississippi, Oxford, MS, USA

Daniel Sousa Health and Clinical Psychology Department, ISPA—University Institute, Lisbon, Portugal

Ernesto Spinelli ES Associates, London, UK

Digby Tantam New School of Psychotherapy and Counselling, Existential Academy, London, UK

Lisa Vallejos The Humanitarian Alliance, Washington, DC, USA

Emmy van Deurzen New School of Psychotherapy and Counselling, Existential Academy, London, UK

Clarifying and Furthering Existential Psychotherapy: An Introduction

Stefan E. Schulenberg

A few years ago, the editor of the *Journal of Contemporary Psychotherapy*, Jim Overholser, approached me about guest editing a special issue on existential psychotherapy. The impetus for the project was the announcement of the first World Congress for Existential Therapy that was to be held in London in May of 2015 (see van Deurzen and Tantam 2016, this volume). It sounded like a great idea. I viewed it as an opportunity to clarify and further existential psychotherapy. As for my background, I consider myself a cognitive-behavioral logotherapist. I was learning extensively about logotherapy, an existential-humanistic perspective, at the same time I was learning extensively about cognitive-behavioral therapy while a graduate student at the University of South Dakota in the mid to late 1990s.

Why logotherapy? Frankl's perspective was my initial, primary contact with existential psychotherapy. I first read *Man's Search for Meaning* (Frankl 1959/1985) while an undergraduate student at the University of Houston in 1994. I had the good fortune of being randomly assigned the text as a book report for an undergraduate course in personality theories. I was struck by the elegant, compelling nature of the writing so much so that I looked for ways to integrate it into my graduate studies. Soon after I began to study Rollo May, Irvin Yalom, James Bugental, Kirk Schneider, and many other authors of existential psychotherapy books and articles. As I studied, many questions came to mind. What is existential

---

ORIGINAL PAPER. Published online: 26 August 2014

S.E. Schulenberg (✉)
Department of Psychology, Clinical-Disaster Research Center (CDRC), The University of Mississippi, Oxford, MS, USA
e-mail: sschulen@olemiss.edu

S.E. Schulenberg (ed.), *Clarifying and Furthering Existential Psychotherapy*,
DOI 10.1007/978-3-319-31086-2_1

psychotherapy? How does existential psychotherapy relate to existential philosophy? Who practices existential psychotherapy? How does existential psychotherapy fit with cognitive-behavioral therapy and other schools of thought? How many existential psychotherapy schools are there? What are the similarities and differences of the various existential psychotherapy perspectives? How do you take such abstract concepts and put them into practice, or research them? It seemed to me that these were essential questions to answer. While the questions appeared straightforward, the answers were not. Existential psychotherapy books and articles are often difficult to read given their abstract nature and their being suffused with technical jargon (an observation that many graduate students in training have helped to confirm over the years, and an observation also often noted by critics).

Frankl "spoke" to me the most. I was particularly enamored by the idea that you could address adversity, even severe forms of adversity such as terminal illness or large-scale disaster, through your attitudinal stance. His perspective was that meaning could be found under any circumstances. His work emphasized meaning, resilience, and empowerment, and was a precursor to many other therapeutic approaches (Schulenberg et al. 2008). Inspired, I read everything by Frankl that I could find. He was really on to something, and speaking in a language that made sense on both personal and professional levels (although at times here, too, one finds abstract concepts and technical jargon that one must work through). We have since incorporated logotherapy and related existential ideas into our work in the area of disaster mental health, meaning's significance serving as a prime focus (e.g., Aiena et al. in press; Schulenberg et al. 2014, in press; Weathers et al. in press; see also Park and Folkman 1997; Park 2010, in press). There is a congruence of fit between these literatures.

Existential psychotherapy perspectives, logotherapy being one example, have much to offer. They are just as relevant to problems encountered today as they were to problems described in years past. The purpose of the initial special issue of the *Journal of Contemporary Psychotherapy* (March 2015, Volume 45, No. 1) on existential psychotherapy was to educate, and more importantly, to clarify, in order to move the literature forward by addressing essential questions about these valuable perspectives. Contributions to the original special issue covered a wide range of contexts, countries, and schools of thought. The works represented an international perspective, with submissions from the United States (Louis Hoffman, Lisa Vallejos, Heatherlyn P. Cleare-Hoffman, and Shawn Rubin; Todd DuBose; Kirk Schneider), the United Kingdom (Emmy van Deurzen; Edgar Correia, Mick Cooper, and Lucia Berdondini), Colombia (Efren Martinez and Ivonne Andrea Florez), the Russian Federation (Dmitry Leontiev), and Portugal (Daniel Sousa). These original articles are reproduced for this book, and two new chapters have also been added. The first selection is a new work by Ernesto Spinelli (United Kingdom) on the nature of change in existential therapy. The second selection is co-authored by Emmy van Deurzen and Digby Tantum (United Kingdom), and focuses on their efforts to develop the World Congress for Existential Therapy. Readers of this book will be able to see themes across the various chapters, such as efforts to clarify what is meant by existential psychotherapy, its utility and congruence of fit with different theoretical perspectives, and its growing empirical support. Efforts are also made to elucidate abstract concepts, making them easier to grasp, with examples of the application of various techniques in different settings.

The original special issue of the *Journal of Contemporary Psychotherapy*, and this expanded book, represent the combined energies of many individuals. I'd like to acknowledge and express appreciation to the contributors. I'd also like to extend my gratitude to the many individuals who provided helpful feedback to the authors, ensuring the integrity of the peer-review process. These individuals include Ernesto Spinelli, Paul T. P. Wong, Michael Winters, Kirk Schneider, Dmitry Leontiev, Efren Martinez, Emmy van Deurzen, Louis Hoffman, Todd DuBose, Daniel Sousa, Edgar Correia, Ed Mendelowitz, Ilene Serlin, Jackson Rainer, Susan Reviere, Shawn Rubin, Edwin Hersch, Brent Potter, and Xuefu Wang. The special issue is also indebted to the graduate student team members of the Clinical-Disaster Research Center at The University of Mississippi, who contributed by providing constructive feedback on many of the submissions. These individuals include Bethany Aiena, Stephanie (Stevie) Wood Campbell, Jennifer Marie Ladner Graham, Ivonne Andrea (Andrea) Florez, Matt Tkachuck, and Lauren Weathers. Their perspectives were invaluable, facilitating many meaningful discussions. Finally, I'd like to offer thanks and appreciation to the editor of the *Journal of Contemporary Psychotherapy*, Jim Overholser, for the opportunity to serve as guest editor for the original special issue, as well as for his encouragement throughout the editorial process.

It was through the combined efforts of many individuals that this book came to fruition. A major goal was to yield a work with a high degree of usefulness to graduate students and experienced clinicians alike, regardless of theoretical orientation, and across a range of settings. With this goal in mind, I believe this text represents a measure of success. It is my hope that readers will agree, finding something of value within these pages that resonates both personally and professionally.

References

Aiena, B. J., Buchanan, E. M., Smith, C. V., & Schulenberg, S. E. (in press). Meaning, resilience, and traumatic stress following the Deepwater Horizon oil spill: A study of Mississippi coastal residents seeking mental health services. *Journal of Clinical Psychology*. doi:10.1002/jclp.22232

Frankl, V. E. (1959/1985). *Man's search for meaning* (Rev. ed.). New York: Washington Square Press.

Park, C. L. (2010). Making sense of the meaning literature: An integrative review of meaning making and its effects on adjustment to stressful life events. *Psychological Bulletin, 136*, 257–301. doi:10.1037/a0018301

Park, C. L. (in press). Meaning making in the context of disasters. *Journal of Clinical Psychology*.

Park, C. L., & Folkman, S. (1997). The role of meaning in the context of stress and coping. *Review of General Psychology, 1*, 115–144. doi:10.1037/1089-2680.1.2.115

Schulenberg, S. E., Drescher, C. F., & Baczwaski, B. J. (2014). Perceived meaning and disaster mental health: A role for logotherapy in clinical-disaster psychology. In A. Batthyany & P. Russo-Netzer (Eds.), *Meaning in positive and existential psychology* (pp. 251–267). New York: Springer.

Schulenberg, S. E., Hutzell, R. R., Nassif, C., & Rogina, J. M. (2008). Logotherapy for clinical practice. *Psychotherapy: Theory Research, Practice, Training, 45*, 447–463. doi:10.1037/a0014331

Schulenberg, S. E., Smith, C. V., Drescher, C. F., & Buchanan, E. M. (in press). Assessment of meaning in adolescents receiving clinical services in Mississippi following the Deepwater Horizon oil spill: An application of the Purpose in Life test-Short Form (PIL-SF). *Journal of Clinical Psychology*. doi:10.1002/jclp.22240

van Deurzen, E., & Tantam, D. (2016). Creating the World Congress for Existential Therapy. In S. E. Schulenberg (Ed.), *Clarifying and futhering existential psychotherapy: Theories, methods, and practices* (pp.145–156). Switzerland: Springer International Publishing.

Weathers, L. N., Aiena, B. J., Blackwell, M. A., & Schulenberg, S. E. (in press). The significance of meaning to conceptualizations of resilience and posttraumatic growth: Strengthening the foundation for research and practice. In P. Russo-Netzer, S. E. Schulenberg, & A. Batthyany (Eds.), *Clinical perspectives on meaning: Positive and existential psychotherapy*. Switzerland: Springer International Publishing.

Existential Psychotherapy: An International Survey of the Key Authors and Texts Influencing Practice

Edgar A. Correia, Mick Cooper and Lucia Berdondini

Existential psychotherapy is one of the longest-established forms of psychotherapy, dating back to the 1920s (Besora 1994; Cooper 2012; Straus 1959). In 1991, 3 % of American Psychological Association (APA) Division 29 psychologists identified existential psychotherapy as their main theoretical orientation (Norcross et al. 1993). In recent years, it has been claimed that the approach is growing (Barnett and Madison 2012; Cooper 2012; Deurzen 2012; Deurzen and Young 2009; Groth 1999, 2000; Schneider 2008a), and recent research indicates it is now spread across 48 countries in six continents (Correia et al. 2014).

But what is existential psychotherapy and what are its principal practices? Over the years, several attempts have been made to give existential psychotherapy a coherent conceptual framework (e.g., Boss 1963, 1979; Deurzen 2010; Frankl 1969; Schneider and Krug 2010) and, more recently, a rationale for an existential practice (e.g., Deurzen and Adams 2011; Längle 2013; Schneider 2008b; Spinelli 2007). Despite these efforts, authors show different (and sometimes opposing) perspectives on what existential psychotherapy is (Cooper 2003; Keshen 2006), and

Ethical standards This investigation was granted ethical approval under the Counselling Unit research projects generic ethical approval (UEC0405/38) by the University of Strathclyde ethics committee.

ORIGINAL PAPER. Published online: 26 August 2014 © Springer Science+Business Media New York 2014.

E.A. Correia (✉) · L. Berdondini
Department of Counselling, University of Strathclyde, Glasgow, UK
e-mail: edgar.agrela@gmail.com

E.A. Correia
Rua de Cabo Verde, Nº 10 2º Dto., 1170-067 Lisbon, Portugal

M. Cooper
Department of Psychology, University of Roehampton, London, UK

S.E. Schulenberg (ed.), *Clarifying and Furthering Existential Psychotherapy*,
DOI 10.1007/978-3-319-31086-2_2

a definitive conceptual framework has yet to be established (Cooper 2012; Mahrer and Boulet 2004).

To a great extent, this diversity of perspectives is consistent with the core epistemological principles of existential philosophy, which strives to acknowledge the ambiguity and uncertainty of existence (Spinelli 2007). Congruent with their theoretical background, existential therapists tend to be sceptical and averse to any attempts to standardize theory or practice (Cooper 2012). But without a clear definition of what existential therapy is and what could be recognized as its core practices, it may be difficult to develop programs of research (Mahrer and Boulet 2004), evidence for effectiveness, and to clarify its place among other psychotherapeutic orientations.

Norcross (1987) attempted to establish a common theoretical framework for existential psychotherapy by analysing 80 publications. Eight unifying theoretical themes emerged from these texts: ontology, intentionality, freedom, choice/responsibility, phenomenology, individuality, authenticity, and potentiality. However, Norcross did not make explicit the methodology used for his content analysis (described as "informal") nor the rationale for his choice of texts, leaving doubts as to how far these data were representative of 1980s existential therapy.

New research, therefore, needs to be undertaken to help develop a theoretical framework for existential psychotherapy, and to find out its common core practices. To assure rigor, a valuable first step is to identify the authors and texts that are considered, by existential therapists, to be most influential on their practice. This can then serve as the basis for extracting understandings and competences that may allow for a clearer definition of existential therapeutic work.

In terms of the authors and texts identified in previous literature, in 1970, Keen presented as suggested readings in existential psychology Bugental's *The Search for Authenticity*, van Kaam's *Existential Foundations of Psychology*, van den Berg's *The Phenomenological Approach to Psychiatry* and May, Angel and Ellenberger's *Existence*.

Besora (1994), in his article about the historic development of existential psychotherapies, presented the "most representative authors" (pp. 15–16) of each of the 11 existential psychotherapy "systems" that he found. According to Besora, the most representative authors for German daseinsanalysis are Binswanger, Boss, Kuhn and Storch; logotherapy's key authors are Frankl, Caruso and Allers; for the UK anti-psychiatry movement Laing and Cooper; and, for the US's existential clinical psychology and experiential psychotherapy, May, van Kaam, Ellenberger, Nedelman, Bugental, Gendlin, Hora, Mahrer and Yalom. Similarly, Cooper (2003) suggests that the main authors from the daseinsanalytic branch are Binswanger and Boss; Logotherapy's is Frankl; for the existential-humanistic approach, May, Bugental, Yalom and Schneider; and Laing is identified as preceding the British School of Existential Analysis, whose main authors are van Deurzen, Spinelli and Cohn.

Angerami-Camon (2007) considers Binswanger, Boss, van den Berg and Laing as the main authors on bringing the existential thought to the therapeutic practice and suggests some of their main books. Viktor Frankl is presented as an important author but only "tangentially touching the existential thought" (p. 105), while Rollo

May is categorically excluded from the existential paradigm for embracing psychoanalytic ideas and practices.

Truscott (2010), in an APA book about theories for a therapist, suggests as recommended readings for existential psychotherapy Cooper's *Existential Therapies*, Frankl's *Man's Search for Meaning*, May's *Existential Psychology*, van Deurzen's *Existential Counselling & Psychotherapy in Practice* and Yalom's *Existential Psychotherapy*. As illustrative case studies he recommends Bugental's *Intimate Journeys*, du Plock's *Case Studies in Existential Psychotherapy and Counselling*, Schneider and May's *The Psychology of Existence* and Yalom's *Love's Executioner*.

From this brief review, it is clear that different authors, from different times, geographies and different conceptual backgrounds, have given different suggestions for the most important or representative authors and texts in the existential psychotherapy field. None of these suggested lists, however, have been developed from an empirical basis. Thus, these data cannot stand as a sustainable basis for a rigorous analysis of the core encompassing concepts and practices of existential psychotherapy.

As existential therapy is a clinical discipline, the authors or texts that best represent existential therapy are the ones that are actually informing and influencing practice. The present research, therefore, is an empirical inquiry with existential practitioners on the authors and texts that they consider most to have influenced their practice.

A worldwide survey was designed in order to have different geographical, cultural and ideological accounts, so data could represent an encompassing selection for different existential therapies.

Methods

Procedures

Design

This study adopts a survey design. The "online" questionnaire platform "SurveyMonkey" was used. Data were analysed using descriptive statistical procedures.

Instruments

Two list-style, open-ended questions were formulated, asking existential counsellors and psychotherapists their most influential existential therapy authors and texts. These questions were, respectively, numbers seven and nine of a 10-item questionnaire. This questionnaire was designed to study the practices, influences and characteristics of existential psychotherapists around the globe. All questions were previously tested with a sample of 23 existential therapists to identify areas for improvement.

The question about authors was "As an existential/existentially-informed counsellor or psychotherapist, which three authors on existential therapy have most influenced your practice?" Participants were asked to complete up to three open-ended answer boxes labelled: "Author 1," "Author 2," and "Author 3."

The question about texts was "As an existential/existentially-informed counsellor or psychotherapist, which three specific texts (book, book chapter, or journal article) on existential therapy have most influenced your practice?" Participants were asked to complete up to three pairs of open-ended answer boxes, labelled "Author 1/Text 1," "Author 2/Text 2," "Author3/Text 3."

The questionnaire design, structure and implementation procedures were developed taking into account the investigations held by Dillman and colleagues about surveys' development and application (Dillman et al. 2009). To increase the response rate (Dillman et al. 2009; Millar and Dillman 2011) each potential participant received an initial "invitation email," followed by two "reminder emails," nine and 23 days after the first email. These emails contained a link which directed the interested participant directly to the online survey. The questionnaire was available in three different languages (English, Spanish and Portuguese) and application took place between March 5 and July 20, 2012—for full questionnaire design and procedures see Correia et al. (2014).

Analysis

Responses were downloaded from SurveyMonkey to an SPSS database, where data codification and statistical descriptive analysis were conducted.

Participants' responses to authors and texts questions had been written in different languages and with many different spellings and terminology for authors and books. To make statistical analysis possible, each response was first scrutinised, translated into a standard author or text name, and then codified into a numeric code. In this process of standardization, authors and texts responses were checked by an Internet search on Google, Google Scholar, Amazon and/or BookFinder, to identify and confirm its existence or its translation. In nine out of 3108 responses to the authors' question it was not possible to identify the author and these were codified as "Others." For the texts question, it was not possible to identify 155 responses due to insufficient, unidentified or unsuitable information, and these were codified as "missing values."

Sampling Procedures

Participants were recruited by email. Contacts were made either directly: to email contacts gathered from an extensive internet search of existential practitioners (counsellors or psychotherapists); or indirectly: through the 40 existential therapy institutions (societies and/or training centres) from all over the world who agreed to forward the invitation email to its members and/or students/trainees. This was on the basis of a systematic online search of existential institutions around the globe that had been conducted previously (see Correia et al. 2014).

Participants

A total of 572 counsellors or psychotherapists were contacted directly, and 5109 invitations were sent out through the 26 institutions that had provided forwarding e-mails. It was not possible to accurately calculate the survey response rate, as 14 (35 %) institutions did not provide information about the number of members that they had contacted.

A total of 1382 participants from all over the world accessed the questionnaire and 1358 gave their informed consent. The number of participants who considered their therapeutic practice as existential or primarily informed by existential ideas and practices was 1264.

A total of 1085 participants, from 48 different countries, gave at least one influential author for their existential practice; and 853, from 45 countries, gave at least one influential text.

Participants who responded to the two questions analysed in this paper were counsellors, psychotherapists or trainees in counselling or psychotherapy. In total, 53.9 % of respondents to the authors' question, and 55.5 % of the respondents to the text question, considered their practice as "existential." The remaining respondents considered their practice "primarily informed by existential ideas or practices" (see Table 1).

More than 90 % of respondents had, or were having, specific institutional training as an existential/existentially-informed counsellor or psychotherapist and around 40 % were in training by the time they filled in the questionnaire (see Table 1). The more experienced practitioners (>10 years of practice) constituted less than 30 %.

Wherever possible, respondents were identified with a particular branch of existential therapy. This was on the basis of their institutional existential therapy training or affiliation. Just over 50 % of the sample had trained or were members of institutions aligned with the existential-phenomenological branch of existential therapy. Slightly more than 25 % were associated with logotherapy and/or existential analysis; approximately 8 % with existential-humanistic; and less than 3 % with daseinsanalysis (see Table 1). It was not possible to associate around 10 % of respondents to any branch and less than 2 % were associated to other psychotherapeutic paradigms (e.g., Gestalt therapy, psychoanalysis).

Most participants were from Europe (51 %, both questions) or Latin America (authors: 25.8 %; texts: 27.6 %). However, responses were received from all inhabited continents (see Table 2): Africa (0.2 %, both questions), Asia (authors: 4.8 %; texts: 4.1 %), Australia (authors: 7.5 %; texts: 7.1 %) and North America

Table 1 Frequencies and percentages of participants' characteristics for both questions

Demographics	Authors		Texts	
	n	%	*n*	%
Practice				
Existential	585	53.9	473	55.5
Existentially-informed	500	46.1	380	44.5
Institutional training				
Yes	983	90.9	782	91.9
No	99	9.1	69	8.1
Currently student				
Yes	424	39.1	341	40.0
No	661	60.9	512	60.0
Years of practice				
<10 years	769	71.4	598	70.7
>10 years	308	28.6	248	29.3
Branch				
Daseinsanalysis	26	2.4	26	3.0
Existential-humanistic	79	7.3	69	8.1
Existential-phenomenological	551	50.8	454	53.2
Logotherapy	290	26.7	216	25.3
Other	19	1.8	9	1.1
None attributed	120	11.1	79	9.3
Total	1085	–	853	–

(authors: 9.8 %; texts: 9.9 %). These percentages of participants by continent are in line with the percentages of existential therapy institutions by continent (see Correia et al. 2014); this may indicate good sample representativeness by continent.

The United Kingdom was the best represented country, constituting slightly more than 21 % of the authors and texts total answers (see Table 2). Next came Brazil (authors: 15.8 %; texts: 17.1 %), Austria (authors: 13.6 %; texts: 12.2 %), the United States (authors: 8.9 %; texts: 8.8 %), Australia (authors: 7.4 %; texts: 6.9 %) and Mexico (authors: 4.8 %; texts: 4.7 %), all of them with more than 40 practitioners, who gave their account of the most influential authors and texts for their existential practice. There were 15 countries with 10 or more existential practitioners answering both questions.

Reflexive Statement

The first two authors are existential psychotherapists and the third author is a Gestalt psychotherapist. This research was conducted to develop a deeper understanding of the influences on, and nature of, existential therapeutic practice and to

Table 2 Frequencies and percentages of participants by continent and country (the 15 most representative)

Continents	Authors		Texts	
Countries	*n*	%	*n*	%
Africa	**2**	**0.2**	**2**	**0.2**
Asia	**52**	**4.8**	**35**	**4.1**
Israel	30	2.8	21	2.5
China	15	1.4	10	1.2
Australia	**81**	**7.5**	**60**	**7.1**
Australia	80	7.4	59	6.9
Europe	**557**	**51.3**	**434**	**51.1**
United Kingdom	227	21.1	184	21.6
Austria	147	13.6	104	12.2
Portugal	30	2.8	23	2.7
Russia	30	2.8	20	2.4
Sweden	19	1.8	14	1.6
Lithuania	16	1.5	13	1.5
Greece	14	1.3	14	1.6
Latin America	**280**	**25.8**	**235**	**27.6**
Brazil	170	15.8	145	17.1
Mexico	52	4.8	40	4.7
Argentina	28	2.6	23	2.7
Chile	16	1.5	14	1.6
North America	**106**	**9.8**	**84**	**9.9**
United States	96	8.9	75	8.8
TOTAL	**1,085**	**---**	**853**	**---**

try to develop greater transparency in the existential psychotherapy field. Although the second author is a writer on existential therapy and closely associated with the "British School," we were not aware of holding any assumptions or biases as to who might be identified as the most influential authors and texts in this field.

Results

Authors Influencing Practice

A total of 1085 participants gave 3108 responses. This amounts to a mean of 2.86 choices per respondent. There were 221 different authors reported as the most influential for the respondent's existential practice.

Table 3 Frequencies and percentages of the 20 most influential existential therapy authors and the amount of times their texts were chosen as the most influential to participants' existential practice

Authors	Participants direct choice		Amount of times their texts were chosen	
	n	% within therapy authors	*n*	% within therapy texts
Frankl, Viktor	395	16.6	352	18.3
Yalom, Irvin	369	15.5	308	16.0
Spinelli, Ernesto	251	10.6	178	9.3
Deurzen, Emmy van	238	10.0	166	8.6
Längle, Alfried	206	8.7	163	8.5
May, Rollo	139	5.9	90	4.7
Bugental, James	57	2.4	53	2.8
Laing, Ronald	57	2.4	46	2.4
Boss, Medard	50	2.1	41	2.1
Lukas, Elisabeth	49	2.1	17	0.9
Cohn, Hans	47	2.0	40	2.1
Rogers, Carl	37	1.6	26	1.4
Binswanger, Ludwig	31	1.3	16	0.8
Cooper, Mick	23	1.0	26	1.4
Schneider, Kirk	21	0.9	24	1.2
Strasser, Freddie	20	0.8	23	1.2
Feijoo, Ana Maria	15	0.6	23	1.2
Tutsch, Lilo	14	0.6	1	0.1
Strasser, Alison	12	0.5	1	0.1
Robles, Yaqui	12	0.5	19	1.0

In 733 (23.6 %) responses, participants cited 53 existential philosophers or other non-therapy related figures. The seven most common being Heidegger ($n = 223$, 30.4 % within philosophers), Sartre ($n = 143$, 19.5 %), Kierkegaard ($n = 87$, 11.9 %), Buber ($n = 53$, 7.2 %), Nietzsche ($n = 41$, 5.6 %), Merleau-Ponty ($n = 38$, 5.2 %), and Husserl ($n = 36$, 4.9 %). As the question had specifically requested authors "on existential therapy," these responses were removed from further analysis.

The 168 remaining authors (psychologists, psychiatrists and/or psychotherapists) were cited between one and 395 times. Only 33 of the authors were cited six or more times. The six most influential authors were Frankl ($n = 395$, 16.6 % of all author citations), Yalom ($n = 369$, 15.5 %), Spinelli ($n = 251$, 10.6 %), van Deurzen ($n = 238$, 10 %), Längle ($n = 206$, 8.7 %), and May ($n = 139$, 5.9 %) (see Table 3).

Texts Influencing Practice

In total, the 853 participants cited 2415 identified texts. This amounts to a mean of 2.83 choices per respondent. A total of 467 different texts from 227 authors were reported by participants as the most influential on their existential practice.

Table 4 Frequencies and percentages of the 20 most influential existential therapy texts

Texts	*n*	% within therapy texts
Frankl, V. *Man's Search for Meaning*	180	9.4
Yalom, I. *Existential Psychotherapy*	176	9.2
Spinelli, E. *Practising Existential Psychotherapy*	67	3.5
Frankl, V. *The Doctor and the Soul*	67	3.5
Deurzen, E. van *Everyday Mysteries*	66	3.4
Deurzen, E. van *Existential Counselling & Psychotherapy in Practice*	62	3.2
Spinelli, E. *The Interpreted World*	51	2.7
Yalom, I. *The Gift of Therapy*	50	2.6
Yalom, I. *Love's Executioner*	38	2.0
Längle, A. *Sinnvoll Leben*	36	1.9
Laing, R. *The Divided Self*	29	1.5
Längle, A. *Lehrbuch zur Existenzanalyse*	27	1.4
Spinelli, E. *Demystifying Therapy*	27	1.4
Cohn, H. *Existential Thought and Therapeutic Practice*	27	1.4
Cooper, M. *Existential Therapies*	24	1.2
May, R., Angel, E., and Ellenberger, H. *Existence*	21	1.1
Spinelli, E. *Tales of Unknowing*	20	1.0
Bugental, J. *The Art of the Psychotherapist*	19	1.0
Frankl, V. *Man's Search for Ultimate Meaning*	19	1.0
Längle, A., Holzhey-Kunz, A. *Existenzanalyse und Daseinsanalyse*	18	0.9

In 492 (20.4 %) cases, respondents cited existential philosophy texts or other non-therapy related texts. The seven most common were Heidegger's *Being and Time* (*n* = 135, 27.4 % within non-therapy related texts), Sartre's *Being and Nothingness* (*n* = 67, 13.6 %), Buber's *I and Thou* (*n* = 35, 7.1 %), Sartre's *Existentialism is a Humanism* (*n* = 20, 4.1 %), Merleau-Ponty's *Phenomenology of Perception* (*n* = 17, 3.5 %) and two of Kierkegaard's books, *The Concept of Anxiety* and *The Sickness Unto Death* (*n* = 15 for each, 3 %).

The remaining 1923 texts were cited between one and 180 times. There were 62 texts chosen six or more times by the respondents. Two books were cited substantially more than any others (see Table 4): Frankl's *Man's Search for Meaning* (*n* = 180, 9.4 %) and Yalom's *Existential Psychotherapy* (*n* = 176, 9.2 %). The next most influential texts were Spinelli's *Practising Existential Psychotherapy* and Frankl's *The Doctor and the Soul* (*n* = 67, 3.5 %), followed by van Deurzen's *Everyday Mysteries* (*n* = 66, 3.4 %) and *Existential Counselling & Psychotherapy in Practice* (*n* = 62, 3.2 %).

Discussion

In terms of the authors most influential to existential practice, a high level of triangulation was found between those directly identified and those who had written the most influential existential texts. As can be seen in Table 3, Frankl's texts were chosen 352 times (18.3 %) as the most influential, followed by Yalom's 308 (16 %), Spinelli's 178 (9.3 %), van Deurzen's 166 (8.6 %) and Längle's 163 (8.5 %) times.

When asked about the authors and texts that most influenced their practice, existential counsellors and psychotherapists chose Viktor Frankl and Irvin Yalom and, respectively, their books *Man's Search for Meaning* and *Existential Psychotherapy*. Two authors (Spinelli and van Deurzen) from the recent British School (Cooper 2003, 2012) come next in popularity, their books being the 3rd, 5th, 6th and 7th most influential, corroborating Miles Groth's (2000) statement about the importance of this existential school for contemporary existential psychotherapy. Längle and his texts also showed considerable influence, mainly among logotherapy and existential analysis practitioners, while May maintains his status as a key influence in the existential psychotherapy world.

Although it was specifically asked for authors and texts "on existential therapy," slightly more than 20 % of responses reported philosophical or other non-therapy related authors. This number of responses may indicate the considerable and direct influence that existential philosophy has on the actual practice and in its theoretical framework. Here, Heidegger's *Being and Time* was overwhelmingly identified as the most influential text.

When compared with the literature review concerning the most important or representative authors and texts, these data corroborate some consensus around Frankl and Yalom (Cooper 2003; Jacobsen 2007; Truscott 2010) and gives strength to the more recent lists where authors and texts from the British School tend to appear (Cooper 2003; Jacobsen 2007; Truscott 2010).

Boss and Binswanger were also identified in the review (Angerami-Camon 2007; Besora 1994; Cooper 2003; Jacobsen 2007), but were only the 9th and 13th most influential authors for existential practitioners, respectively. This could have two main explanations: (a) These authors are associated with the daseinsanalytic branch, and its worldwide representation, as reflected in the sample, is very small currently (Correia et al. 2014); (b) The historical relevance of these figures may influence the reviewed authors' choice, but these authors may not have the equivalent weight to influence the contemporary practitioner's practice.

If this last explanation is correct (and the same phenomena happened with van Kaam and van den Berg), then a choice of authors and texts made by a study of the most cited authors and texts in the bibliographic references will probably end up with a different list of the most influential. Historical and academically influential authors and texts, present on bibliographical references, may not always correspond to the ones that most influence practitioners' current conceptual and practical framework. If the aim is to study the practical and clinical sides of existential therapy, then data collected from actual practitioners may give us a more representative pool of texts and authors.

Limitations

Data concern practitioners' *self-reported* perceived influence upon their own practice, and it may be that the *actual* authors and texts that influence their practice are different. Results also aim to reflect the main influences upon *contemporary* existential practitioners' practice and it cannot be assumed to be representative of the most influential authors and texts for the historical, conceptual and clinical development of existential psychology, psychiatry and psychotherapy.

Another important limitation is that those who responded to the questionnaire may not be representative of the actual global population of existential counsellors and psychotherapists. Not only because the option for an online questionnaire may have excluded existential psychotherapists without access to this technology, but also due to language constraints, as this research was biased towards English, Spanish and Portuguese speakers.

Percentages of participants by continent are in line with the percentages of existential therapy institutions by continent (see Correia et al. 2014), but there were no previous studies about the actual distribution of existential therapists worldwide. As a result, no guarantees can be given about the representativeness of this sample either by continent, country or by branch of existential psychotherapy.

Implications for Practice

Despite the limitations, this study gives the first empirically-based understanding of the authors and texts that are most influential on the work of existential therapists around the globe. There is now available evidence of who and which texts are informing existential practitioners' practice. This helps to develop an understanding of the nature of existential therapy, and also sets a basis for future analysis of the conceptual and practical frameworks of contemporary existential practice.

Training institutes, practitioners or trainees interested in deepening their knowledge of existential practice now have a basis for the main references being used by today's existential practitioners worldwide.

Längle is ranked as one of the most influential authors, but his books are currently only in German. This suggests there is a need to translate more of these texts into English and other languages.

Further Research

Recent developments within existential therapy could eventually dictate rapid changes to this list. Future studies of the most influential authors and texts may indicate the impact of contemporary developments within existential psychotherapy.

Existential philosophy's great influence upon existential practitioners' practice, revealed in this study, raises several interesting and intriguing research questions: How do existential therapists translate a philosophical/theoretical thought into a practical intervention? What practices are these? And what is the therapeutic impact of the approach and benefit for the client? Further inquiry should also be made into the philosophical authors and texts that most influence existential practice.

Conclusion

This pool of existential therapy's authors and texts stems from more than 850 respondents worldwide who identify their practice as existential or primarily informed by this paradigm. An empirical base of the most influential authors and texts upon contemporary existential practice is now available for future literature/bibliographic research on existential psychotherapy. This kind of research may help us to deepen the understanding of the similarities and differences between the most influential perspectives and to clarify existential therapies' common theoretical and practical grounds.

Acknowledgments This research was supported by a scholarship (SFRH/BD/71484/2010) from the FCT—Fundação para a Ciência e a Tecnologia, Ministério da Educação e Ciência, Portugal.

References

Angerami-Camon, V. A. (2007). *Psicoterapia existencial* (4th ed.). São Paulo: Thomson.

Barnett, L., & Madison, G. (Eds.). (2012). *Existential therapy: Legacy, vibrancy and dialogue*. London: Routledge.

Besora, M. V. (1994). Las psicoterapias existenciales: Desarollo historico y modalidades conceptuales. In J. A. C. Teixeira (Ed.), *Fenomenologia e psicologia* (pp. 11–23). Lisboa: ISPA.

Boss, M. (1963). *Psychoanalysis & daseinsanalysis*. New York: Basic Books.

Boss, M. (1979). *Existential foundations of medicine and psychology*. New York: Jason Aronson.

Cooper, M. (2003). *Existential therapies*. London: Sage Publications.

Cooper, M. (2012). *The existential counselling primer: A concise, accessible and comprehensive introduction*. Ross-on-Wye: PCCS.

Correia, E., Cooper, M., & Berdondini, L. (2014). The worldwide distribution and characteristics of existential counsellors and psychotherapists. *Existential Analysis, 25*(2), 321–337.

Deurzen, E. V. (2010). *Everyday mysteries: A handbook of existential psychotherapy* (2nd ed.). Hove: Routledge.

Deurzen, E. V. (2012). *Existential counselling & psychotherapy in practice* (3rd ed.). London: Sage Publications.

Deurzen, E. V., & Adams, M. (2011). *Skills in existential counselling & psychotherapy*. London: Sage Publications.

Deurzen, E. V., & Young, S. (Eds.). (2009). *Existential perspectives on supervision: Widening the horizon of psychotherapy and counselling*. Hampshire: Palgrave Macmillan.

Dillman, D. A., Smyth, J. D., & Christian, L. M. (2009). *Internet, mail, and mixed-mode surveys: The tailored design method* (3rd ed.). Hoboken: Wiley.

Frankl, V. E. (1969). *The doctor and the soul: From psychotherapy to logotherapy* (A. Knopf, Trans.). London: Souvenir Press.

Groth, M. (1999). The background of contemporary existential psychotherapy. *The Humanistic Psychologist, 27*(1), 15–22.

Groth, M. (2000). Existential psychotherapy today. *Review of Existential Psychology & Psychiatry, 25*(1–3), 7–27.

Jacobsen, B. (2007). *Invitation to existential psychology: A psychology for the unique human being and its applications in therapy*. Chichester: Wiley.

Keen, E. (1970). *Three faces of being: Toward an existential clinical psychology*. New York: Meredith Corporation.

Keshen, A. (2006). A new look at existential psychotherapy. *American Journal of Psychotherapy, 60*(3), 285–298.

Längle, A. (2013). *Lehrbuch zur existenzanalyse: Grundlagen*. Wien: Facultas.wuv.

Mahrer, A. R., & Boulet, D. B. (2004). How can existentialists do research on psychotherapy? *Existential Analysis: Journal of the Society for Existential Analysis, 15*(1), 15–28.

Millar, M. M., & Dillman, D. A. (2011). Improving response to web and mixed-mode surveys. *Public Opinion Quarterly, 75*(2), 249–269.

Norcross, J. C. (1987). A rational and empirical analysis of existential psychotherapy. *Journal of Humanistic Psychology, 27*(1), 41–68. doi:10.1177/0022167887271005

Norcross, J. C., Prochaska, J. O., & Farber, J. A. (1993). Psychologists conducting psychotherapy: New findings and historical comparisons on the psychotherapy division membership. *Psychotherapy: Theory, Research, Practice, Training, 30*(4), 692–697. doi:10.1037/0033-3204.30.4.692

Schneider, K. J. (2008a). Introduction. Existential-integrative psychotherapy: A new era. In K. J. Schneider (Ed.), *Existential-integrative psychotherapy: Guideposts to the core of practice* (pp. 1–11). New York: Routledge.

Schneider, K. J. (2008b). Part 2: Guideposts to an existential-integrative (EI) approach. In K. J. Schneider (Ed.), *Existential-integrative psychotherapy: Guideposts to the core of practice* (pp. 31–96). New York: Routledge.

Schneider, K. J., & Krug, O. T. (2010). *Existential-humanistic therapy*. Washington, DC: American Psychological Association.

Spinelli, E. (2007). *Practising existential psychotherapy: The relational world*. London: Sage Publications.

Straus, E. (1959). The fourth international congress of psychotherapy Barcelona, Spain, September 1 through 7, 1958. *Psychosomatic Medicine, 21*(2), 158–164.

Truscott, D. (2010). Existential. In D. Truscott (Ed.), *Becoming an effective psychotherapist: Adopting a theory of psychotherapy that's right for you and your client* (pp. 53–66). Washington, DC: American Psychological Association.

Emotion, Relationship, and Meaning as Core Existential Practice: Evidence-Based Foundations

Louis Hoffman, Lisa Vallejos, Heatherlyn P. Cleare-Hoffman and Shawn Rubin

A primary challenge in considering the evidence-based foundations to existential therapy is that one first must determine which existential psychotherapy is being discussed. Although common themes across the existential psychology approaches exist, there remain important distinctive features (Cooper 2003; Hoffman 2009a). Hoffman (2009a) suggested that, when talking about existential therapy as a whole, it is best to think of it as a mosaic, or a collection of themes, approaches, and values, that most existential therapists tend to agree upon. Within this mosaic, there are few aspects that all existential therapists agree upon; however, individuals identifying as existential therapists tend to incorporate most of the mosaic into their own approach.

The fluidity of the existential approach establishes it as an ideal foundation for an integrative approach to therapy (see Schneider 2008; Wampold 2008). It can be readily adapted to individual and cultural differences as well as integrating other approaches to therapy, such as cognitive-behavioral therapy (Bunting and Hayes 2008; Wolfe 2008) and psychoanalytic psychotherapy (Dorman 2008). The ability for it to be adapted does not mean this is easy or something that all practitioners can

ORIGINAL PAPER. Published online: 26 August 2014

L. Hoffman (✉)
Department of Humanistic and Clinical Psychology, Saybrook University,
475 14th Street, 9th Floor, Oakland, CA 94612, USA
e-mail: lhoffman@saybrook.edu

L. Vallejos · S. Rubin
The Humanitarian Alliance, Washington, DC, USA

H.P. Cleare-Hoffman
University of Colorado at Colorado Springs, Colorado Springs, Colorado, USA

S.E. Schulenberg (ed.), *Clarifying and Furthering Existential Psychotherapy*,
DOI 10.1007/978-3-319-31086-2_3

do. As with any therapy orientation, a foundation of knowledge, experience, and skill is necessary to appropriately adapt therapy approaches.

Despite limited research directly on existential therapy (Hoffman 2009a; Walsh and McElwain 2001), Hoffman and colleagues (Cleare-Hoffman et al. 2013; Hoffman 2009a; Hoffman et al. 2012) maintain that existential therapy can be rightly claimed as an evidence-based practice. The common factors literature in psychology (Duncan et al. 2009; Elkins 2009; Wampold 2009a, 2015) support the assertion that the primary change agents in psychotherapy are connected to various common factors embedded in most therapy approaches. This suggests that while researching particular psychotherapies has an important utility, it is not necessary to rely upon narrowly defined specific outcome research on specific approaches to determine if it fits evidence-based practice.

When the mosaic of existential psychology is examined in the light of psychotherapy research, the strong empirical support for its efficacy is evident. In this chapter, we examine the evidence basis for three central components of existential therapy practice closely associated with existential-humanistic psychotherapy: relationship, emotion, and meaning. This school of existential therapy follows in the tradition of May and Bugental (1987, 1999) and is exemplified in the contemporary writing of Schneider (2008) and Schneider and Krug (2009).

Evaluating the Evidence

Therapists and researchers have engaged in extensive debate about what constitutes an "evidence-based" approach to therapy (see Norcross et al. 2006). As noted by Wampold et al. (2007), evidence is an ambiguous word that can include different sources of data including quantitative research, qualitative research, scholarship, and clinical expertise. Evidence-based approaches are more inclusive, adaptable, and rigorous than other more narrowly defined ways of considering therapy efficacy, including the empirically supported treatments that were myopically tied to specific methods of outcome evaluation. Although existential therapists have been leery of Evidence-Based Practice in Psychology (EBPP), as long as EBPP is understood broadly and inclusively it is not a threat to existential practice (Cleare-Hoffman et al. 2013; Hoffman et al. 2012). Instead, existential therapists should engage in the dialogue about EBPP to assure it continues to be defined in a broad, inclusive manner.

The American Psychological Association (APA) Presidential Task Force on Evidence-Based Practice (2006) identified three aspects of EBPP: (1) research, (2) clinical expertise or competency, and (3) patient characteristics, culture, and preferences. EBPP is not strictly tied to a therapy modality, but rather focuses on an appropriately skilled therapist implementing a valid approach of therapy. Hoffman et al. (2012) advocated that existential therapists should engage EBPP through demonstrating that existential therapy is already an evidence-based practice. It would behoove existential therapy to continually examine weaknesses in its evidence-based foundation while seeking to address these limitations. There are three important aspects of this. First, existential therapists should examine where the evidence is weak and seek to gather further evidence to support existential therapy. Second, weaknesses in the existential approach should be identified and addressed. Third, existential therapists should engage the EBPP literature to see where it can inform the future development of existential practice.

In unpacking the three pillars of existential practice, the first task is to address the research. EBPP practice encourages the utilization of various types of research. Although this can include outcome studies and randomized clinical trials, this is not the only method for establishing an evidence-basis. The type of research should be geared to the research question, not an arbitrary choice of preferred methodology imposed upon all contexts and therapy modalities.

Second, clinical expertise or competency refers to assessment and diagnosis, treatment planning, interpersonal expertise, utilizing appropriate research to inform therapy, offering a cogent rationale for treatment approach, assessing progress, and other foundational competencies (APA Presidential Task Force on EBPP 2006). Many of these factors should be interpreted broadly. For example, diagnosis does not need to be restricted to a DSM-5 diagnosis. Rather, this refers to working with the client to agree upon a statement of the problem from which a cogent plan to address the problem can be developed. Existential therapy relies upon a competency approach that is, in reality, quite similar to the conception advocated by the APA Presidential Task Force on EBPP. Norcross (1987) notes, "Perhaps more than any other clinical approach, existential psychotherapy depends upon a set of individual skills and characteristics—the therapist him or herself" (p. 53).

These competencies are consistent with the expectations for basic skills all psychologists should have entering independent practice. One must have certain foundational therapeutic competencies to be competent in any particular approach to therapy. These competencies vary in accordance with the different therapy modalities. Hoffman et al. (2012) advocated that existential-humanistic psychology could claim to have an evidence-based foundation relevant to the clinical expertise dimension if (a) there is sufficient demonstration that various clinical competencies are utilized within the framework of existential therapy, and (b) approaches to existential-humanistic psychology have been appropriately vetted in the peer-reviewed literature by experts in the field.

The competencies refer more to the therapist than the therapy modality. For existential therapy to meet this standard of EBPP it is necessary that the foundational competencies fit with, can be adapted to, and can be integrated into an existential therapy approach.

Third, patient characteristics, culture, and preferences require that existential therapy be adapted to individual as well as group contexts and needs. Although the nature of existential therapy is readily adaptable to individual and cultural differences, it has struggled in actualizing this value. Recent advancements helped address this including the identification of indigenous Chinese (Bao 2009; Wang 2011) and Greek (Dallas et al. 2013) approaches to existential therapy, international applications (Hoffman et al. 2009b), and new conceptions of the self (Hoffman et al. 2009a).

Relationship

Research evidence supports that one of the primary determining factors for successful psychotherapy is the client-therapist relationship (Elkins 2009; Norcross 2009; Wampold 2001, 2009a; see also Norcross 2002), which can be conceived in various ways. Rogers (1961) described the ideal relationship between client and therapist as having three conditions: genuineness, unconditional positive regard, and empathy. Bugental (1987) described presence, which is a quality of being engaged and participating on a deep level, as a foundation of relationship. Bugental (1978) also emphasizes the therapy alliance, which he described as comprising "mutuality, honesty, respect [and is] dynamic, vital and trusting" (p. 70). As Schneider (2008) notes, European existentialists call the quality of presence "Dasein" (p. 60) or "being there."

Yalom (1980) focused on the "interpersonal" nature of relationship with the therapist and client. Often, the therapeutic relationship comprises a microcosm of what's happening in the client's world outside of therapy. Bugental focused more on the intrapersonal relationship, where what is happening within each individual in relationship with the other is primary (Krug 2009). Despite differences such as these, most existential therapists agree that it is the interpersonal nature, or the relationship, between therapist and the client that promotes healing conditions.

Research. Much of the existing research on existential therapy has been clinical experience where experienced therapists documented their findings in a systematic manner; however, more attention recently has been directed to empirical research. Wampold (2001, 2009a, b), whose findings supported the supposition that the relationship is foundational to healing, is one of the leading empirical researchers of therapy outcomes. Wampold (2009b) writes, "there are hundreds of studies that show that a purposeful collaborative relationship between a therapist and the patient—what we call the therapeutic alliance—is related to therapeutic progress" (Sect. 3, Para. 2).

A review of the literature shows that psychotherapy is effective and that one therapy is not superior to others (Elkins 2009; Wampold 2001, 2009a, b). Studies conducted by van Hees et al. (2013) demonstrate that differences based upon therapy approach "are small and they are often not significant" (p. 7) and therefore should be adjusted to client preferences. Norcross and Lambert (2010) indicate psychotherapy is beneficial to clients in 75–80 % of cases across therapeutic models and, based upon a meta-analysis sponsored by two APA divisions, the primary tool for effective psychotherapy is the client-therapist relationship (Norcross and Lambert 2010).

Research by Norcross (1987) indicated most existential therapists rated the relationship values of warmth, empathy, and authenticity extremely high on the therapeutic interventions commonly used, indicating the intricate link between existential psychotherapy principles and the research on therapy effectiveness. Wampold (2008) states that "it could be argued that an understanding of the principles of existential therapy is needed by all therapists, as it adds a perspective that might… form the basis of all effective treatments" (Para. 15). Moreover, recent research in neuropsychology demonstrates "a positive and attuned interpersonal relationship enhances neural plasticity [the brain's ability to change and learn new patterns] and learning" (Cozolino 2002, p. 292), which adds neuropsychological support for the therapy relationship.

Clinical Expertise/Competency. A significant portion of the competencies identified by the APA Presidential Task Force on EBPP (2006) focus on the therapeutic relationship. Given that existential therapy emphasizes the relationship, there is a strong convergence between existential therapy and the relational competencies of EBPP. Bugental (1978) describes important therapist qualities as including: "The therapist's own well-being, commitment to being a 'pro', dedication to the healing/growth process, presence, cultivated sensitivity and lastly, skills" (p. 43). Bugental's emphasis on therapist well-being emerges from the existential viewpoint that the person of the therapist is the primary therapeutic tool that the therapist brings (see also Hoffman 2009a). The therapist's well-being fits well with the EBPP competencies of interpersonal skills, self-reflection, acquisition of skills, working with cultural and individual differences, and seeking out appropriate consultation and/or supervision as needed (APA Presidential Task Force on EBPP 2006).

Schneider and Krug (2009) identify existential stances, which are not techniques, but rather a set of skills that, when cultivated, provide the necessary environment for change. Those stances include, "the cultivation of therapeutic presence, the cultivation and activation of therapeutic presence through struggle, the encounter with the resistance to therapeutic struggle, and the coalescence of the meaning, intentionality, and life awakening that can result from the struggle" (p. 35). Schneider and Krug (2009) describe presence as something that can concurrently hold and illuminate what is relevant within the client and in the therapeutic relationship. Although this is a complex relational skill, it includes relational factors identified by Norcross (2009) as important aspects of effective therapy relationships, including empathy, positive regard, cohesion, openness, genuineness, and being collaborative.

A second existential stance is the ability to facilitate the client's experiential awareness by using such techniques as *invoking the actual* (Schneider and Krug 2009). Invoking the actual is calling "attention to the part of the client that is attempting to emerge" (p. 114). This can be done in a myriad of ways including the therapist pointing out what is happening in the present moment or calling attention to the physical responses the client is demonstrating such as moistening eyes or tightening of facial features. This complex relational skill converges with the relational factors identified by Norcross (2009) of listening to the client and privileging their experience.

Third, Schneider and Krug (2009) discuss vivifying and confronting resistance as a skill that helps therapists reflect what clients reveal pertaining to resisting or deflecting difficult emotional material. This confrontation is not harsh and must be approached cautiously to avoid re-traumatizing clients. It draws upon various relational skills identified as part of effective therapy (see Norcross 2009) including establishing a basis of unconditional positive regard and collaboration, which allow the therapist to encourage the client to safely engage more difficult emotional material.

Unlike other therapies, existential therapy does not offer a manual on how to conduct therapy. Yalom (1980) suggests therapists create and adapt a new therapy for each client. The skills required to be an effective existential therapist are a highly tuned, oft-practiced, and carefully cultivated way of being. Similarly, Norcross (2009) notes that excessive rigidity is not effective in psychotherapy, stating, "Using an identical therapy relationship (and treatment method) for all clients is now recognized as inappropriate and, in selected cases, even unethical" (p. 131).

Individual and Cultural Differences. Because of the relational foundation of existential psychotherapy and the valuing of the client's self-and-world constructs, it is well-suited to meet the needs of a variety of clients. It is unique in its approach to individual and cultural differences in that it is not so much the clients' experience that matters as it is the meaning the client attributes to the experience (Schneider and Krug 2009). The therapist and client must attend to the individual and cultural levels of meaning and experience (Hoffman 2009b). Vontress (1979) notes that self-understanding serves as a basis for understanding others, particularly clients with different cultural backgrounds. Engaging in a deep self-exploration assists therapists avoid what Vasquez (2007) calls *psychotherapy bias*, wherein the therapist has difficulty "staying present and empathic with a person who is struggling with a painful discriminatory event" (p. 881).

As previously noted, existential psychology needs to continue to advance in integrating the cultural and social aspects of the client in a more explicit and direct manner. Existential scholarship historically has neglected this issue. However, numerous recent publications have established a strong foundation for adaptations of existential therapy in working with diverse clientele (Alsup 2008; Brown 2008; Cleare-Hoffman et al. 2013; Comas-Dias 2008; Hoffman and Cleare-Hoffman 2011; Hoffman et al. 2009a, b, 2014; Monheit 2008; Rice 2008; Serlin 2008; Wang 2011).

Emotion

Emotion is central to all approaches to psychotherapy. A primary reason most individuals enter therapy is to deal with emotional struggles. Diverse therapy approaches conceive of and approach emotions differently. Some therapy modalities focus on controlling and coping with emotions while other approaches facilitate emotional experiencing and expression. Much of the contemporary field of psychology tends to pathologize certain emotions, such as anger, anxiety, and sadness, while others emphasize that all emotions have value and, at their base, are normal. Every therapy modality has an implicit or explicit theory of emotions influencing how therapy is applied. From an existential perspective, all emotions are normal with the potential to be healthy, but sometimes become problematic for individuals because of the way the person is relating to or experiencing the emotions (Hoffman 2009a). Therefore, existential therapy seeks less to change emotions than some other approaches while focusing more on changing the way people experience their emotions.

Existential therapy encourages clients to welcome their emotions, experience them more deeply, and make meaning from them (Hoffman 2009a; Hoffman and Cleare-Hoffman 2011). To accomplish this, therapists develop a strong therapeutic alliance, create a safe environment for the clients to enter their emotions, and encourage clients to move into their emotions at a safe pace. At times, this means developing coping skills or other strategies to help clients feel confident managing their emotions as they move more deeply into them. As the clients engage their emotions, therapists facilitate understanding their meaning and using emotions to create meaning.

Research. Greenberg et al. (2001) note that a wealth of research supports the importance of emotional expression as well as the physical and psychological risks of ignoring, denying, or suppressing emotions. Whelton (2004), reviewing research on emotions in therapy across modalities, states, "There is accumulating evidence that both the in-session activation of specific, relevant emotions and the cognitive exploration and elaboration of the significance and meaning of these emotions are important for therapeutic change" (p. 58). Regardless of the approach to therapy, experiencing and exploring emotions is an important change factor.

Client-centered and experiential therapies, like existential therapy, are classified under the umbrella of "humanistic." These approaches tend to approach emotions in similar ways, including encouraging experiencing, processing, and finding meaning in emotion. In their review of research on person-centered and experiential therapies, Watson et al. (2010) state that the research indicates that experiencing emotions has a clear relationship with successful therapy outcomes, even if that relationship is "never 'very high'" (p. 139).

One aspect of experiencing is emotional arousal. Emotional arousal and the ability to tolerate moderate to high levels of emotion is associated with better therapy outcomes (Watson et al. 2010). Some clients enter therapy with this ability; however, for others, increasing their ability to be comfortable with or tolerate the emotional arousal is an important part of the healing process in therapy. Therapists play an important role in facilitating and processing emotions. Bugental (1987, 1999) was highly focused on the emotional aspects of therapy. Similar to Rogers, Bugental recognized that therapist responses to their clients influence their going deeper into their experience or shifting away from their emotions. He was critical of therapists that targeted getting to the emotions as if this was some type of therapeutic gold or magic bullet. Instead, he advocated for a nuanced way of moving in and out of the emotions balancing emotional experiencing, cognitive reflections on the emotion, and creating meaning from the emotional experience. This moving in and out of emotions (i.e., emotional processing) is key to Bugental's existential approach.

Bugental drew his conclusions about processing emotions from clinical experience; however, research has supported his approach. Watson et al. (2010), drawing directly from the research, summarize that activating and expressing intense emotions during therapy is a good predictor of successful outcomes, but not if the client remains in this level of emotional expression for too long. Adams and Greenberg (as cited in Watson et al. 2010), in research tracking emotion in therapy sessions, noted that therapists' experiential focus, or focus on the depth of emotional processing, influenced the client's experiencing of emotion and successful therapy outcomes.

Clinical Expertise/Competency. Various clinical competencies help establish a basis for clinical practice when working with emotions. In this section, we focus on (a) self-reflection, (b) interpersonal expertise, (c) assessment, and (d) providing a cogent rationale for treatment.

Self-awareness is a foundation for existential therapy practice (Bugental 1987, 1999; Hoffman 2009a). Therapists need to be comfortable with their own intense emotions as well as those of their clients. When therapists are not comfortable with these emotions, they struggle to facilitate client emotional processing and expressions, and may even intentionally or unintentionally discourage these emotions. Self-awareness, then, provides a basis for interpersonal practice. In order to facilitate emotional expression and processing, therapists create a safe space to enter these emotions. Bugental (1987) and Hoffman (2009a) discuss specific skills that can further help clients gently move deeper into their emotions or come out of more intense emotional arousal.

Although existential therapists are not prone to using DSM-5 diagnosis, they do work with clients to develop an understanding of the problem from the client's perspective. Typically, this focuses on the client's lived experience of the problem. For instance, clients struggling with anxiety may focus on how the anxiety is impacting them in their relationships or work. While many therapy modalities are quick to identify symptoms and then chart a plan to cope with, reduce, or eliminate them, existential approaches do not assume clients are seeking symptom reduction. When it is a goal of the client, it is often not the sole or primary goal. Prior to developing a treatment plan, the therapist helps the client explore possible desired outcomes, which, at times, means helping the client understand a variety of options. From an existential perspective, treatment plans are fluid and there is concern that a rigidly adhered to treatment plan may prevent the therapist and client from recognizing or considering emergent problems (Elkins 2009; Hoffman 2009a). From an existential approach, it is important to regularly discuss the treatment process and direction in order to maintain a cogent, agreed upon treatment approach.

Individual and Cultural Differences. Hoffman and Cleare-Hoffman (2011) note, "mainstream Western psychology has often approached most, if not all, emotions as a problem to be solved or a spurious aspect of human nature that needs to be controlled" (p. 261). Embedded in much of Western psychology is an implicit theory of emotions that tends to impose upon clients without consideration being given pertaining to the client's view of emotions. There are wide cultural and individual differences pertaining to experiencing and expressing emotion. Without consideration and sensitivity given to these differences, it is easy for therapists to impose a value system related to emotions upon clients.

Kang et al. (2003) note that cultural variation in emotional expression does not necessitate cultural variation in the intensity or experiencing of emotions. Regardless of culture, people have emotions and may have similar levels of intensity of emotion. However, Kang and colleagues found that the way the person relates to emotions has varied implications for aspects of well-being, such as relational well-being. Their study found emotional expressiveness to be more important in predicting relational health in individualist cultures whereas emotional differentiation (i.e., making subtle distinction between emotions) was a better predictor of relational health in collectivist cultures.

While research has suggested that experiencing emotional arousal and processing emotion is consistently associated with better therapy outcomes, this does not necessitate a particular way of experiencing or expressing emotions. Hoffman and Cleare-Hoffman (2011) note that different types of emotional experiencing and expression are healthy for different cultures. To impose a particular way of experiencing and expressing emotions upon a client may be detrimental. Therapists ought to be able to work with emotional experiencing and expression in various ways.

Meaning

Although meaning is a central concept throughout existential thought, it is more explicitly central in certain approaches (Frankl 1959/1984; Hirsch 2009; Hoffman 2009a, b; Wong 2012a, b; Yalom 1980). Frankl (1959/1984) discusses the role meaning plays in coping with and transforming suffering. Regarding coping, Frankl was fond of quoting Nietzsche: "He who has a *why* to live for can bear almost any *how*" (as cited in Frankl 1959/1984, p. 109). Frankl more frequently spoke to the transformative role meaning can play in people's lives: "suffering ceases to be suffering at the moment it finds a meaning" (p. 117). Wong (2012a) extended Frankl's work on meaning incorporating a dual-systems model. While much of existential psychology focused on making meaning through suffering, Wong advocates for the importance of balancing this with the more positively rooted ways of seeking meaning that also promote well-being.

Yalom (1980) identified meaning as one of the existential givens. For Yalom, there is no meaning that innately exists in the world for one to discover, but rather meaning comes from being engaged and committed in the world. For some existentialists, Yalom's focus on the meaningless aspect is considered too pessimistic (Greening 1992). May (1991) identified meaning as embedded in myths (see also Hoffman 2009b), which are understood as pertaining to how individuals organize their meaning systems. Myths are not untrue, but rather highly symbolic beliefs or beliefs systems that cannot be proven to be true. Myth and meaning often rely upon a type of faith, trust, or belief, though not necessarily spiritual. While abstract, May also recognized that myths are lived out in the world. While meaning is approached from various perspectives in existential thought, the idea of meaning being connected to one's lived experience is a consistent theme. As Wong (2012a) states, "Every philosophy of life leads to the development of a certain mindset—a frame of reference or prism—through which we make value judgments" (p. 5).

Existential therapists engage in various approaches to work with meaning in therapy, including integrative approaches (Schneider 2008; Wong 2012a, b). Relationships are key to helping clients engage meaning in their lives; including using the therapy relationship as the primary vehicle of change as well as identifying relationships as one of the deepest and most sustaining forms of meaning (Frankl 1959/1984; Hoffman 2009a, b; Schneider and Krug 2009; Yalom 1980). Existential therapists encourage clients to explore and analyze the meaning in their lives, including reflecting upon what guides their decisions, behaviors, and priorities (Frankl 1959/1984; Hirsch 2009; Hoffman 2009a; May 1991; Wong 2012a, b; Yalom 1980). Because of their inherent similarities in reference to meaning, narrative (Richert 2010) and constructivist (Raskin 2008) approaches are frequently integrated with existential therapy.

Research. Research evidence supports the relationship between meaning or purpose in life and psychological well-being (Addad and Himi 2009; Dezutter et al. 2013; Halama 2009; King and Hicks 2012; Maddi et al. 2011; Neimeyer et al. 2006; Scannell et al. 2002; Solomon 2012; Steger 2012; Tavernier and Willoughby 2012). Increasing research demonstrates a link between meaning and physical health (Krause 2012; Roepke et al. 2013; Thompson et al. 2003). Meaning, or purpose in life, has been found to be a protective factor in situations of psychological and physical distress or trauma (Mascaro and Rosen 2006; Stark et al. 2009; Thompson et al. 2003). Given the preponderance of theory and research supporting the importance of meaning for psychological and physical health, this aspect of existential theory is clearly established. The association between meaning and well-being does not answer the question of how therapy helps clients discover, create, or enhance meaning in their lives or whether existential therapy is effective in accomplishing this goal.

Salvatore et al. (2010) conducted a particularly relevant study utilizing a case study model to examine meaning over the course of therapy. Although the identified therapy was constructivist, it was consistent with existential therapy including a relational/intersubjective focus, intentional examination of one's meaning systems, and seeking to change the client's experience as opposed to focusing on symptoms or solely on cognitions. The results demonstrated that the client initially showed a decrease in meaning; however, by the end there was an overall increase. Although this was a single-subject case study and needs further replication, it does show the potential for therapies to increase meaning. The U-shaped process in which meaning may initially decrease could prove important in understanding how meaning changes through therapy. Hoffman (2009c), for example, discusses how existential therapy often involves a process of deconstructing and re-constructing meaning.

Fillion et al. (2009) examined the impact of meaning-centered interventions on job satisfaction and quality of life with palliative care nurses. While there were increases in the perceived meaning of working on a palliative care unit, there were not significant changes in job satisfaction and quality of life. The intervention was brief (4 weeks) and largely psychoeducational. It is not clear that the intervention was able to impact the experiential or lived level that Frankl, Schneider, and others emphasize. Furthermore, the focus was on a very narrow aspect of meaning. Breitbart and colleagues (2010) examined meaning-centered interventions in a group setting with patients with advanced cancer. The results found an increase in spiritual well-being and meaning as well as a decrease in psychological distress. Compared with the Fillion study, Breitbart and colleagues used an 8-week group intervention and focused on less discrete outcome measures.

Holland et al. (2007) reviewed the efficacy of personal construct therapy (PCT), which bears many similarities to existential therapy pertaining to meaning. Although noting they found weaker results than previous reviews, overall their results supported the efficacy of PCT when compared to other forms of therapy or a control group pertaining to increases in meaning as well as more traditional outcome measures, such as depression.

Clinical Expertise/Competency. Meaning, as a factor consistently associated with better psychological well-being, can be integrated into psychological assessment, treatment planning, and developing a cogent rationale for treatment strategies. Examining meaning or purpose in life and working to facilitate its development for clients has a long and established history in the peer-reviewed literature (Bugental 1990; Hoffman 2008; May 1991; Schneider 2012; Spinelli 1997; Yalom 1989, 1999). One competency identified by the APA Presidential Task Force on EBPP (2006) was the evaluation and use of appropriate research. The strong research support for the importance of meaning in psychological well-being demonstrates it is an important factor to consider in psychotherapy. Related to assessment, meaning is an important factor for therapists to assess (Leitner et al. 2000). If clients are struggling in identifying or living in accordance with meaning in life, this may contribute to psychological difficulties. It also can be part of treatment planning and developing a rationale for treatment. Clients generally can readily understand that a lack of meaning contributes to their psychological difficulties.

Individual and Cultural Differences. May's (1991) work on myth, though largely contained to Western myths, provides a foundation for analyzing meaning systems in the context of culture. Expanding upon May, Hoffman (2009b) states: "myths represent the universality of the existential givens and the particularity of cultural responses to those givens" (p. 264). Meaning systems require consideration of cultural and individual aspects of meaning. As an illustration, Hoffman et al. (2009) discuss *myths of self*. The self is conceived of differently in different cultural contexts, yet consistently is connected to the way meaning is understood and experienced. Although no universal agreement on what the self is exists, much of Western psychology is built upon an individualistic conception of the self that does not fit well with all cultures. Hoffman and colleagues argue that different conceptions of the self may be associated with psychological well-being in different cultures. Psychological models must be adaptable to different views of the self.

Conclusion

Existential therapy has a strong evidence-based foundation when considering the principles of EBPP. Yet, EBPP in psychology is about more than the therapy approach, as it also considers the competency of the therapists. It could be maintained that existential therapists competent in the general practice of psychotherapy and existential psychotherapy in particular are practicing consistent with the standards of EBPP. Existential practitioners ought to not feel apologetic or defensive about their approach. While there are places where existential therapy ought to strengthen its evidence-based foundation, there is already in place a solid foundation to existential therapy. Existential therapists need not fear the EBPP movement in psychology as it poses no threat to existential therapy and, in fact, provides a solid support for its practice.

References

Addad, M., & Himi, H. (2009). Logotherapy—theoretical aspects and field studies in Israel. In A. Batthyany & J. Levinson (Eds.), *Existential therapy of meaning: Handbook of logotherapy and existential analysis* (pp. 445–461). Phoenix, AZ: Zeig, Tucker & Theisen.

Alsup, R. (2008). Existentialism of personalism: A Native American perspective. In K. J. Schneider (Ed.), *Existential-integrative psychotherapy: Guideposts to the core of practice* (pp. 121–127). New York, NY: Routledge.

American Psychological Association Presidential Task Force on Evidence-Based Practice. (2006). Evidence-based practice in psychology. *American Psychologist, 61*, 271–285.

Bao, Z. (2009). Zhungzi's view of freedom. In L. Hoffman, M. Yang, F. J. Kaklauskas, & A. Chan (Eds.), *Existential psychology east–west* (pp. 221–231). Colorado Springs, CO: University of the Rockies Press.

Breitbart, W., Rosenfeld, B., Gibson, C., Pessin, H., Poppito, S., Nelson, C., et al. (2010). Meaning-centered group psychotherapy for patients with advanced cancer: A pilot randomized controlled trial. *Psycho-Oncology, 19*, 21–28.

Brown, L. S. (2008). Feminist therapy as a meaning-making practice: Where there is no power, where is the meaning? In K. J. Schneider (Ed.), *Existential-integrative psychotherapy: Guideposts to the core of practice* (pp. 130–140). New York, NY: Routledge.

Bugental, J. F. T. (1978). *Psychotherapy and process: The fundamentals of an existential-humanistic approach*. New York, NY: McGraw-Hill.

Bugental, J. F. T. (1987). *The art of the psychotherapist: How to develop the skills that take psychotherapy beyond science*. New York, NY: Norton & Company.

Bugental, J. F. T. (1990). *Intimate journeys*. San Francisco, CA: Jossey Bass.

Bugental, J. F. T. (1999). *Psychotherapy isn't what you think: Bringing the psychotherapeutic engagement into the living moment*. Phoenix, AZ: Zeig, Tucker, & Co.

Bunting, K., & Hayes, S. C. (2008). Language and meaning: Acceptance and Commitment Therapy and the EI model. In K. J. Schneider (Ed.), *Existential-integrative psychotherapy: Guideposts to the core of practice* (pp. 217–234). New York, NY: Routledge.

Cleare-Hoffman, H. P., Hoffman, L., & Wilson, S. S. (2013). Existential therapy, culture, and therapist factors in evidence-based practice. In K. Keenan (Ed.), *Evidence in support of existential-humanistic psychotherapy: Revitalizing the third force*. Symposium presented at the 121st annual convention of the American Psychological Association, Honolulu, HI.

Comas-Diaz, L. (2008). Latino psychospirituality. In K. J. Schneider (Ed.), *Existential-integrative psychotherapy: Guideposts to the core of practice* (pp. 100–109). New York, NY: Routledge.
Cooper, M. (2003). *Existential therapies*. Thousand Oaks, CA: Sage.
Cozolino, L. (2002). *The neuroscience of psychotherapy*. New York, NY: W.W. Norton & Company.
Dallas, E., Georganda, E. T., Harisiadis, A., & Zymnis-Georgaios, K. (2013). Zhi Mian and "oistios" of life. *Journal of Humanistic Psychology, 53*, 252–260.
Dezutter, J., Casalin, S., Wachholtz, A., Luyckx, K., Hekking, J., & Vandewiele, W. (2013). Meaning in life: An important factor for the psychological well-being of chronically ill patients? *Rehabilitation Psychology, 58*, 334–341.
Dorman, D. (2008). Dante's cure: Schizophrenia and the two-person journey. In K. J. Schneider (Ed.), *Existential-integrative psychotherapy: Guideposts to the core of practice* (pp. 236–245). New York, NY: Routledge.
Duncan, B. L., Miller, S. D., Wampold, B. E., & Hubble, M. A. (Eds.). (2009). *The heart and soul of change: Delivering what works in therapy* (2nd ed.). Washington, DC: American Psychological Association.
Elkins, D. N. (2009). *Humanistic psychology: A clinical manifesto. A critique of clinical psychology and the need for progressive alternatives*. Colorado Springs, CO: University of the Rockies Press.
Fillion, L., Duval, S., Dumont, S., Gagnon, P., Tremblay, I., Bairati, I., & Breitbart, W. S. (2009). Impact of meaning-centered intervention on job satisfaction and on quality of life among palliative care nurses. *Psycho-Oncology, 18*, 1300–1310.
Frankl, V. E. (1984). *Man's search for meaning: An introduction to logotherapy* (3rd ed.). New York, NY: Simon & Schuster. (Original work published in 1959).
Greenberg, L. S., Korman, L. M., & Paivio, S. C. (2001). Emotion in humanistic psychotherapy. In D. J. Cain & J. Seeman (Eds.), *Humanistic psychotherapies: Handbook of research and practice* (pp. 499–530). Washington, DC: American Psychological Association.
Greening, T. (1992). Existential challenges and responses. *The Humanistic Psychologist, 20*(1), 111–115.
Halama, P. (2009). Research instruments for investigating meaning of life and other logotherapeutic constructs. In A. Batthyany & J. Levinson (Eds.), *Existential therapy of meaning: Handbook of logotherapy and existential analysis* (pp. 415–444). Phoenix, AZ: Zeig, Tucker & Theisen.
Hirsch, B. Z. (2009). Logotherapy—the theory—the logotherapist—the client. In A. Batthyany & J. Levinson (Eds.), *Existential therapy of meaning: Handbook of logotherapy and existential analysis* (pp. 39–52). Phoenix, AZ: Zeig, Tucker & Theisen.
Hoffman, L. (2008). An existential approach to working with religious and spiritual clients. In K. Schneider (Ed.), *Existential-integrative psychotherapy: Guideposts to the core of practice* (pp. 187–202). New York, NY: Routledge Press.
Hoffman, L. (2009a). Introduction to existential psychotherapy in a cross-cultural context: An east–west dialogue. In L. Hoffman, M. Yang, F. J. Kaklauskas, & A. Chan (Eds.), *Existential psychology east–west* (pp. 1–67). Colorado Springs, CO: University of the Rockies Press.
Hoffman, L. (2009b). Gordo's ghost: An introduction to existential perspectives on myths. In L. Hoffman, M. Yang, F. J. Kaklauskas, & A. Chan (Eds.), *Existential psychology east–west* (pp. 259–274). Colorado Springs, CO: University of the Rockies Press.
Hoffman, L. (2009c). Knowing and the unknown: An existential epistemology in a postmodern context. *Humana. Mente, 11*, 97–110.
Hoffman, L., & Cleare-Hoffman, H. P. (2011). Existential therapy and emotions: Lessons from cross-cultural exchange. *The Humanistic Psychologist, 39*, 261–267.
Hoffman, L., Cleare-Hoffman, H. P., & Jackson, T. (2014). Humanistic psychology and multiculturalism: History, current status, and advancements. In K. J. Schneider, J. F. Pierson, & J. F. T. Bugental (Eds.), *The handbook of humanistic psychology: Theory, research, and practice* (2nd ed., pp. 41–55). Thousand Oaks, CA: Sage.

Hoffman, L., Dias, J., & Soholm, H. C. (2012). Existential-humanistic therapy as a model for evidence-based practice. In S. Rubin (Ed.), *Evidence in support of existential-humanistic psychology: Revitalizing the 'third force'*. Symposium presented at the 120th annual convention of the American Psychological Association, Orlando, FL.
Hoffman, L., Stewart, S., Warren, D., & Meek, L. (2009). Toward a sustainable myth of self: An existential response to the postmodern condition. *Journal of Humanistic Psychology, 49*, 135–173.
Hoffman, L., Yang, M., Kaklauskas, F. J., & Chan, A. (Eds.). (2009b). *Existential psychology east–west*. Colorado Springs, CO: University of the Rockies Press.
Holland, J. M., Neimeyer, R. A., Currier, J. M., & Berman, J. S. (2007). The efficacy of personal construct therapy: A comprehensive review. *Journal of Clinical Psychology, 63*, 93–107.
Kang, S. M., Shaver, P. R., Sue, S., Min, K. H., & Jing, H. (2003). Culture-specific patterns in the prediction of life satisfaction: Roles of emotion, relationship quality, and self-esteem. *Personality and Society Psychology Bulletin, 29*, 1596–1608.
King, L. A., & Hicks, J. A. (2012). Positive affect and meaning in life. In P. T. P. Wong (Ed.), *Meaning: Theories, research, and applications* (2nd ed., Chapter 6, Kindle version). New York, NY: Taylor & Francis.
Krause, N. (2012). Healthy aging. In P. T. P. Wong (Ed.), *Meaning: Theories, research, and applications* (2nd ed., Chapter 19, Kindle version). New York, NY: Taylor & Francis.
Krug, O. (2009). James Bugental and Irvin Yalom: Two masters of existential therapy cultivate presence in the therapeutic encounter. *Journal of Humanistic Psychology, 49*(3), 329–354. doi:10.1177/0022167809334001
Leitner, L. M., Faidley, A. J., & Celentana, M. A. (2000). Diagnosing human meaning making: An experiential constructivist approach. In R. A. Neimeyer & J. D. Raskin (Eds.), *Constructions of disorder: Meaning-making frameworks for psychotherapy* (pp. 175–203). Washington, DC: American Psychological Association.
Maddi, S. R., Khoshaba, D. M., Harvey, R. H., Faxel, M., & Resurreccion, N. (2011). The personality construct of hardiness, V: Relationships with the construction of existential meaning in life. *Journal of Humanistic Psychology, 51*, 369–388.
Mascaro, N., & Rosen, D. H. (2006). The role of existential meaning as a buffer against stress. *Journal of Humanistic Psychology, 46*, 168–190.
May, R. (1991). *The cry for myth*. New York, NY: Delta.
Monheit, J. (2008). A lesbian and gay perspective: The case of Marcia. In K. J. Schneider (Ed.), *Existential-integrative psychotherapy: Guideposts to the core of practice* (pp. 140–146). New York, NY: Routledge.
Neimeyer, R. A., Baldwin, S. A., & Gillies, J. (2006). Continuing bond and reconstructing meaning: Mitigating complications in bereavement. *Death Studies, 20*, 715–738.
Norcross, J. C. (1987). A rational and empirical analysis of existential psychotherapy. *Journal of Humanistic Psychology, 27*(1), 41–68.
Norcross, J. C. (Ed.). (2002). *Psychotherapy relationships that work: Therapist contributions and responsiveness to patients*. New York, NY: Oxford University Press.
Norcross, J. C. (2009). The therapeutic relationship. In B. L. Duncan, S. D. Miller, B. E. Wampold, & M. A. Hubble (Eds.), *The heart and soul of change: Delivering what works in therapy* (2nd ed., pp. 113–141). Washington, DC: American Psychological Association.
Norcross, J. C., Beutler, L. E., & Levant, R. F. (Eds.). (2006). *Evidence-based practices in mental health: Debate and dialogue on the fundamental questions*. Washington, DC: American Psychological Association.
Norcross, J. C., & Lambert, M. J. (2010). Evidence-based therapy relationships. In J. C. Norcross (Ed.), *Evidence-based therapy relationships*. Retrieved from http://www.nrepp.samhsa.gov/Norcross.aspx
Raskin, J. D. (2008). The evolution of constructivism. *Journal of Constructivist Psychology, 21*(1), 1–24.

Rice, D. L. (2008). An African American perspective: The case of Darrin. In K. J. Schneider (Ed.), *Existential-integrative psychotherapy: Guideposts to the core of practice* (pp. 110–121). New York, NY: Routledge.

Richert, A. J. (2010). *Integrating existential and narrative therapy: A theoretical base for eclectic practice*. Pittsburgh, PA: Duquesne University Press.

Roepke, A. M., Jayawickreme, E., & Riffle, O. M. (2013). Meaning and health: A systematic review. *Applied Research in Quality of Life*. Advance online publication. doi:10.1007/s11482-013-9288-9

Rogers, C. (1961). *On becoming a person: A therapist's view of psychotherapy*. Boston, MA: Houghton-Mifflin Company.

Salvatore, S., Gelo, S., Gennaro, A., Manzo, S., & Radaideh, A. A. (2010). Looking at the psychotherapy process as an intersubjective dynamic of meaning-making: A case study with discourse flow analysis. *Journal of Constructivist Psychology, 23*, 195–230.

Scannell, E. D., Allen, F. C. L., & Burton, J. (2002). Meaning in life and positive and negative well-being. *North American Journal of Psychology, 4*, 93–112.

Schneider, K. J. (Ed.). (2008). *Existential-integrative psychotherapy: Guideposts to the core of practice*. New York, NY: Routledge.

Schneider, K. J. (2012). The case of Allison: An existential-integrative inquiry into death anxiety, groundlessness, and the quest for meaning and awe. In P. R. Shaver & M. Mikulincer (Eds.), *Meaning, mortality, and choice: The social psychology of existential concerns* (pp. 339–352). Washington, DC: American Psychological Association.

Schneider, K. J., & Krug, O. T. (2009). *Existential humanistic therapy*. Washington, DC: American Psychological Association.

Serlin, I. (2008). Women and the midlife crisis: The Anne Sexton complex. In K. J. Schneider (Ed.), *Existential-integrative psychotherapy: Guideposts to the core of practice* (pp. 146–163). New York, NY: Routledge.

Solomon, S. (2012). The social psychology of meaning, mortality, and choice: An integrative perspective on existential concerns. In P. R. Shaver & M. Mikulincer (Eds.), *Meaning, mortality, and choice: The social psychology of existential concerns* (pp. 401–417). Washington, DC: American Psychological Association.

Spinelli, E. (1997). *Tales of un-knowing: Eight stories of existential therapy*. Washington Square, NY: New York University Press.

Stark, P. L., Ulrich, B., & Duffy, M. E. (2009). The meaning of suffering experiences. In A. Batthyany & J. Levinson (Eds.), *Existential therapy of meaning: Handbook of logotherapy and existential analysis* (pp. 487–502). Phoenix, AZ: Zeig, Tucker & Theisen.

Steger, M. F. (2012). Experiencing meaning in life: Optimal functioning at the nexus of well-being, psychopathology, and spirituality. In P. T. P. Wong (Ed.), *Meaning: Theories, research, and applications* (2nd ed., Chapter 8, Kindle version). New York, NY: Taylor & Francis.

Tavernier, R., & Willoughby, T. (2012). Adolescent turning points: The association between meaning-making and psychological well-being. *Developmental Psychology, 48*, 1058–1068.

Thompson, N. J., Coker, J., Krause, J. S., & Henry, E. (2003). Purpose in life as a mediator of adjustment after spinal cord injury. *Rehabilitation Psychology, 48*, 100–108.

van Hees, M. M., Rotter, T., Ellermann, T., & Evers, S. A. (2013). The effectiveness of individual interpersonal psychotherapy as a treatment for major depressive disorder in adult outpatients: A systematic review. *BMC Psychiatry, 1*, 1–10. doi:10.1186/1471-244X-13-22

Vasquez, M. T. (2007). Cultural difference and the therapeutic alliance: An evidence-based analysis. *American Psychologist, 62*, 878–885. doi:10.1037/0003-066X.62.8.878

Vontress, C. E. (1979). Cross-cultural counseling: An existential approach. *Personnel & Guidance Journal, 58*(2), 117–122.

Walsh, R. A., & McElwain, B. (2001). Existential psychotherapies. In D. J. Cain & J. Seeman (Eds.), *Humanistic psychotherapies: Handbook of research and practice* (pp. 253–278). Washington, DC: American Psychological Association.

Wampold, B. E. (2015). *The great psychotherapy debate: The evidence for what makes psychotherapy work* (2nd ed.). New York, NY: Routledge.

Wampold, B. E. (2008). Existential-integrative psychotherapy: Coming of age. *Psyccritiques, 53* (6), doi:10.1037/a0011070

Wampold, B. E. (2009a). Research evidence for the common factors models: A historically situated perspective. In B. L. Duncan, S. D. Miller, B. E. Wampold, & M. A. Hubble (Eds.), *The heart and soul of change: Delivering what works in therapy* (2nd ed., pp. 49–81). Washington, DC: American Psychological Association.

Wampold, B. (2009b). How psychotherapy works. Retrieved from http://www.apa.org/news/press/releases/2009/12/wampold.aspx

Wampold, B. E., Goodheart, C. D., & Levant, R. F. (2007). Clarification and elaboration on evidence-based practice in psychology. *American Psychologist, 62*, 616–618.

Wang, X. (2011). Zhi mian and existential psychology. *The Humanistic Psychologist, 39*, 240–246.

Watson, J. C., Greenberg, L. S., & Lietaer, G. (2010). Relating process to outcome in person-centered and experiential psychotherapies: The role of the relationship conditions and clients' experiencing. In M. Cooper, J. C. Watson, & D. Holldampf (Eds.), *Person-centered and experiential therapies work: A review of the research on counseling, psychotherapy and related practices* (pp. 132–163). Ross-on-Wye, UK: PCCS Books.

Whelton, W. J. (2004). Emotional processes in psychotherapy: Evidence across therapeutic modalities. *Clinical Psychology and Psychotherapy, 11*, 58–71.

Wolfe, B. E. (2008). Existential issues in anxiety disorders and their treatment. In K. J. Schneider (Ed.), *Existential-integrative psychotherapy: Guideposts to the core of practice* (pp. 204–216). New York, NY: Routledge.

Wong, P. T. P. (2012a). Toward a dual-systems model of what makes life worth living. In P. T. P. Wong (Ed.), *Meaning: Theories, research, and applications* (2nd ed., Chapter 1, Kindle version). New York, NY: Taylor & Francis.

Wong, P. T. P. (2012b). From logotherapy to meaning-centered counseling and therapy. In P. T. P. Wong (Ed.), *Meaning: Theories, research, and applications* (2nd ed., Chapter 28, Kindle version). New York, NY: Taylor & Francis.

Yalom, I. D. (1980). *Existential psychotherapy*. New York, NY: Basic Books.

Yalom, I. D. (1989). *Love's executioner and other tales of psychotherapy*. New York, NY: Harper Perennial.

Yalom, I. D. (1999). *Momma and the meaning of life: Tales of psychotherapy*. New York, NY: Perennial.

The Case for Existential (Spiritual) Psychotherapy

Kirk J. Schneider

Many, if not most of our troubles as human beings are traceable to one overriding problem: our suspension in the groundlessness of existence. This is the conclusion of a long line of existential-spiritual thinkers, from Tillich (1952) to Becker (1973), and Buber (1965) to Laing (1969)—(see also Schneider 2013; Stolorow 2011 for elaborations).

When a loved one dies, or we are attacked, or we fall ill, it often feels like the bottom has dropped out—and there is nothing left to hold us up. Like the astronaut who's cut from his tether, or the tight rope walker who slips, we suddenly come face to face, not just with our particular difficulty, but with the difficulty of existence itself.

This "difficulty" is eloquently portrayed in the opening credits of the award-winning US television series *Mad Men*. In that signature scene, a male character is depicted in a free fall. We know very little about this character except that he is successful—and almost totally bereft of his moorings.

Trauma is a lot like this free fall—it makes us aware of what most of us, most of the day, contrive to deny—that we're all in suspense. Right now, for example, you're probably in a comfortable chair that rests on a floor in a building that feels solidly anchored to the ground, but this is not at all the complete picture. What is more fully taking place is that you're in a comfortable chair in a building that rests

ORIGINAL PAPER. Published online: 26 August 2014 © Springer Science+Business Media New York 2014.

K.J. Schneider (✉)
Saybrook University, Oakland, CA, USA
e-mail: kschneider56@gmail.com

K.J. Schneider
Columbia University, New York, NY, USA

K.J. Schneider
Existential-Humanistic Institute, San Francisco, CA, USA

S.E. Schulenberg (ed.), *Clarifying and Furthering Existential Psychotherapy*,
DOI 10.1007/978-3-319-31086-2_4

on a gigantic ball that is whirling around the sun at 67,000 miles per hour. This ball, moreover, is situated in a galaxy that's hurtling through space–time at 1.2 million miles an hour, to a destination that is completely unknown. And as if that is not enough, you don't really know where you came from to get to this chair and building. Although you may retort that you made a thousand arrangements to arrive at this particular place and time, and that you can trace them all back to your past, this does not really clarify much; nor does the ostensibly established presumption that well before you arranged anything you were the "happy" product of a stray sperm and a receptive egg. The fact is that so much of what we take for granted, even today, is a culturally sanctioned artifact—a stop-gap—set against a sea of bewilderment.

Now trauma, which literally means shock, has a way of stripping bare this culturally sanctioned frame. It has a way of rupturing our culturally agreed upon security systems—for example, our bodies, our jobs, and our identities—and exposing us to our foundationless depths. And what happens when we come face to face with these depths? Depending on our own traumatic histories, this encounter tends to jar us in either of two directions—toward expansive grandiosity to overcompensate for the fragility we feel, or toward constrictive withdrawal to overcompensate for the unsustainability of grandiose expansion. Yet either way we are imprisoned by these extremes, and both sabotage our growth (Schneider 1999, 2008, 2013).

The idea here then is not so much to "get rid of" a condition that's inherently human but to help people to develop a new relationship to that condition. Helping people develop a new relationship to a shocking part of themselves is not easy, but this is precisely what existential oriented therapy attempts to promote. It attempts to help people face and gradually realign themselves with the groundlessness of their existence. What does such realignment look like? It looks like an improved ability to experience choice within that groundlessness—an experiential "home," and to engage one's capacity to respond to rather than simply react against its ferocity. Finally, the realignment can also sometimes manifest as "awe"—the humility and wonder, or sense of adventure, toward all living things (Schneider 2004, 2008).

The chief and ongoing question of an existentially oriented therapy is "How is one willing to live, in this remarkable moment, with this exceptional opportunity to encounter one's pain?" As my client Janice[1] sat across from me one Friday afternoon, I tried my best to appreciate the struggle she experienced, and the awkwardness with which she attempted to convey it. It was the first time Janice and I met and from the moment we shook hands, I could sense a cloud over her demeanor.

Janice was a 45-year-old White, working-class female with a history of severe emotional and sexual abuse. Her father was an inveterate alcoholic with an explosive temper, and her grandfather sexually molested her when she was eight years old. When Janice was four, she would be regularly left alone with a

[1]The case of Janice is a composite drawn from my practice combined with elements of my work with a client in the APA video series *Existential-Humanistic Therapy Over Time* (Schneider 2009), and not reflective of any individual client.

"schizophrenic" aunt. These visits terrified Janice, but apparently, there was no parental recognition of this sentiment. When Janice was five, her mother suddenly died. This left Janice with her volatile alcoholic father, her rapacious grandfather, and her psychotic aunt. How Janice even partially emerged from these circumstances is still a mystery to me, but somehow she managed.

As Janice and I greeted each other, I was struck by her composure, and bright, articulate style. Janice told me that although she had brief brushes with therapy in her past, she did "tons" of work on her own. I emphatically believed that. Although Janice ostensibly came to therapy because of her lack of assertiveness with men, I sensed—and in her tacit way, she conveyed—that the assertiveness issue was not her ultimate concern.

In keeping with my "existential-integrative" style (Schneider 2008), I first worked with Janice to help her build confidence when she confronted men. I invited her to engage in role plays with me where I would stand in for the menacing fellow, e.g., her boss or husband, and she would play herself in a particular dilemma. I also worked with Janice to cognitively restructure her thinking about how these men perceived her (e.g., see Beck 1979). Would she really be seen as a "bitch" if she clarified her needs to them, I would ask. And even if she was seen that way, would that make her one? As we deepened and rehearsed these scenarios, Janice was gradually able to develop new skills that would help her confront and successfully assert herself with the aforementioned men.

At the same time as she worked with these cognitive and behavioral restructuring skills, however, something else began to happen to Janice: she began to acknowledge, and I encouraged her to stay present to, fears that went beyond feeling intimidated by men. These fears related to a sense of being intimidated by life.

In this context, she began to share powerful dreams with me, like a dream she had recently of feeling like a burned out tree; and another about a monster attacking her home. In time I took the risk to invite Janice, not just to "talk about" such dreams and fantasies, but to experience them here and now with me (see Krug 2009). I invited her, in other words, to become more present to how she felt, sensed, and pictured these dreams and fantasies. I also invited her to share her responses about what it was like to interact with me, and to experience the difficult sides of herself, like shame or weakness, in my presence. This brought the work alive between me and Janice and significantly deepened our bond. It also enabled Janice to plumb depths only hinted at during our cognitive restructuring exercises. Finally, it moved Janice to realize how her suffering stemmed not just from her relationships with men (and sometimes women), but also from her relationship with life's uncertainties, and from the need for courage in the face of them.

In this vein, Janice began to allude to a whole new language in our work together; this was a language that emphasized her concerns about existence, not just specific aspects of existence. For example, she started speaking about "unnamable fears" and a part of herself that felt like a "black hole." She told me she had never acknowledged these feelings with anyone before, but that she had often glimpsed them, especially when stressed. She also began talking about wonderments that she had rarely ever disclosed—such as her fascination with the occult and her resonance with ancient Mayan culture. When I shared my puzzlement about these identifications, given her background, she quipped: "They are freeing, and in tune with the natural world."

In my experience, these ranges of resonance are not all that extraordinary in depth existential therapy. As people feel safer to explore, they begin to unveil the parts of themselves that both torment, and potentially, set them free. These parts are not necessarily Freudian in nature. They don't necessarily evoke sexual or aggressive conflict or frustrated parental attachments, but they do in my experience stir very primordial undercurrents, some of which pertain directly to sexual, aggressive, or attachment conflicts. To put it succinctly: these undercurrents strike me and others who witness them as emphatically existential in nature—pertaining not just to turbulent sexual-aggressive drives or attachments to parental figures, but fears and desires toward the uncontrollability of existence itself. For example, behind the fear (and sometimes attraction) of aggression can be an even deeper anxiety about imminent disarray, uncontrollability, and ultimately chaos. Or beneath the terror of parental devaluation can be the thornier challenge of one's significance in existence (e.g., see also Binswanger 1958; Laing 1969).

These were precisely the mooring points I faced with Janice on a fateful afternoon some 6 months following our initial meeting. Janice was on the brink of a breakthrough, and we both knew it. On the other hand, she also grappled with great fears and the need to come to terms with those fears. On this basis, I invited Janice to simply close her eyes and become aware of her breathing. As she seemed ready, I then invited her to become aware of any tension areas she experienced in her body—any areas that felt tight or blocked, and that she was willing to describe. She began by identifying a tension in her neck area, which loosened as she stayed present to it. Then she began perceiving an image of a tiny little girl trapped in a well. She couldn't identify where this well was, or how it got there, but she was clear that it felt fathomless with no end in sight. As I continued to invite her to stay present to this well, she began to feel the girl's terror. "It's like she's sinking," Janice told me, "and she doesn't know where she's going." Gently I supported her to continue with the experience, while at the same time reassuring her that if she needed to stop, she could do so at any time. She chose to proceed.

At about halfway into our session, Janice noticed that the little girl was fading, while the darkness around her grew. At times, the little girl struggled to unfold herself and peek out of the darkness, but invariably she sank back in. To this point Janice said very little about her relationship to the little girl, but as she "stayed with" her, her sense of connection grew. Suddenly, Janice panicked. She could no longer find the little girl!

Yet at that very same moment, tears welled up in Janice's eyes. I asked her what brought on the tears and after a long silence she whispered: "I reached out into the dark to touch her, and she reached out into the dark to touch me."

With this simple yet profound image, Janice began a remarkable self-transformation. She moved from a position of abject terror to one of wonder to one of love. Through embracing the little girl, Janice at the same time embraced the void in which the little girl (as well as adult Janice) had languished for many years; and now she found solace there, and an awe-inspired renewal.

I won't say that this moment completely changed Janice's life, but it went a long way toward freeing her and relieving her panic. Although the specifics of Janice's life—for example, her long-time employment and her involvement with her family —essentially remained the same, what she brought to those specifics altered dramatically. She now had an expanded capacity to feel, for example, particularly when she encountered children, a deepened experience of the moment, and a broader appreciation of life's possibilities. In the end, Janice learned much more than assertiveness skills, or an ability to think more "rationally." She discovered how to be present to her life; and this presence enabled her to more fully experience her life–to experience life's awesome paradoxical range (see Bugental 1987; Geller and Greenberg 2012; May 1983; on the power of presence to deepen life experience; not merely attain isolated goals).

Coda

Psychologists today can talk until they're blue in the face about pat formulas and programmatic treatments. They can cite chemical imbalances in the brain (e.g., Kramer 1997), for example, or the lack of ability to regulate emotions (e.g., Siegal 2007), or the irrationality of conditioned thoughts (e.g., Beck 1979) as the bases for our disorders. However, until psychologists get down to the fundamental problem which fuels all these secondary conditions—our precariousness as creatures (e.g., Becker 1973)—they will be operating at a very restrictive level (see also Wolfe 2016). The work I did with Janice had elements of this very restrictive level—and that was important work to accomplish. However, the question needs to be continually raised, is helping a person to change behavior patterns and recondition thoughts enough? Or do we owe it to that person to make available to him or her a deeper dimension of self-exploration? Do we owe it to that person to enable him or her to discover what really matters about his or her life, wherever that may lead? I believe Janis would answer in the affirmative to that question—as would I, and many others I've known throughout my 35 year clinical career. In a recent review of my book on *Existential-Integrative Psychotherapy*, leading psychotherapy researcher Wampold (2008) offered a bold conjecture. "It could be," he wrote "that an understanding of the principles of existential therapy is needed by all therapists, as it adds a perspective that might… form the basis for all effective treatments" (p. 6). Isn't it time that we took such propositions seriously? Or must we continue to sacrifice depth for expedience in psychotherapy; the transformed life for the alteration of routine?

References

Beck, A. T. (1979). *Cognitive therapy and the emotional disorders*. New York: Meridian.
Becker, E. (1973). *Denial of death*. New York: Free Press.
Binswanger, L. (1958). The case of Ellen West. In R. May, H. Ellenberger & L. Binswanger (Eds.), *Existence: A new dimension in psychiatry and psychology* (pp. 237–364). New York: Basic Books.
Buber, M. (1965). *Between man and man*. New York: Macmillan.
Bugental, J. F. T. (1987). *The art of the psychotherapist*. New York: Norton.
Geller, S. M., & Greenberg, L. S. (2012). *Therapeutic presence: A mindful approach to effective psychotherapy*. Washington, DC: APA Press.
Kramer, P. (1997). *Listening to Prozac*. New York: Penguin.
Krug, O. T. (2009). James Bugental and Irvin Yalom: Two masters of existential therapy cultivate presence in the therapeutic encounter. *Journal of Humanistic Psychology, 49*, 329–354.
Laing, R. D. (1969). *The divided self: An existential study in sanity and madness*. Middlesex: Penguin.
May, R. (1983). *The discovery of being*. New York: Norton.
Schneider, K. J. (1999). *The paradoxical self: Toward an understanding of our contradictory nature* (2nd ed.). Amherst: Humanity Books.
Schneider, K. J. (2004). *Rediscovery of awe: Splendor, mystery, and the fluid center of life*. St. Paul: Paragon House.
Schneider, K. J. (2008). *Existential-integrative psychotherapy: Guideposts to the core of practice*. New York: Routledge.
Schneider, K. J. (2009). *Existential-humanistic therapy over time*. [DVD] American Psychological Association Systems of Psychotherapy Series (Speaker). http://www.apa.org/videos
Schneider, K. J. (2013). *The polarized mind: Why it's killing us and what we can do about it*. Colorado Springs: University Professors Press.
Siegal, D. J. (2007). *The mindful brain*. New York: Norton.
Stolorow, R. D. (2011). *World, affectivity, trauma: Heidegger and post-Cartesian psychoanalysis*. New York: Routledge.
Tillich, P. (1952). *The courage to be*. New Haven: Yale University Press.
Wampold, B. (2008, February 6). *Existential-Integrative psychotherapy comes of age. (Review of the book Existential-integrative psychotherapy: Guideposts to the core of practice). PsycCritiques, 53*, Release 6, Article 1.
Wolfe, B. E. (2016). Existential-humanistic therapy and psychotherapy integration: A commentary. *Journal of Psychotherapy Integration, 26*, 56–60.

Engaged Understanding for Lived Meaning

Todd DuBose

Any cursory review of current affairs will find blatant existential concerns in everyday encounters, concerns that are on the rise. The call is for existential care to address these concerns, but what is "existential care," and more importantly, what does it look like in therapeutic situations? Existential practices of therapeutic care are numerous: daseinsanalysis, integrative humanistic-existential, the British school, the new school, the new existentialists, logotherapy, existential-phenomenology, and a myriad of other hybrid practices such as existential psychoanalysis, just to name a few options (Barnett and Madison 2012; Burston and Frie 2006; Cohn 1997; Cooper 2003; Halling 2008; Laing 1967; Spinelli 2006).

The challenge for any one of us lies in how to clarify what we do in therapeutic care for those not familiar with this way of caring, though intuitively seek it, and to better inform practitioners of other orientations who want to dialogue with us. Yet, this paper is not intended to be another explication of the philosophical and historical foundations of this position. Instead, these reflections aim to describe a therapeutic process and atmosphere for change, acceptance, reconfiguration, and/or understanding to take place, where the art of "being-with" is central to its process. The further temptation here is to go into several pages of classifying myself regarding this or that particular existential orientation, the very act of abstract categorization that I try to de-construct in therapeutic care, so I won't; the influences on me should be obvious, for which I owe my lifelong gratitude.

At the very least, though, I will say that my way of practicing therapeutic care arises out of the human science tradition of existential-phenomenological

ORIGINAL PAPER. Published online: 26 August 2014 © Springer Science+Business Media New York 2014.

T. DuBose (✉)
Department of Clinical Psychology, The Chicago School of Professional Psychology, 325 North Wells, Suite 316, Chicago, IL 60654, USA
e-mail: tdubose@thechicagoschool.edu

S.E. Schulenberg (ed.), *Clarifying and Furthering Existential Psychotherapy*,
DOI 10.1007/978-3-319-31086-2_5

psychology, which is also and always hermeneutical, or about the art of understanding through interpretation, and influenced by years of training and work in pastoral care, both of which I integrate into a practice of existential therapy I describe as *engaged understanding for lived meaning*. I hope my explication of this phrase becomes clearer through many, and varied, examples of therapeutic care.

I prefer to present snippets of situations rather than an entire, singular case so as to better guard the confidentiality of the dear souls who have entrusted their care to me. The identifying factors of their names and circumstances have been changed, and any resemblance to those persons whom the reader may know or speculate about is unintentional and accidental.

On a final note about style, I may often use "we" and "our" when discussing how *I* work, a pronoun switching that is intended only as an invitation to and/or recognition of those who share similar values and practices, and not to speak for anyone else. Now, to our project: What, then, is this often used, centrally placed, though exquisitely ambiguous, non-negotiable aspect of our shared human condition, and magnificent, therapeutic art of "being-with?"

Being-with, originally taken from Heidegger's (Heidegger 1962) description of the human condition as a with-world, denotes how any experience or event occurs in relationship—again, a very, very long philosophical discussion that exceeds the bounds of this discussion. Suffice it to say here that being-with is ontological, or what inherently makes us human beings, as we are always and already in relationship, mutually shaping and being shaped by others; there is no non-relational situation. *Who* we are is *how* we are in relationship. If this is our human condition, our shared ontological condition, then it is congruent for our ways of understanding and caring to focus on ontic, or particular, ways of caring as expressions of being-with as well. *Being-with* others in therapeutic care includes *being-for*, *being-alongside*, and *being-otherwise*. These phrases will become clearer below as shown in various examples of how each one is practiced in therapeutic care, including how these ways of being-with are inter-related and simultaneously co-constitute each other. Therefore, regarding *any* presenting concern in therapeutic care, from *any* person, of *any* age or life situation, I will *being-with* him or her in ways that: (1) radically validate *any* way of being-in-the-world as significant, or *being-for* another, while (2) sharing a common, human condition, de-construct-ing abstractions to see meaning as lived in particular situations, and re-context-ualizing thoughts, feelings and actions, which are integrated comportments, in light of the human condition and/or life projects, or *being-alongside* another, while (3) hospitably inviting otherness of many sorts, including what has not been attended to, ontological limits that cannot be surmounted, possibilities overlooked, ways of relating that have yet to be considered, and the irreducible mystery, uncertainty, immeasurability, invisibility that is a part of each and every moment, into an intimate participation of commensality, a dining with otherness, or *being-otherwise* with another.

These steps are simultaneous and imply value stances that are quite different from the more familiar and commonplace practice of care that view persons, illness, health and therapy from what could be called a "deficit-correction" perspective. The deficit-correction model of care aims at treating, curing, fixing, and/or enhancing one's present lived situation, viewing it as "lesser than" what could or should be a "better" way of living. An understanding-collaboration model of care, to which my way of practicing belongs, aims at "walking with" (*therapeia*) another fellow human being through engaged, collaborative understanding of meaning as lived in particular life circumstances and situations. Being-for, being-alongside, and being-otherwise are ways of being-with that create a therapeutic atmosphere of engaged understanding for lived meaning.

Radical Validation, or *Being-for*

Radical validation of *any* way of being-in-the-world is akin to the practice of bracketing, horizontalization, and descriptive clarification inherent in the phenomenological process for the sake of and in honor of the lived meaning disclosed in this process (Spinelli 2005). Bracketing, horizontalization and descriptive clarification are traditionally understood as practices in phenomenology in order to allow a particular experience and its meaning for those going through it to be understood as the experience is intended and lived. Bracketing entails holding at bay our presumptions, biases, prejudices and what everyone else has said about or thinks about the experience being explored so as to experience it more fully. Bracketing does not mean eliminating our assumptions, but not allowing the ways we engage the world and how things matter to us foreclose on alternative understandings. An example would be to not assume that all mourning must be expressed through painful sobbing. Individuals mourn in different ways. Yet, loss is an experience of the human condition and one that we can gain access to simply having lived through loss in our everyday existence, even if the losses experienced are different.

Following the example of mourning to better explicate horizontalization, a child may mourn a lost stuffed animal in a fire as well as a parent or sibling. Being horizontal means not imposing on the child a rank-ordering of what counts as meaningful and what weight should be given to the parent or sibling over the stuffed animal. Losing the stuffed animal, the parent and the sibling are all meaningful, albeit with different significance. Nevertheless, difference does not mean either deficient or exclusive in relation to every other meaning one may hold in any given situation. Our task is to respectfully note any and all meaning lived by those entrusted to our care.

Descriptive clarification, a phrase Spinelli hones for his own theory and practice, is at the core of phenomenological process as a counter alternative to "explanation." Explanation presumes causation and impact of one variable to another, whereas the phenomenological task is to describe an experience that is lived in a way that highlights nuance, clarification of detail and significance, and the unique ways some event is lived out. The very clarification brings to life an event's vibrancy and lived meaning without needing to explain causes or justify any particular way of being in a situation.

Continuing with the example of mourning, descriptive clarification would not focus on why the child is mourning as much as "how" and "that" she is mourning, or the ways in which she is mourning. In clarifying the ways in which she is mourning we may stumble on how she feels responsible for the fire as she was thinking of a campfire scene on vacation with her family the night before the house fire occurred. This "unveiling" of concern would not surface if we merely and generically concluded she "has to" be mourning due to the loss of her family in a fire. Such conclusions beg the questions: How does she experience the loss? In what way is she mourning? How does she understand and live in a world without her family, stuffed animal or home?

Radical validation, therefore, is 'radical' in that it acknowledges the "root" of who a person is, which is his or her lived meaning, through bracketing, horizontalization and descriptive clarification. Soul *is* lived meaning, a living out what matters most to a person in any given moment, which, in turn, is more fully understood in relation to our shared human condition and our larger purposes and projects in life. Soul, or better, soul-ing in the world, is a qualitative experience where any expression, whether a thought, action, feeling, gesture, or embodied movement, is intentional and concerned in significant ways. Even despair and meaninglessness disclose the significance of agonizing absence. The word, 'validation,' does not mean granting value or permission to be; quite the opposite. Validation, as used in this chapter, is the respectful recognition of how one lives in the world as significant, as mattering.

A person, thing, event, action, or feeling having its "say," that is, experiencing its existence in its significance, *is* the validation itself. Our ontic, or particular, ways of being-in-the-world are radically incomparable, even as shared with other ways of being-in-the-world in a common human condition. Being-in-the-world means being-together in a "context of signification" (Hofstader, as cited in Heidegger 1975, p. 334), that is significant in the ways it takes up shared, nonnegotiable ontological givens such as our temporality, spatiality, mooding, co-existence, historicity, bodyhood, and mortality (Boss 1994, pp. 85–126). Erik Craig has noted that an ontological given is "that which is the case in any situation, for everyone, in every moment" (Craig 2012, p. 12).

So, ontological givens are what make up what we call our shared, human condition, whether we are professors in Chicago, welders in Atlanta, soldiers in the Middle East, or a Maasai Chief in Kenya. At the same time, how each of us lives out these shared givens of the human condition are potentially as different as not only persons living them out, but also the divergent situations in which any one person may live out in his or her existence. The ontological is not the "thing in itself" behind an ontic expression; this would slip us back into a familiar dualism. The ontological is experienced through ontic situations, while ontic experiences find their significance through their expression of their ontological givenness.

Any expression, any thought, any feeling, or any action is a confession of what the human condition means to a person and how it is particularly taken up and lived out. The ontological is not "behind" the ontic, and seeing it as such perpetuates the very Cartesian dualism Heidegger sought to resolve. The ontological is "invisible" in itself and only "seen" in ontic comportments of lived meaning in concrete, existential situations (Heidegger 2001, p. 7). Being-for someone is a discernment of what "matters" in what one is saying or doing, that is, the "point" of a person's communication of any form, such as what she needs me to receive and see and be influenced by given her discourse, practices, moodings, and direction in life.

Being given the very space to experience my "am-ness," or that I exist at all, rather than not, as Heidegger posed the inquiry, and exist in my particularity, if not in my peculiarity, *is* lived validation (Heidegger 1962). What is intended by radical validation is to witness what matters to someone for its own sake, without being e-valuative or de-valuative based on rank-ordered, instrumental or commodifying scales of measurement. In other words, *radical validation "sees" what is, as it is, and appreciates whatever "is" for its own sake, without "why" or "for the sake of," or "in order to," and beyond rank-ordered classifications of human worth, such as appropriate or inappropriate, civil or crass, good or evil.*

Radical validation requires that we give up imposing essentialist ways of living on others, or privileging one allegiance of values as either better or worse than any others. This stance is highly influenced by a Nietzschean transvaluation of all values, most particularly discussed in *The Antichrist*, which deconstructs *all* rank-ordered scales of e- and de-valuation of ways of being-in-the-world, including Nietzsche's own hierarchy of nobility over weakness (Nietzsche 1982). The transvaluation of values dismantles any and all criteria used to impose one valued way of living over others. If we were to say, "Caring for others is 'right,'" this is itself yet another valuation that presumed a scale of measurement of right or wrong. The transvaluation of this scale of measurement challenges that anyone can decide for all others what is right or wrong, good or bad, appropriate or inappropriate—attempts to do so are merely privileges of certain values over others and not an objective seeing of ontological values established for all persons at all times.

This is not to say that we do not privilege values. Nietzsche himself privileged the noble hero over the weak coward, thus deconstructing his own proposal to transvalue. What the transvaluation of all values does suggest is that my or your privileging cannot be imposed on everyone else, but, alas, here is another privileged value to transvalue. A final aspect of the transvaluation of all values is to keep in mind the situatedness of knowledge and truth: what is true depends on context, situation and circumstance. As these situations are relative, so are truths as values.

Transvaluation of values as it relates to radical validation is a way of being-for another that values what "is" simply for its "is-ness," that values and beholds being *qua* being as a part of Being, instead of assigning rank-ordered usefulness or exchangeability. Perhaps one of our deepest needs is to matter to someone else, simply as we are, and, if so, feel truly understood. Of course, given our different pre-understandings of phenomena, we don't experience things in the raw, but only out of how we allow things to matter to us. Hence, part of what "is" as it is, is taken up and co-constituted by those in the encounter or event. Each relational "is-ness" is itself radically incomparable, even among differences in the sharing. *Different* ways of living, though, are not *deficient* or *efficient* ways of living, just *different allegiances and privileges of lived values*, even if they clash with other lived values.

Someone who chooses to eat delicious, artery clogging food is not "less than" someone who eats salads and smoothies. Choosing a lifestyle of eating fattening country cooking may indeed shorten one's life, but owning such a life, through informed consent, that one will take a shorter life of eating smothered fried chicken and pecan pie over a longer life of eating salads does not make one set of lived values better or worse than another. One choice values particular culinary tastes over the other's value of healthy arteries. They are differently lived values, sometimes not mutually exclusive, both with gains and losses.

No doubt any way of being-in-the-world *is* a stance of chosen values and allegiances, as is any stance a therapist takes in relationship to such stances. Yet, again, *there is no objective place from which to essentially judge one way of being-in-the-world as better than another one without enforcing one's values as essentialist on others in hegemonic ways.* It no longer follows, then, that we can regard any way of being-in-the-world as ill or healthy, crazy or sane, dangerous or safe, healthy or ill, *in itself*—such categories are secondary demarcations established by collectives servicing imposed standards and desired, essentialist outcomes. The therapeutic hour, however, can offer a different transvalued valuation. We are equipped to do so when heeding the wisdom of the ancient Roman playwright Terrence: "I am human, nothing human is alien to me."

Without the space to have one's soul-as-lived-meaning heard, or for one's tears, fists, laughter, addiction, fear, conviction, violence, love, or apathy to show their respective lived meanings, we will by default negate the expressions of soul-as-lived-meaning, and thus engage, perhaps unwittingly, in soul murder. Whenever we ignore, negate, belittle, demean or dismiss lived meaning we are committing soul-icide.

The meaning that is validated is neither made, lost, nor found, but *lived.* Meaning is lived each moment, with each particular moment standing on its own in its significance as well as living out an aspect of the person's larger project(s) in life. If we want to know what matters to a person, then look at how one is living one's life in any given moment. Each step we take serves a significant "about" or "toward" project that is a response to some calling or purpose in life, no matter how insignificant any momentary comportment may seem to others. Our task here is to allow ourselves to reach a place of understanding for *any* way of being-in-the-world as "making sense," and not in a way that suggests only that we see how someone else sees it, but in a way that communicates: as one human being sharing a human condition with another, I can see how this path was chosen and for what kinds of meaningful values. The human condition provides the basis of coming to this place with another person, which in turn provides the possibilities of understanding, empathy, compassion, forgiveness and love.

What helps facilitate one's being-for through radical validation, particularly with more disturbing, lived values, is the vital importance of starting and ending with our shared, ontological condition as human beings, and not as an abstract anthropological science, but as how meaning is bodied forth in our vulnerable yet resilient ways, and how it touches us. We cannot "be-for" someone without being free in the sense Heidegger meant when he wrote that "freedom is to be free and open for being-claimed by something" (Heidegger 2001, p. 217). Whatever someone does, even if destructive, is a response to a difficulty with the human condition, a condition we share with the very one we hate, love, fear, or admire. Entry into the lived experience of being-for begins with allowing ourselves to notice how we are claimed by those for whom we care.

Being-for as a *lived* phenomenon, rather than as just a nice idea or moral prescription, comes through the moving experiences of seeing the tenderness in the moist eyes of a hardened face, the bowed head in shame, or red ears of embarrassment, or when recognizing the worry and concern that is attempted to be overcome by the highbrow or the meek voice, or to see how pain is literally carried in the slouched posture or limp, or how important being appreciated comes in the excessive cologne, comic performance, or through sweet eyes of trepidation that wonder about adequacy in another's eyes. It means to see the determination in the furrowed brow of the bullied one, or clenched teeth in chronic pain, the surrender of resignation in blank eyes, or the aspirated voice in love. These manifestations are confessions of what it means to exist in particularly meaningful ways within our throwness. Being-for through radical validation heeds the profundity of nuance, when no one else notices or cares and knowing that the existential vulnerability of the other is shared by us as well.

Being-for through being-horizontal in practice means not dismissing what is manifest as less than what is latent, or what is surface as less profound than what is deep, or what is external as less important than what is internal. Reducing what shows itself as *merely* a condensation, or hidden symbolization, or *epi*phenomenon, or *nothing but* neurological discharge or historical causes or *just* the expected outcomes of socio-politio-economic forces, is disrespectful of the integrity of a phenomenon's showing here and now. This hermeneutic of suspicion breeds mistrust and is a practice of being-suspicious rather than being-for. If we view a phenomenon as hiding its full disclosure, being distrustful of it, or worse, suggesting it is lying, does not help its trust of us.

Angie, a four-year old, lost her stuffed alligator, Herman, and mourned him. From this perspective as practiced, the alligator does not mean the desire to master the father's oral tendencies, or a projection of her own disowned aggression, or merely neurological discharge of cortisol misnamed as grief, or an inability to supersede an animated, anthropomorphized composite of cotton, cloth, and button eyes, or an obvious distraction from the horrors of social violence going on outside her window in a dangerous neighborhood. All of these framings dismiss the integrity of this event for *her*, that she finds herself (*befindlichkeit*) in a world having lost her friend. Reminding Angie that there are other stuffed animals available to her, or advising her to stop being melodramatic about it, or that Herman isn't real, are comments that are not horizontally attuned to the matterings of Angie's existential situation, and hence, are not being-for her in radically validating ways. Moreover, these comments impose privileged essentialisms and norms on Angie that she does not share, or at least does not own by choice.

It may be uncomfortable for us to bear witness to the tears of a little girl, or, on the contrary, find it difficult to take her suffering seriously given other kinds of suffering around the world, but being-for through radical validation means staying with her in disciplined vigilance regarding her lived meaning on the level of significance she ascribes to it. Our being-with her as being-for her means engaging her as if nothing else in the world mattered at that moment.

All that "is" regarding a person as being-in-the-world shows itself in the decisive instant (Kierkegaard 1846/1941): one's past that brought him there, one's hopes or dreads of a chosen or desired future, how meaning works for him, the limitations and possibilities couching his deliberations, who he is, others are, and how life functions, which values are privileged, how he understands agency, what is lost and gained, all the persons and events that have shaped him and how he is living their influences out in his projects—all show up in the decisive instant. Significance is not first thought of and then only subsequently applied in action. Action *is* lived meaning. Meaning is not a philosophy of life that seeks pragmatic ways to be implemented.

A stance of radical validation also suggests very different approaches to pathology and change. Affirming each and every moment of our lives as meaningful is different from a deficit-correction model of pathology and change where symptoms are things to be jettisoned as contaminants or troubles toward an a/symptomatic existence. Symptoms, viewed from an understanding/collaborative model, however, are not "sins" from which to be washed clean, but disclosures of soul to be deeply understood–though *not* respected and deeply understood *in order to* fix, correct, or eliminate them. Eliminating our symptoms eliminates *us*; symptoms are not "things we have," but ways we *are*.

Although we may self-congratulate for not categorizing or classifying others with diagnostic labels proper, *anytime we privilege where one should be as "better than" where one is or has been we are nonetheless pathologizing*; we are rank ordering the goal of "should-ness" over the "is-ness" of someone's life. As long as we continue doing this, then de-stigmatization is impossible. Existential therapists are not immune to this challenge: we privilege freedom over constriction, authenticity over inauthenticity (mistaking what both mean), responsibility and accountability over irresponsibility and unaccountability, and growth over stagnation. Being-with as being-for also means doing so when those we care for do not want to grow, prefer to stay closed, constricted and/or irresponsible, without being pathologized. There are meanings in these comportments as well, and, again, not as pathologies that we secretly want to be corrected for more proper living. Nietzsche's eternal return and its emphasis on *amor fati*, is helpful here: to embrace what is ugly until there is no more demarcation of beautiful or ugly (Nietzsche 1967, p. 714).

Take, for instance, Janelle, a five-year-old girl whom I saw in therapeutic care for being kicked out of kindergarten for disrupting class and whose father was dying of kidney failure. After reprimands from her teacher and worries for her father, she took control by being selectively mute. She moved from her selective mutism, though, with the help of my puppet, Orville, an alligator who thinks he is a dragon but has trouble owning his facticity that he can't fly, but who also has extraordinary skills to be-with as being-for children in pain. At the end of one session in which she and Orville were finishing a reverie of broad and colorful markings on a large paper tablet, she quietly commented, "In here, I don't get in trouble."

Being-for someone mitigates against seeing someone as "compromised." We all have thrown limits by which we process experiences and live in the world, but norming one way of being-in-the-world as better than others ignores the radical incomparability of anyone's way in the world—particularly when assessing and assigning human worth. Alyssa, a 29-year-old artist and song-writer who has suffered from Trigeminal Neuralgia since she was 14, quaked when meeting me out of fear that I would dismiss her pain as nothing but anxiety driven or was merely "all in her head."

Trigeminal Neuralgia, a painful neurological disorder usually located in the facial nerves (i.e., Trigeminal nerve), is known as "the suicide disease" given that it is considered one of the most painful experiences a human being can encounter. Often sufferers contemplate ending their lives rather than chronically endure its brutality.

Alyssa came to me wondering if there were any possibilities of living creatively within these cruel limitations, as well as to explore the ways she waits longer than necessary to stay ahead of the pain when administering Morphine so as not to be stigmatized, and, finally, to understand how she pushes herself beyond her limits if feeling creative and social, and subsequently contributing to the potential of another "episode." A common trope for her is "23 min," 23 min of hell: the time it takes for the Morphine to start working after administering it at the start of the unpredictable attacks. 23 min is the only certainty she has during a maelstrom of variable intensity with the pain.

I did not pathologize her concerns as "projections," but, instead, validated both horns of her dilemma by seeing the profundity of her lived dys-ability given her particular kind of throwness in the world, while affirming the gifts that are a part of who she is in the world when granted the space of brief respites from the pain. Whether she used Morphine or not I would be there to walk with her through how to take up the ontological throwness with which she was faced, and, likewise, what I had to face in regards to my helplessness in caring for her, without viewing her as broken, directing how she should live, nor minimizing the pain or what is necessary to manage it. She is now finding a gradual decrease in Morphine use, is connecting with friends more, and for the first time in a long time bought a dress so as to "feel pretty" out on a date with her husband.

Rather than framing ways of being-in-the-world as compromised *or* competent, which are categories of a deficit-correction model of care, being-for views any way of being-in-the-world in its own right and by its own criteria. Any way of being-in-the-world is, admittedly, in context with other ways of being-in-the-world as we are inescapably relational beings. This brings us to the next discussion of being-alongside, or the process of sharing, de-construct-ing and re-context-ualizing ways of being-in-the-world.

Sharing, De-Construction, and Re-Contextualization, or *Being-Alongside*

Being-alongside, as used in this chapter and in a somewhat different way than Heidegger used it as a description of being "absorbed" or "concerned" in the world, though concernment as disclosing how things matter to someone in situations is, of course, what we are trying to understand (Heidegger 1962, pp. 80–81). Being-alongside, as used here means acknowledging and embracing a shared human condition that is nonetheless lived out in unique, incomparable ways, and only understood in context. Being-alongside deconstructs abstractions so as to see how meaning is lived in concrete situations, and recontextualizes isolated thoughts, feelings or behaviors as expressions of how the ontological givens are taken up and serve larger life projects.

Being-alongside as sharing is a radically egalitarian view of the therapeutic process. As differentiated from symptom or problem-centered, or person-centered, or even relationship-centered, this way of caring is *human condition-centered.* This phrase means that whatever suffering or joy we experience comes off of, and points to, a shared, ontological reality of human existence. Being-alongside does not mean analyzing and "treating" (i.e., correcting, fixing) the compromised person-as-object "over there" by the detached and healed expert, "over here." The task is to explore together and through our "meetings" how to tackle life dilemmas. Life dilemmas are not problems to be solved, as Ernesto Spinelli reminds us, but lived (Spinelli 2001, pp. 9–10).

Lived engagements are understood by de-construct-ing abstractions (e.g., "I am doing ok"), diagnostic categorizations (e.g., "Clearly this is depression"), and classifications ("He's an attorney"), while re-contextualizing meaning as lived to find its fit, or niche, within a shared web of meaning: "If I were to see you being ok, what would I see?" "Would you consider our interaction ok in the same way?" "When you are being depressed, or depressing in the world, what is happening?" "How is he an attorney in that situation and how does that sit with you?" Our movement is toward contextualized uniqueness. For instance, when referrals and presenting problems come my way I have many questions to ask: Who is referring and for what reasons? What is problematic and for whom, and in which situations? If someone comes in who "has depression," I try to discern through how she engages me what is presumed about therapy, who I am as a therapist and how she views suffering and care, while deconstructing 'depression' in such a way that I can see it lived.

"Depression" is an abstraction; we can't see it. As Kierkegaard pointed out, existence is "something particular, [as] the abstract does not exist at all" (Kierkegaard 1846/1941, p. 295). What we *can* see is someone weeping intermittently for no apparent reason, sleeping either too much or too little, eating too much or too little, with no interest in much of anything but lying fallow. Even then, we can't visually "see" the meanings disclosed in these comportments; they make sense in relation to larger, lived projects, shared webs of meaning, and in how ontological givens are addressed.

Exploring Angie's sleepless night in which she stays up writing a song calls for discernment of whether doing so is something she enjoys or feels obligated to do, whether she can't go to sleep or doesn't want to go to sleep, as well as which projects this particular song writing on this particular night serves for her and for those in relation to her, all in relation to the ontological givenness of a bodying forth in the world that has limits of how much she can function without sleep.

Approaching care in this way calls for us to release what she *should* do according to numerous eagerly offered norms of ways to live, such as promoting good sleep hygiene, and take her way of being-sleepless-in-the-world seriously and with deep respect. More often than not exploring her lived meaning this way will allow her to go to sleep, but going to sleep is not our aim. Our aim is being-with her in engaged understanding of her project of staying awake. She is not going to sleep because she is called for one meaningful reason or another to stay awake. Agency is always and already active, even in unacknowledged ways, and is always and already "about" or "toward" some purpose or intention.

As Heidegger noted, "…we understand ourselves and our existence by way of the activities we pursue and the things we take care of" (Heidegger 1975, p. 159). How we understand someone is disclosed in how we care for them. Asking question after question about whether someone is using heroine again communicates my lack of trust. When we pontificate to others about "how life is," we are communicating that we think they are naïve and myopic as well as that what we are offering is needed and true. When we sit quietly and reverently with someone crying through a terrible loss, we are communicating that they can make it through this pain without us rescuing them.

Being-alongside is not a prelude to the *real* intervention, or something instrumentally set up to soften the client for more rigorous confrontation. It *is* the intervention itself. Selene survived a week of being held captive and sexually tortured. She noted that she "went a little crazy" by only allowing herself road kill to cook and eat for "being so stupid" in traveling to meet the person who would become her kidnapper and attacker, and with whom she had only internet contact. As she was living, not just cognitively structuring, the hermeneutical context of her existential situation, she saw herself as the cause of her assailant's attacks and undeserving of subsequent, healthy nurturance, pained all the more by her guilt given how her betrayed husband who remained by her, preventing her from poisoning herself with road kill, literally and existentially, from becoming the rot she felt herself to be. During one meeting, I mentioned to her that even if she took all her clothes off and threw herself at her assailant's feet, he still had choices of what to do in response to her, one of which could have been, "Come on now, we are not going to do this, get dressed and let's take this relationship in a different way."

The hermeneutical reframe invited her to be released from one particular past as lived to embrace an alternative one without over-responsibility for being abused. The hermeneutical reframe invites perspective through unfolding the broader contextualization in which someone finds herself. This may include a different view of the matter that punctuates other values differently or how an invitation to review how situations are constructed by those participating in it. Much of what is brought in for a hermeneutical reframe is what is forgotten or unattended to or devalued by the one experiencing an event, something we will explore more when we get to "being-otherwise." What is vital here, though, is that the hermeneutical reframe not suggest the reframed way of viewing matters is "better than" another way, particularly the way the one suffering views a circumstance. It is merely an expanded and alternative way to take in the full contextualization of a person's existential situation, as well as highlight that what "is" cannot be separated from how what "is," is understood.

This realization discloses how there are histories (as well as futures), rather than one fixed past or future, which is why practicing from a grounding in unilinear causality is inadequate; how things are depends on how they matter to us and, hence, are co-constituted. This understanding is not just intellectual gymnastics. I could literally see blood come back into Selene's face, her respiration grow deeper, and tears and smiles occur simultaneously during the hermeneutical reframe; not just her thoughts were altered, but an entire world changed.

Keep in mind, though, that being-alongside, although inviting specificity in lived meaning and context, still, in honor of being-for, respects a person's choice to be vague or ambivalent or generic without pathologizing them, realizing that these comportments are also lived meanings, and if protective, for instance, such protectiveness isn't pathologized as lesser than openness and encounter. But with all ways of being-in-the-world, any chosen pathway occurs in relation to otherness: other people, other contingencies and the otherness of what is uncontrollable and immeasurable. This calls for another way of being-with as being-otherwise.

Hospitable Commensality with Otherness, or *Being-Otherwise*

Hospitable commensality is the ancient tradition of hosting and dining with others, particularly guests and strangers. More specifically, the guests and strangers in our lives as represented by being-otherwise include: being a resolute other with whom to relate (e.g., allowing tears to show the impact of a situation on me); giving voice to the unattended other persons in our lives (e.g., the pain that suiciding or affairs may have for those who love us); reminding us of forgotten ontological givens and/or contingencies in situations (e.g., that time together is limited or that we can't control how others will view us); inviting a way of relating that expands possible ways of being-in-the-world beyond what is familiar and sedimented (e.g., relating differently with a partner in other than sedimented, critical or avoidant ways); and, finally, being-otherwise as a pointing to that which is uncontrollable and invisible and immeasurable in each decisive moment (e.g., recognizing the uncertainty of longevity).

We "dine" with all these otherwise experiences and persons in our lives in respectful, hosting ways, hearing out what they have to say about our existential situations and life projects. What is important to note here is that our task is not to *require* others to "be nice to strangers." Being-otherwise isn't the practice of shaming one's myopia or subtly suggesting that what one wants to do in life should be ignored if someone else doesn't like it. Being-otherwise does, however, remind us all of what hasn't been considered given our perspectival limitations and our deeply lived convictions.

Being otherwise is more than pointing to the otherwise experiences in the lives of those for whom we care, but *being*-otherwise in light of those experiences in the therapeutic relationship itself. We may ask, "What will your children eat if you gamble your salary and lose it all at the horse track?" "If you want to pass the course have you allotted enough time to complete your final paper?" "As good as the carrot cake is, if your goal is to lose two pounds a week how will you compensate at the gym?" We may bring in the otherwise quality of our relationship by saying, "Our time is up," "I see it differently," "I will only be in the office two days a week during the holidays," or "Here is the total balance due." *Being-otherwise will not be received if being-for and being-alongside do not leave the person feeling deeply cared for and non-manipulated.* This is why being-for, being-alongside and being-otherwise are not linear and progressive steps, but are simultaneously lived out, one way of being-with taking precedence in one moment but not without or at the expense of the other ways of being-with. Being-otherwise, if saddled with being-for and being-alongside, should not be heard as prescriptive of living life one way or another, but as an even deeper respect that takes seriously life in its unforeseen detail.

As Heidegger and Buber noted, we cannot meet another in such detail except through our resoluteness (Buber 1971; Heidegger 1962). Without the definitive other meeting us, even if fleeting from moment to moment, we cannot understand ourselves in action regarding how we are with others as congruent with or distinctive from how we think we are with others. Although we are very much imprinted with imposed values that we should keep ourselves out of a person's way in therapeutic care, this stance misunderstands the ontological reality that we are all co-constituted and there is no you without me or me without you in any given situation.

Guided by Cicero's question, "Cui bono?," or "For whose sake?," we are nonetheless always and already engaged and understand ourselves in relationship to one another. What shows itself as it is often does not show itself until engaged. The "clearing," (*Lichtung*), as Heidegger noted, is whatever allows for this unveiling to occur, sometimes it is with silence, sometimes with engagement (Heidegger 1962). It is not as if we know what is there, as this position privileges unknowing as a virtue in itself and not just the privation of knowing. We may mention "shaggy dog" and unwittingly evoke a sad story. Not saying shaggy dog for fear of evoking a sad story presumes the situation at hand as one that only happy stories are allowed and that either the other person cannot handle sadness or that we can't work it out together if it shows up. Being-otherwise as a resolute other may very well entail offering my concerns, frustrations, irritations, delights and other experiences, owning those experiences as mine and not as definitions of who someone else is, and still show validating understanding of the significance as lived by someone else, particularly if living contrary to how we would prefer him or her to live.

Jaylin, who was a member of a well-known gang, had something stolen from him and was considering how he was going to retaliate. We "walked together" and explored what it is like to be robbed and to seek revenge, but I also shared that I was concerned and would be pained if he were caught and had to spend 10 years in a small cell, robbing him of the freedom that he so desired. I was also concerned about whom he was targeting and to protect the other person would warn him if identified. He knew I did not agree with his pending aim toward retaliation, his way of taking up the ontological givenness of uncertainty about what someone could do to you, but he also knew I would not shame or judge how he was *making sense* of his situation or his pending choices. I also told him that I would stay in contact with him if he found himself in prison, as I do with others who have chosen that path; the therapeutic frame is different for two human beings than it is for a doctor and a patient.

Being-otherwise also means being-with those we see in therapy in a way that invites, though does not require, a way of living beyond sedimented, constricted, fixed, or hardened ways of relating with which a client comes into therapy (Spinelli 2007). It is very important here not to subtly nudge clients into being in the world in one way over another with accusing inflections and dancing brows when discussing responsibility and accountability. Besides, we are always and already responsible and accountable, even though we may be responding to and are accounting for other values than expected, including the paradoxical *choice* to displace or blame. Sedimentation and constrictions are valuable in their own right and not as pathologies; here is where being-for helps balance being-otherwise, and vice versa. The new way of relating does not correct the old way. The old way may very well be helpful in other situations. New ways of living can come in actions, attitudes or values (Frankl 1963, 1986), *if chosen*.

Eleazar and Patricia come into counseling after Eleazar had an affair, both finding themselves stuck in a loop of accusation and evasion. She cross examines him to see if she can catch him lying to her again, which invites him to withdraw from such suspicious surveillance. His withdrawal in turn invites further inquiry and suspicion. Both inquiry and withdrawal are self-protective, not pathologies, but could prevent the very closeness they want. Being-otherwise with Eleazar and Patricia means being-with them in ways that neither accuses nor withdraws while inviting them to consider whether their sedimented ways of relating with one another helps them move toward each other in the way they prefer. In doing so, I am being-otherwise in several ways. I model a way of relating beyond accusation and withdrawal in my *own* relationship with each of them and with their co-constituted couplehood. I do this without privileging one way of relating over another, but inviting experimentation of being-otherwise with each other and with me. In this process, Patricia turned to me and said, "I can never be sure he won't have another affair." I simply said, "Yes. That is correct."

Here, being-otherwise brings into awareness the "other" of our ontological condition that highlights what cannot be avoided or controlled, which, in this situation, is the uncertainty of what a partner may decide to do. Nevertheless, encouraging Patricia to reflect on "what if" he had another affair, or didn't, and the options available to her in those situations also invites further reflection on being-otherwise. Balancing being-otherwise with being-for means not to privilege fidelity or infidelity, but clarifying the lived meaning of either choice, including the contingencies, gains and losses that accompany either choice. Being-alongside acknowledges that situations are co-constituted, and thus, blame is moot. Although one cannot make one's partner be a certain way, one is 100 % responsible for their 50 % co-constitution of shared events, even if their participation is in how they want to make sense of what their partner has done to them.

Finally, being-otherwise embraces that which cannot be embraced, comprehended, controlled or coerced. It is striking how many people come to therapy worried they will not be able to handle the uncertainty and unpredictability of life circumstances, or how they don't have the courage to risk or they can't find the strength to trust—all the time doing so each and every moment of their lives. We know on some level that the next moment is not guaranteed. Each time we step out into the world, get in our cars, step onto the commuter train, ride the elevator, walk down the street, or begin a workout, we are not guaranteed that we will arrive safely home that night. Even if we are fortunate enough to find ourselves in worlding situations such that probabilities of safety and nurturance are on our side, certainties are not for any of us. As we have tragically witnessed, not even kindergarten classrooms are immune from unexpected tragedy.

So much is out of our hands that nonetheless impact us, yet we live into them all the time. Take the well-known paradox of someone telling us (in trusting ways) that he or she does not trust anyone. Being-otherwise means to bring to mind what cannot be controlled or predicted or measured or seen, but also to bring to mind how these ever present realities of faithful risking in daily experiences are taken up by us in unique ways. Trying to force someone's love nullifies love, as we know it must be given by choice. This leaves us with the possibility that love may never come or could at any moment be withdrawn, but it could come nonetheless given our lack of coercing it to do so. Although daunting at times, that which is uncontrollable and unpredictable also brings moment to moment possibilities of transcendence. Transcendence is not an escape from our facticity, but the possibility of transformation, that is, to do or see something differently, even if it means seeing and embracing the familiar in a new way, or even newly owning that one does *not* want to do something new. So being-otherwise brings to heart and mind overlooked limitations as well as the surprise of possibilities heretofore unconsidered.

Conclusion

A final word on the evidence-based expectations in relation to this way of caring is in order. I have written elsewhere about my stance on this process (DuBose 2013a, b), so I won't go into detail of that argument. Here, I will note that nothing can be evidence-based given that each moment is inherently and inescapably lived with uncertainty, with evidence showing up only *after* the fact. Even if a plan for the upcoming situation is based on prior situations that have worked, each moment stands alone and still, as Kierkegaard knew, is indeed a risk of faith. Even given the benefit of the doubt that we want to care well, hence the concern for evidence-based foundations that something "works," this still begs the questions of what works, and for whom. Moreover, the evidence sought by evidence-based protocols does not have room in its criteria for that which is invisible, immeasurable, and incomparable, namely, *meaning*, in spite of our being creatures that live meaning, and do so with diverse understandings of "the good life." As Heidegger advised, "One must abandon the belief that only what can be proved is true" (Heidegger 2001, p. 217).

That said, caring through an engaged understanding for lived meaning *is* an evidence-based way of practicing care *if* we reframe what evidence, science, measurement, data, and outcomes mean, back to, not instead of, their genealogical origins. Even as evidence-based protocols are currently and hegemonically determined by experimental research values, meta-analyses over and over again still show that the most important variable in successful therapeutic outcome is the quality of the therapeutic relationship (APA 2006). Interestingly enough, most factors related to successful therapy are not therapy related, but are life circumstances (APA 2006). With these conclusions, the existential stance holds steady. Being-with as *both* an ontological given *and* as a congruent, ontic focus of care based on such givens, is as empirical as it gets, and, hence, the most evidence-based anyone could be. Moreover, it is the most respectful stance given our differences as human beings and thus most sensitive to diversity.

Being-with as *being*-for, *being*-alongside and *being*-otherwise are comportments of *engaged* understanding for lived meaning, which is different from *talking about* lived meaning; this is the difference being what distinguishes *addressing* existential issues from *being* existential with those we care for in therapeutic practice. As an understanding-collaboration model of care it calls us to release our needs for imposed, essentialist framing of ways to be-in-the-world. It can be quite unsettling for us to take an experience, person, or situation as it is in its own way, and do so as resolute stewards of soul-as-lived-meaning. It costs us much: persons can no longer be seen as isolated things to be algorithmically engineered to status quo ways of living by way of calculated and enforced standards of care. In fact, if care is "best" when well matching the uniqueness of one's way of being-in-the-world, then the genericity of the word, "standard," must give way to a relativity of diverse ways of being-in-the-world that are neither better nor worse than each other on rank-ordered scales of measurement, but simply "are," as different. We share an ontologically given human condition which provides any and all events in which we experience each moment together. But we take up these experiences in incomparable ways, and our care—to be "effective"—must be relative to each existential situation, thus in a most authentic way be a stance of lived multicultural sensitivity. Each encounter is an adventure. What a great way to live out a vocation of existential therapeutic care! What a great way to live!

References

American Psychological Association. (2006). Presidential Task Force on Evidence—Based Practice. Evidence-based practice in psychology. *American Psychologist, 61*, 271–285.

Barnett, L., & Madison, G. (Eds.). (2012). *Existential therapy: Legacy, vibrancy and dialogue*. London: Routledge.

Boss, M. (1994). *Existential foundations of medicine and psychology*. Northvale, NJ: Jason Aronson Inc.

Buber, M. (1971). *I and thou*. New York: Touchstone.

Burston, D., & Frie, R. (2006). *Psychotherapy as a human science*. Pittsburgh, PA: Duquesne University Press.

Cohn, H. (1997). *Existential thought and therapeutic practice: An introduction to existential psychotherapy*. London: Sage.

Cooper, M. (2003). *Existential therapies*. London: Sage.

Craig, E. (2012). Existential psychotherapy, discipline and demarche: Remembering essential horizons. In L. Barnett & G. Madison (Eds.), *Existential therapy: Legacy, vibrancy and dialogue* (pp. 7–19). London: Routledge.

DuBose, T. (2013a). Let the Kierkegaardian comedy resume: Faith-phobia and faithful leaping in evidence-based criteria for therapeutic care. *Existential Analysis, 24*(1), 70–81.

DuBose, T. (2013b). Essentialism. In D. Leeming (Ed.), *Encyclopedia of critical psychology*. Norwell, MA: Springer Science and Business Media.

Frankl, V. (1963). *Man's search for meaning: An introduction to logotherapy*. New York: Washington Square Press.

Frankl, V. (1986). *The doctor and the soul: From psychotherapy to logotherapy* (2nd ed.). New York: Vintage.

Halling, S. (2008). *Intimacy, transcendence, and psychology: Closeness and openness in everyday life*. New York: Palgrave Macmillan.

Heidegger, M. (1962). *Being and time* (J. Macquarrie & E. Robinson, Trans.). New York: Harper and Row.

Heidegger, M. (1975). *The basic problems of phenomenology* (A. Hofstader, Trans.). Bloomington: Indiana University Press.

Heidegger, M. (2001). *Zollikon seminars: Protocols-conversations-letters*. Evanston, IL: Northwestern University Press.

Kierkegaard, S. (1846/1941). *Concluding unscientific postscript* (D. Swenson & W. Lowrie, Trans.). Princeton: Princeton University Press.

Laing, R. D. (1967). *The politics of experience and the bird of paradise*. Harmondsworth: Penguin.

Nietzsche, F. (1967). *Basic writings of Nietzsche* (W. Kaufmann, Trans.). New York: Penguin.

Nietzsche, F. (1982). *The portable Nietzsche* (W. Kaufmann, Trans.). New York: Penguin.

Spinelli, E. (2001). *The mirror and the hammer: Challenges to therapeutic orthodoxy*. London: Continuum.

Spinelli, E. (2005). *The interpreted world: An introduction to phenomenological psychology*. London: Sage.

Spinelli, E. (2006). *Demystifying therapy*. London: PCCS Books.

Spinelli, E. (2007). *Practising existential psychotherapy: The relational world*. London: Sage.

Meaning-Centered Psychotherapy: A Socratic Clinical Practice

Efren Martinez Ortiz and Ivonne Andrea Flórez

Introduction

Meaning-centered psychotherapy, or logotherapy, is a theory of psychotherapy based on Viktor Frankl's theory of meaning and psychopathology (Frankl 1992). It focuses on the clinical problems of individuals, but also has a special emphasis in difficulties associated with meaninglessness, with the ultimate goal of helping individuals discover meaning (Frankl 1992). Research findings in the area of meaning have systematically indicated that the absence of meaning is associated with symptoms of psychopathology such as depression, anxiety, substance use, negative affect, general risk factors for suicidal ideation, and symptoms of post-traumatic stress disorder (PTSD) after a traumatic experience (Martínez et al. 2013). In addition, studies on the importance of meaning have established meaning in life as a factor related to general well-being, life satisfaction, and positive personal resources such as resilience, self-esteem, and positive affect (Debats 1996; DeWitz et al. 2009; Drescher et al. 2012; Halama 2003; Schulenberg et al. 2008; Steger et al. 2008; Zika and Chamberlain 1992).

During the last two decades Meaning-centered therapy has had important developments that have consolidated a strong framework of knowledge capable of meeting the needs of today's clinicians (Martínez et al. 2013). Presently, several

ORIGINAL PAPER. Published online: 26 August 2014 © Springer Science+Business Media New York 2014.

E.M. Ortiz (✉)
Society for the Advancement of Meaning-Centered Psychotherapy,
Cra. 14a #101–11 Oficina 403, Bogotá, Colombia
e-mail: yortizo@hotmail.com

I.A. Flórez
University of Mississippi, University, MS 38677, USA
e-mail: iaflorez@go.olemiss.edu

S.E. Schulenberg (ed.), *Clarifying and Furthering Existential Psychotherapy*,
DOI 10.1007/978-3-319-31086-2_6

logotherapeutic treatment models have been developed to address a wide range of psychological disorders and symptoms (Henrion 2004; Martínez 2011; Rogina and Quilitch 2006, 2010). For instance, logotherapeutic interventions have been developed for the treatment of depression (Henrion 2004; Ungar 2002), substance use disorders (Crumbaugh et al. 1980; Duque 1998; Henrion 2002; Hutzell 1984; Martínez 2002, 2003; Oscariz 2000; Somov 2007), eating disorders (Lukas 2004), anxiety disorders (Frankl 1992, 1995a; Lukas 1992, 2004; Rogina 2002), and PTSD (Southwick et al. 2006), among others. Specific logotherapeutic approaches for the treatment of narcissistic personality disorder (Martínez 2011; Rogina 2004), borderline personality disorder (Rodríguez 2004), avoidant personality disorder (Martínez 2011), obsessive-compulsive personality disorder (Díaz del Castillo 2011), dependent personality disorder (Martínez 2011; Rogina and Quilitch 2006), and histrionic personality disorder (Frankl 1995b; Lukas 1995, 2004; Martínez 2011) have also been designed. Furthermore, logotherapeutic treatments to enhance psychological adjustment associated with terminal illnesses such as cancer (Breitbart and Heller 2003; Breitbart et al. 2012; Greenstein 2000), disabilities (Julom and de Guzmán 2013), grief (Rogina and Quilitch 2006), and care-giving in rehabilitation and palliative care (Leung et al. 2012) have been shown to be promising interventions in alleviating suffering and helping clients find meaning.

Due to logotherapy's ongoing growth in previous decades, several researchers and clinicians have advocated for a greater visibility of logotherapy in mental health practice (Ameli and Dattilio 2013; Fabry et al. 2007; Schulenberg and Florez 2013; Schulenberg et al. 2008). Schulenberg et al. (2008) indicated the potential contributions of a Meaning-centered psychotherapy for the treatment of mental health problems and elaborated on several practical guidelines to conduct logotherapy (see also Ameli and Dattilio 2013; Benware 2003; Fabry et al. 2007; Schulenberg et al. 2008; Sharp et al. 2004). In their paper, Schulenberg and colleagues summarize Frankl's conceptualization of existential vacuum, mental health, as well as well-known logotherapeutic techniques of clinical practice. In addition, a number of other authors have addressed the potential contribution of logotherapy to other well-established treatments such as Acceptance and Commitment Therapy (ACT; Sharp et al. 2004), Cognitive-Behavioral Therapy (CBT; Fabry et al. 2007), Rational Emotive Behavior Therapy (REBT; Hutchinson and Chapman 2005), and Cognitive therapies (Benware 2003). These authors emphasize Frankl's initial conceptualization of logotherapy as a clinical model that can be integrated with other forms of psychotherapy. Moreover, they identify areas in which logotherapy can complement and enhance the efficacy of treatment (see Fabry 1981; Kovacs 1999).

In spite of the growth of Meaning-centered interventions, among mental health professionals there is still a lack of familiarity with logotherapy's working model in clinical practice. Moreover, there remain several misconceptions of the scope and depth of Frankl's theory of psychotherapy as well as a lack of dissemination of concrete guidelines regarding the practical applications of logotherapy. Expanding on the overview presented in Schulenberg et al. (2008), the present chapter aims to complement the theoretical framework of logotherapy for clinical practice as well as to provide some concrete guidelines of the therapeutic process. Additionally, the present chapter introduces Socratic dialogue as a fundamental technique in Meaning-centered psychotherapy and illustrates the use of this technique as a means to facilitate change in the client in both individual and group processes.

Theoretical Fundamentals

To understand Frankl's conception of the origin of mental health issues and the consequent treatment to address psychopathology, it is important to review some of Frankl's theoretical assumptions. Logotherapy relies on the presumption that the individual is composed of three dimensions: the biological dimension (the physical organism), the psychological dimension (basic processes such as attention, memory, and learning capacity), and the spiritual dimension (Ameli and Dattilio 2013; Frankl 1994a, b, c, d; Schulenberg et al. 2008). Without disregarding the importance of the psychological and physical dimensions, logotherapy places special emphasis on the spiritual dimension of the human being. The spiritual dimension is defined as the individual's potentiality of reflecting upon himself or herself, and the human capacity to intentionally have an encounter with others as well as to discover meaning (Frankl 1986, 1994a, b, c, d). For Frankl, the spiritual dimension is not equivalent to a religious dimension or as spirituality. Although being religious and spiritual are potentialities of the spiritual dimension, the spiritual dimension does not only relate to these areas, but it is a broader category that represents what is uniquely human (Frankl 1994a). The spiritual dimension is the core of the individual that remains healthy in spite of biological and psychological conditions. It possesses unique characteristics that enable the individual to face the limitations imposed by the biological and psychological dimensions (Frankl 1994a).

Specifically, the spiritual dimension includes the spiritual resources of *self-distancing* and *self-transcendence* (Frankl 1992, 1999; Martínez 2013). *Self-distancing* encompasses the ability of *self-comprehension* (the ability to objectively see oneself and assume a healthy stance upon such observation), *self-regulation* (the ability of monitoring and regulating emotional and cognitive processes and oppose oneself to the need of fighting against discomfort or of avoiding suffering), and *self-projection* (the ability of perceiving oneself differently in the future) (Frankl 1992, 1999; Martínez 2013). On the other hand, *self-transcendence* refers to the human capacity to intentionally direct attention and efforts to reach something or someone significant other than themselves (Frankl 1988). It encompasses the capacity of *differentiation* (the ability of interacting with the environment while maintaining individuality and recognizing that others might hold different beliefs and emotionality), *affectation* (the ability of being emotionally and motivationally moved by the presence of values and meaning), and *commitment* (the ability of giving oneself to a cause or a higher power that brings a sense of meaning) (Frankl 1988, 1994b, c, d, 1999; Martínez 2007, 2013). The importance of these abilities underlies the assumption that psychotherapy is possible thanks to the spiritual resources that allow individuals to take a different attitude towards their symptoms and engage in behaviors that are in opposition to internal (e.g., urges to drink) and external demands (e.g., parents suffering from alcoholism).

Another important concept in logotherapy refers to the distinction between an authentic personality and an inauthentic personality. According to Frankl, an *authentic personality* occurs when the biological and psychological development are aligned with the spiritual dimension, and accurately mirror the person reflecting his or her individuality and potentiality (Frankl 1992). The authentic personality is the one that is open to the external world and is willing to be affected and moved by experience. An inauthentic personality, conversely, represents a person that is restricted by his or her psychological and biological dimensions and is not able to mirror through his or her personality his or her spiritual resources, and thus, the person that he or she truly aims to be (e.g., a person restricted by the urges of drinking is not capable of superimposing his or her spiritual resources) (Frankl 1992). An inauthentic personality is closed to the external world and unwilling to be affected by others. In the presence of an inauthentic personality, the individual is more vulnerable to develop rigid response patterns and endorse problematic coping strategies to constantly experience pleasure or avoid distress and suffering (Martínez 2007, 2011). From this perspective, mental health problems occur when the spiritual dimension has been restricted by the psychological and biological dispositions and the person becomes inflexible in the coping strategies used to face difficulties, underusing his or her spiritual resources (Martínez 2007, 2011). Moreover, this rigidity and the harmful use of coping strategies perpetuates the same psychological problems the individual is trying to avoid, and further makes the individual more susceptible to experience discomfort and the maintenance of symptoms (Martínez 2007, 2011).

In this model, coping strategies are classified via four levels (Frankl 1992; Martínez 2007, 2011, 2013). The first two levels of coping strategies represent *maladaptive coping strategies* (e.g., self-injurious behavior, self-medication, avoidance, and escape) and the third and fourth levels represent *adaptive coping strategies* (Martínez 2007, 2011, 2013). The first two levels of maladaptive strategies have in common the extreme urge of eliminating any experience of discomfort when facing a threat to one's identity. The difference between first-level strategies and second-level strategies is that with first-level strategies the individual attempts to fight the discomfort through means that involve a direct alteration of the physical organism (self-medicating, purging, self-injury), while in the second level the attempts to eliminate discomfort involve changing the individual's environment (escaping and avoiding). On the other hand, the third and fourth levels of coping strategies represent the use of self-distancing and self-transcendence, respectively, to deal with such threats (Martínez 2007, 2011, 2013). The strategies related to the first and second levels of coping are associated with the expression of an inauthentic personality. Conversely, an authentic personality engages in coping strategies at the third and fourth levels and allows the person to transcend beyond difficulties and assume a healthy attitude in the face of potential threats to identity (Frankl 1992, 1994a, 2001; Lukas 2004; Martínez 2007, 2009a, 2011).

In terms of treatment, to promote change in the client the therapist has to mobilize healthy coping strategies of self-distancing and self-transcendence. Self-distancing is mobilized to promote change in coping strategies and self-transcendence is used to promote meaning-oriented behavior and alleviate difficulties related with loss of purpose in life and existential issues (Martínez 2007, 2013). Therefore, in Meaning-centered psychotherapy, or logotherapy, change occurs when the individual is capable of accepting discomfort and instead of trying to eliminate it or to change his or her environment in an unhealthy way, tries to replace maladaptive coping strategies with the use of existential resources (Frankl 1992, 1994b, c, d, 2001; Lukas 2003; Martínez 2007, 2011, 2013). The ultimate goal of psychotherapy is to facilitate in the individual psychological flexibility, malleability to situations, and an authentic personality open to the world and others (Martínez 2007, 2011, 2013). This in turn will widen the phenomenological field of the individual, enabling him or her to perceive different alternatives and realities of his or her existence, and allow the individual to engage in the alternatives that bring more meaning to his or her life (Martínez 2007, 2011, 2013).

In summary, logotherapy is a Meaning-centered psychotherapy that focuses on the personal spiritual/existential resources of the individual. It is person- and personality-centered, it highlights the role of maladaptive coping strategies on the development of psychopathology, and it promotes change by implementing adaptive coping strategies (Ameli and Dattilio 2013; Martínez 2002, 2003, 2007, 2009a, 2011).

Evaluation and Diagnosis in Clinical Practice

Logotherapy, as a Meaning-centered psychotherapy, has specific principles and technical procedures regarding the nature of the therapeutic relationship (Frankl 1992, 1994b), the process of evaluation and diagnosis, and the intervention techniques used in clinical practice (Martínez 2011, 2013; Schulenberg et al. 2008). In this model of logotherapy, the evaluation process is targeted to the assessment of the individual's biological, psychological, and spiritual resources and restrictions as well as the individual's values and areas of meaning (see Winters and Schulenberg 2006). The ultimate goal of the process of evaluation is to arrive at a clear conceptualization of the client's individuality, and of how he or she perceives the world (Martínez 2011). To meet these goals the therapist makes use of assessment procedures that include the clinical interview and administration of self-report measures (see Melton and Schulenberg 2008; Winters and Schulenberg 2006). During the assessment phase the therapist explores psychological symptoms (related to specific psychological disorders), physiological restrictions (medical conditions), coping strategies, spiritual resources, and motivation to change (Martínez 2009a, b, c, d). The interview allows the clinician to identify areas of meaning, have a comprehensive view of the client's problem, and explore in depth the client's healthy and unhealthy coping strategies (Martínez 2009a, b, c, d; Schulenberg et al. 2008; Winters and Schulenberg 2006).

Regarding *self-report measures,* as of today there are more than 50 instruments developed to assess different areas of meaning (see also Brandstätter et al. 2012; Melton and Schulenberg 2008; Park and George 2013). Although the majority of these instruments have been used mainly in research contexts, some of these measures, such as the Life Regard Index (Battista and Almond 1973), the Personal Meaning Index (Reker 1992), and the Schedule for Meaning in Life Evaluation (SMILE; Fegg et al. 2008), could inform the clinician on the processes of meaning that are present within the client and offer a systematic way of monitoring changes in several areas of meaning in life. In Latin America, the Scale of Noological Resources (Martínez et al. 2010) and the Vital Meaning Scale (Martínez et al. 2011) have been developed and validated in Spanish-speaking populations to assess perception of meaning and level of spiritual resources within clients.

With respect to the diagnosis of psychological symptoms and medical conditions, logotherapy recognizes the importance of a comprehensive evaluation that includes assessment of clinical disorders and a coherent and comprehensive case formulation that assesses symptomatology in depth (Martínez 2007, 2009a, 2011; Winters and Schulenberg 2006). Thus, it is important for the clinician to be familiar with current diagnostic procedures of psychopathology as well as with the administration of psychometrically sound assessment instruments that target specific disorders (Winters and Schulenberg 2006). The process of evaluation and diagnosis determines the route of treatment and the techniques that are going to be used throughout the process. The clinician must prioritize the urgency of symptoms, evaluate his or her own competence to treat such symptoms, and respect the different moments of the therapeutic process, as indicated in the following section.

The Therapeutic Process

The process of psychotherapy requires a general delimitation of the different moments of intervention of the therapeutic process (Martínez 2007, 2009b, c, d, 2011). In logotherapy or Meaning-centered psychotherapy, three fundamental phases of the therapeutic process are recognized.

In the first phase of treatment, the Meaning-centered therapist should develop a clear case formulation and engage in an on-going facilitation of spiritual resources. Specifically, self-distancing (self-comprehension, self-regulation, and self-projection) is mobilized during this first stage. In this phase the client starts to self-comprehend his or her maladaptive coping strategies as well as monitor and regulate his or her symptoms (Martínez 2011). During the first phase of therapy there are six special areas that the therapist should address (Martínez 2011): the therapeutic frame (e.g., the cost, time, place, and rules), a safe environment (e.g., evaluate self-injury behavior, suicidal ideation), assessment and diagnosis (case conceptualization), the consolidation of the therapeutic relationship, the client's motivation to change, and the reduction of symptoms that generate significant distress in the client (see Lukas 2003). Once these areas have been successfully addressed the therapist and the client can move to the second phase of therapy.

In the second phase, three special aspects are considered. The first aspect refers to the maintenance of the therapeutic relationship and the ongoing use of the relationship as a tool to promote change. The second aspect involves promoting a new understanding of the psycho-biological restrictions that limit the individual's freedom (e.g., a disability, a mental illness, a difficult situation) to broaden the perspective and the field of choices and possibilities. The third aspect involves the replacement of second-level maladaptive strategies with third-level adaptive strategies (e.g., instead of avoiding feared situations, using self-distancing to relate differently to symptoms). Once symptoms have been significantly reduced and the client is able to recognize the use of harmful coping strategies, self-regulating techniques are implemented and the client starts to give a new functional order to his or her inauthentic personality and learns new ways to cope with difficulties (e.g., perceiving feared situations as events that can lead to the attainment of meaningful goals). The therapist helps the client to become less rigid and to let go of the closeness of the psychological dimension. In this phase, willingness to be open to uncertainty and discomfort associated with change is promoted as well as adaptive and authentic behavior.

The last and final stage of therapy involves change consolidation, relapse prevention, and the discovery of a meaningful life (Martínez 2007, 2011). In change consolidation, the progress is normalized by the client and change is integrated into his or her life. In this phase of therapy, changes are maintained and the individual expresses satisfaction with the new way of approaching the world. To assure further maintenance of change, relapse prevention is implemented. The therapist and the client anticipate possible obstacles to maintain progress as well as possible setbacks that could trigger previous maladaptive coping strategies. Spiritual unfolding and meaning in life then are further promoted. The therapist focuses in guiding the client to experience the spiritual resources of *affectation* (the ability of being moved by the presence of values and meaning) and *commitment* (the ability of giving oneself to a cause or a higher power that brings a sense of meaning) (Frankl 1988, 1994b, c, d, 1999; Martínez 2007, 2013). At the end of successful treatment, the client displays self-transcendence and engages in a meaningful life (Martínez 2007, 2009a, 2011; Schulenberg et al. 2008).

Methods of Intervention

The therapeutic relationship, or the existential encounter between the individual and the therapist, is the principal technique in the therapeutic process (Frankl 1992, 1994a). An authentic therapeutic relationship facilitates an encounter in which the client is able to display an authentic personality and is willing to experience the unavoidable anxiety of life. In terms of specific techniques to target symptoms and enhance meaning in life, the most well-known techniques in logotherapy are paradoxical intention (Bazzi and Fizzotti 1989; Broomfield and Espie 2003; Frankl 1994d, 1995a; Michelson and Asher 1984), dereflection (Ameli and Dattilio 2013; Frankl 1975; Lukas 2003), and attitude modification (Ameli and Dattilio 2013; Lukas 2006; Martínez 2009d). These techniques are useful in enhancing meaning, promoting self-distancing, and decreasing symptoms (see Ameli and Dattilio 2013; Bazzi and Fizzotti 1989; Frankl 1994d, 1995a; Schulenberg et al. 2008). Because these techniques have been well-documented in the literature of logotherapy (for a review see Schulenberg et al. 2008), the present chapter elaborates specifically on the technique of Socratic dialogue as used in Meaning-centered psychotherapy or logotherapy (Fabry 1994; Guttman 1998).

Socratic Dialogue

Socratic dialogue has been used in several other forms of psychotherapy, in which it is used depending on the therapeutic goals and theoretical fundamentals of each form of therapy (Beck 2000, 2007; Ellis 1999; Martínez 2009c; Overholser 2010; Rudio 2001). In logotherapy or Meaning-centered psychotherapy, the use of Socratic dialogue has gathered special attention as one of the most important techniques to mobilize spiritual resources and facilitate the discovery of meaning in clients through the use of systematic questioning (Bellantoni 2010; Fabry 2001; Freire 2002; Guttman 1998; Lukas 2006; Scraper 2000). This technique was modeled by Viktor Frankl on multiple occasions, in which through Socratic questioning, Frankl helped clients find meaning in difficult situations and discover alternative perspectives to their problems (Frankl 1994b, 2001). In the following section the application of Socratic dialogue in logotherapy is illustrated. In addition, guidelines on the application of Socratic dialogue to enhance meaning perception in individual and group therapy are provided.

Socratic Dialogue in Logotherapy

As mentioned previously, Socratic dialogue is used to mobilize the spiritual resources of the client. In logotherapy, the implementation of Socratic dialogue requires the establishment of a safe environment, a genuine encounter between the therapist and the client, and a caring disposition to listen and discover meaning in the dialogue (Bruzzone 2003; Frankl 1994b; Freire 2002). The therapist has to establish a relationship of trust and give to the conversation a tone of an adequate sense of humor far from a judgmental, moralistic, or exhortative stance (Freire 2002). The first instance of Socratic dialogue is characterized by a naïve and ironic position assumed by the therapist; Frankl recommended this stance constantly (Freire 2002). However, the use of these positions should be used with caution to avoid coming across as disrespectful to the client (Lukas 1983, 2006; Martínez 2002, 2003, 2007, 2009c).

Once a safe environment has been established, the therapist listens in silence so the client can voice his or her problems openly to the therapist (Lukas 1983). Then, assuming a naïve stance, the logotherapist aims to broaden the phenomenological field of the client through questions that aim to define what *it* (client's perceived problem) really is. This means, that during the first part of Socratic dialogue the therapist tries to refute the partial knowledge narrated by the client to get closer to a more essential truth and facilitate the existential resource of self-distancing. Now, let's take a look at some specific examples of how to mobilize self-comprehension, self-regulation, and self-projection in a client. The following vignettes do not contain examples of real cases but rather they show an approximation of examples of how Socratic dialogue is applied in logotherapy (Martínez 2009c).

Self-comprehension: (T = therapist, C = client)

T: How do you react when you are in that situation?
C: I try to pretend I am not nervous.
T: And, why do you do that? (acting naïve)
C: So people don't realize I am embarrassed.
T: And why be ashamed about that?
C: Well, my hands start sweating.
T: Are there any other circumstances when this also happens?
C: Whenever I am in meetings or when too many people are around me.
T: What's going on in those situations that make you have this sensation?
C: Well, it happens when I feel observed.
T: I understand, your hands sweat because you feel observed. However I am curious to know, what is the danger in that situation? I mean, what do you think these people that are observing you are going to find out?
C: Well, that my hands are sweating.
T: Of course, but if your hands are sweating what can people think about you?
C: That I am a nervous person.
T: And, why is it embarrassing to be nervous?
C: They are probably going to think that I am not good at my job.

Self-regulation

T: Interesting, I had not met an enterprise in which hand sweating was an indicator of bad job performance. (ironically)
C: (laugh) That is not what I meant. (laugh)
T: So, how did you get that you are not good at your job?
C: I just have always had that sensation.
T: But why do you think that?
C: I guess I got the sensation because of my father; he was so successful and judgmental…
T: And how have you managed to still hold such an important job position for this long?

C: Well, I guess they have not noticed…
T: What? So the people at your work are so negligent, that they have not even realized how bad you are? (in a naïve manner)
C: It is not that, there are very successful people there.
T: Sure. That is why you are also there.

Self-projection

T: What would be the best thing that would happen to you if you could overcome your shyness?
C: I would be more successful with women. (laugh)
T: If we pretend for a moment that this session is happening two years from now, after you have overcome your shyness, what would you be telling me?
C: Maybe I would not even be here. (laugh) Well, I would be introducing you to my friends…

Socratic dialogue can also be used to promote differentiation. For instance, the following dialogue illustrates an approximation of an example of a client that presents to therapy to address relationship issues with his or her partner.

Differentiation

C: It's just that I feel that he does not love me as much as I love him.
T: What do you mean by that? Could you please be more specific?
C: Well, he is a priority to me. I would like to spend all my time with him and be able to call him more frequently, but it seems to me that he would rather do other things.
T: So, if he would like to spend all his time with you and call you as many times as you would like him to, then you would feel really loved?
C: Yes, exactly.
T: So, if he would stop being himself, and instead he would be just like you are, then you would feel loved.
C: Well, it is not that I would like for him to be just like me.
T: Why not?
C: There are some things that I have that I would not like him to have.
T: For example?
C: For example, I tend to be always in a rush and stressed out about several things.
T: Oh, ok. I understand. There are also some things about you that do not have anything to do with him. What would happen if he would not only love you as you wish he would love you, but if he would also be always in a rush and stress out about things?
C: I think we would have already broken up.
T: So it seems a relief that you both are different.

As can be seen, through the use of Socratic questioning, the therapist leads the client to identify fears and underlying beliefs, information that contradicts these beliefs, client potentialities, and reasons to change. Table 1 provides additional examples of questions that can be used to promote each of these spiritual resources.

Along the same lines, based on Socratic dialogue the logotherapist Elisabeth Lukas (1983, 2000, 2006) has developed the *ironic and naïve questioning technique*. In this technique the therapist, with some level of ingenuousness and irony, pretends to accept the irrationality behind the client's beliefs. Paradoxically, when assuming this position, as a defensive strategy the client tries to re-formulate his or her problem getting closer to the real issues that bring him or her to therapy (Martínez 2002, 2003; Restrepo 2001). In the following vignette a brief approximation of an example of the technique is provided (Martínez 2002).

C: Actually, my problem is not as bad as it sounds, I can control my drug use.
T: (in a naïve manner) What is the thing that you control the most about your drug use?
C: Well, I do not do it as frequently and I do not use drugs so much.
T: (in a naïve manner) Oh, that is good to know, for a moment I thought that you were using drugs at least once a week. So, how frequently do you use drugs?
C: Well, sometimes I do use drugs frequently, but some other times I can go for a while without using.
T: Why did you decide to come to our institution?
C: My wife insisted that I should come.
T: (surprised) Your wife asked you to come!!! She must believe you are not doing very well then.
C: Sometimes she exaggerates.
T: So it must be hard for you to live with a person that does not get it is okay to use drugs once in a while. Have you thought about finding a woman that is okay with you using drugs once in a while?
C: Well, she is right in some of the things she says. If I would have to be by myself, I would probably use more drugs.
T: (in a naïve way) So what is wrong with using drugs?
C: It does have a lot of bad things, you start becoming an irresponsible person, and your relationship with your family starts deteriorating.
T: (in a naïve way)… And do you think that being irresponsible and losing your family and wife are enough reasons for you to stop using drugs?

Therefore, through the use of questions and a naïve/ironic stance the therapist can facilitate self-distancing. Apart from mobilizing the spiritual resources of self-distancing, the Socratic questioning technique is also used to guide the client to identify meaning across various situations.

Table 1 Questions to promote the spiritual resources of self-comprehension, self-regulation, self-projection, and differentiation

Self-comprehension	Self-regulation	Self-projection	Differentiation
– When you think about it what do you feel? – When you start feeling like that, what is going through your head? – How does your body behave when you are feeling like that? – What is going on in that situation that upsets you so much? – In what other situations do you feel like that? – How would you describe that sensation in another way? – How does this start to happen? – What is the price that you have to pay if you continue like this? – When that situation occurs, what do you usually do? – When you react that way, how do other people usually react? – From where did you get that things should be that way? – Can you think of any metaphor to help me understand what happens to you? – What do you tell yourself when this occurs? – If your life was a book, what would be the title of the current chapter? What are those mistakes or errors you would like to edit? What is the best part of the book?	– What is the price of changing? – When that situation occurs, what other different things can you do? – How do you withhold yourself? – How do you force yourself to be able to stop yourself in that situation? – How does the conversation that you have with yourself to make that decision go? – Where do you get the strength to maintain that decision from? – What did you do to overcome that situation? – What is stopping you? – Is there any way you can regulate your excessive regulation? – I do not understand. Do you really think you can force him or her to change? – How do you cope with what you feel? – How do you resist that urge? – What do you tell yourself to withhold from doing that? – How can you disagree with what others expect from you? – How do you manage to contradict what your thoughts are telling you to do?	– So why do you want that? – How would you like to live the rest of your life? – If you decide to change, how would everything look? – What is the version of yourself that you would like to have? – Is it worth the effort to obtain that? – What obstacles are you going to face to obtain what you want? – What are you going to lose if you chose to live differently? – Are you willing to accept the price of changing? – What is your goal in this process? – Why would you bet on it? – How do you imagine yourself when all of this is in the past? – What is the best thing that could happen to you if you overcome this? – In the future, how would you tell your children or grandchildren that you overcame this? – How can you continue changing, even if some people would benefit more if you do not change?	– What have you kept doing as a result of past relationships? – Where did you get that things should happen this way and not any other way? – Why don't you like others to think for themselves? – What is it that you get by not allowing him or her to feel that way? – How did you get to the conclusion that everyone should behave the same way you do? – So is there only one way to approach that situation? – Would you be comfortable if he/she just pretends to enjoy those places? – What would you lose if you just let him/her be who they are? – What is so scary about his/her feelings? – What are some goals that are only yours? – Apart from discrediting what he/she says, in what other way could you express that you disagree?

Training in Meaning Perception Through Socratic Dialogue

The training in meaning perception is Socratic in essence. Through this method the client is trained to recognize personal sources of meaning and to be aware of meaningful moments in his or her life (Martínez 2009a). This method is developed through four instances that need to be addressed when training in meaning perception in a specific situation.

1. *The emotional perception*: the first step is centered on identifying the affectivity evoked by the presence of meaning. It is a moment that intends to describe the emotional resonance of meaning. For instance:
   T: I can see that your face changes when you talk about that. What exactly are you feeling?
   C: I feel good about going back to college.
   T: What do you mean when you say "I feel good"? What is that?
   C: Well, I feel happy, satisfied.
   T: And, what is feeling happy?
   C: Being content, I am excited about coming back.
   T: Could you describe the sensation?
   C: I feel complete, calm, and relief.
2. *The cognitive perception*: this relates to the rationale and the usefulness that is perceived in a particular source of meaning. It involves the thoughts and significance generated by the presence of a value or a valuable person. For example:
   T: What kind of thoughts do you have regarding this situation you are experiencing?
   C: It just makes me want to change even more.
   T: And, why keep changing?
   C: So I can get along with everyone as I have been doing lately.
   T: And, what is good about it?
   C: It motivates me to keep making progress.
3. *The values perception*: within every perceived situation there are values immersed. In this step the therapist guides the client to perceive those values and find out what is most important to him or her. Consider this example:
   T: And, who benefits from your feelings of satisfaction and motivation to change?
   C: Everyone.
   T: Could you give me some examples?
   C: My father seems calmer, my brothers are happy, I am happy…
   T: Among all the alternatives that you have, is there any other better option than what you are doing right now?
   C: At this moment, I don't think so…

4. *Value attraction*: for a value to become meaningful it has to be accompanied by an act. In this instance, the client is invited to experience the value and act upon it. For instance:
   T: What is it that you find so appealing in that option?
   C: Well, I am going to be able to return to my previous life.
   T: How do you notice that is what you want?
   C: Just thinking about it excites me.
   T: So what specific acts do you have to do to get what you want?

Therefore, with the training in meaning perception the client is helped to recognize sources of meaning, personal values, as well as the acts that allow him or her to attain meaning and realize such values. Finally, Socratic dialogue is not only limited to individual therapy, but can also be applied in group therapy to empower clients and facilitate group dialogue.

Group Logotherapy Through Socratic Dialogue

There is evidence that group therapy benefits from the application of logotherapy. Specifically, there have been important developments for the group treatment of individuals with cancer (Hoseinyan et al. 2009), addictions and relapse prevention (Crumbaugh et al. 1980; Martínez 2002, 2006, 2009d), somatic disorders (Lukas 2006), grief therapy (Berti and Schneider-Berti 1994), and war veterans (Martínez 2009a). In group logotherapy, Socratic dialogue is also a useful technique. Through this technique the facilitator promotes an environment in which the participants are the ones that discover the solutions to the problems, and therefore are empowered. The use of Socratic questioning can be systematically used in three distinct moments of group therapy: the initial moment, the moment of refutation, and the moment of discovery (Martínez 2009d).

The initial moment: the first moment of group Socratic dialogue consists in the active and ongoing listening of the participant's discourse to identify their phenomenological field. The fundamental question in this moment is: *What is it that we are talking about?* In other words, how is the specific subject (cancer, addiction, death, war, symptoms) defined by the group members? The Socratic facilitator initiates the group conversation with a trigger question and then listens to participant opinions and captures how they perceive the subject being discussed and the beliefs underlying the topic of conversation. Meanwhile, the facilitator assumes a receptive attitude and refrains from questioning participant beliefs. His or her role in this moment is to occasionally summarize what is being said in the group. Once the facilitator has summarized participant responses, he or she can either re-phrase the original trigger question to obtain more information or ask a new question to move to another area of interest. It is the role of the facilitator to assure that all of the group members have had the opportunity of participating. Some specific recommendations of the initial moment are to conduct the group with approximately 12 participants (more than 12 can be difficult to manage and less than 12 can make the group too tense), to provide feedback every four or five responses without attempting to interpret or question participant opinions, to focus on capturing the phenomenological field of each participant while also fostering a genuine and trustworthy environment, and to place the group members that participate the most to the right side and left side of the facilitator, while placing the members that talk the least in front of the facilitator (Martínez 2002, 2006, 2009d).

The moment of refutation or contradiction: once the facilitator has identified the phenomenological field of the group members and has listened to their arguments and beliefs, he or she begins asking questions that will challenge participant beliefs. In this moment it is important to also take into account the strategies used in the initial moment. However, questions such as *How so?* are used to introduce doubt in the group members (e.g., How is it that when people get sad they have to drink alcohol?). *What for?* or *Why?* questions are used to query the meaning attributed to a behavior (e.g., Why is it that you have to escape when you encounter a situation?). Such questions tend to have more importance. By refuting or providing arguments against their beliefs in the form of questions, the facilitator attempts to generate a process of meaning incongruence that further leads them to doubt their assumptions and the beliefs that underlie them. This is the moment of Socratic irony and/or the naïve questions that aim to facilitate in the group the discovery of inconsistencies and contradictions. In this moment, the facilitator can also introduce facts from reliable sources that challenge their arguments, lectures, talks or conferences, alternatives on how other people have perceived or approached the same subject (e.g., stories of people that have overcome cancer), and also present hypothetical situations that promote perspective taking and allow the participants to be flexible in the way they approach a situation. It is recommended that the facilitator introduce the material appearing objective, neutral, and without overemphasizing particular information (Martínez 2002, 2006, 2009d).

Finally, *the moment of discovery* focuses on broadening the phenomenological field of the group members. Once the participants have doubt in their assumptions and beliefs, the facilitator then guides them to discover new conclusions and new alternatives when facing a particular situation. This process is conducted through questions that promote the consideration of other possibilities and that allow for the development of healthy coping strategies. In this moment, the facilitator also guides the group members to identify the meaning and the values underlying the range of possibilities and to engage in the solution that is most meaningful and valuable to them. The ultimate goal is for their beliefs, values, and goals to be aligned with what is meaningful for them (Martínez 2002, 2006, 2009d).

To conclude, Socratic dialogue in a Meaning-centered psychotherapy is a valuable tool to promote spiritual resources in the client, to generate meaning dissonance and motivate change, and to guide the discovery of a meaningful life. This approach is not only of benefit to logotherapist clinicians but it is also useful across a range of orientations and settings that emphasize the need to facilitate value clarification, goal setting, motivation to change, and the discovery of a life worth living (Ryan et al. 2011; Steffen 2013; Wollburg and Braukhaus 2010). Thus, the described approach warrants further exploration and validation as a technique used within various therapeutic models and mental health settings.

Final Comments

Logotherapy is considered one of the most sound and useful therapies among existential treatments (Vos et al. 2014). The principles and fundamentals that underlie logotherapy have expanded beyond Meaning-centered therapy, and have been addressed in other theories of psychotherapy that recognize the role of meaning in treatment (Duckworth et al. 2005; Martínez 2013; Wong 2011). However, there is still a lot of work that needs to be done to position logotherapy in a place that allows for wider applicability and recognition (Schulenberg and Florez 2013). Specifically, a research agenda to validate the techniques and potential effectiveness of the application of a logotherapeutic model across various settings, populations, and disorders, continues to be a priority for the Meaning-centered practitioner (Schulenberg and Florez 2013). The new demands and advances in the field of mental health require treatments with empirical support and data that validate the usefulness of the practices and encourage researchers and clinicians to contribute to the understanding of active components of therapy, mechanisms of change, and treatment generalization within every theory of psychotherapy (Spring 2007).

Therefore, it is important for researchers interested in meaning to focus more on the empirical validation of this paradigm and enhance efforts in dissemination of the clinical model (see Schulenberg and Florez 2013). Specifically, efforts are needed to conduct rigorous randomized controlled trials to test the effectiveness and efficacy of treatment protocols, to train researchers interested in the advancement of logotherapy, and to develop and describe parsimonious interventions, techniques, and instruments that are testable and replicable. Along the same lines, it is recommended that Meaning-centered psychotherapists work to attempt to make logotherapy more visible and accessible to the academic world that exists beyond logotherapy and existential therapies (Schulenberg and Florez 2013; Vos et al. 2014).

Viktor Frankl himself encouraged clinicians to conduct research to strengthen a Meaning-centered psychotherapy (Frankl 1995a). He developed a strong and promising theory of psychotherapy that allowed the consolidation of a science of meaning and of a growing body of research supporting meaning's clinical utility (Frankl 1994b). Frankl's goal was to disseminate a model of therapy that focuses on facilitating meaningful lives (Frankl 1995a). To attain this goal it is necessary for logotherapists to engage in scientific efforts to confirm the validity and utility of Meaning-centered psychotherapy to then be recognized and tested against therapeutic models that are well-known for their strong research framework. The final objective is for logotherapy to hold the highest standards of clinical practice and to be open to rigorous scientific evaluation that leads to research-informed practices (Schulenberg and Florez 2013).

References

Ameli, M., & Dattilio, F. M. (2013). Enhancing cognitive behavior therapy with logotherapy: Techniques for clinical practice. *Psychotherapy, 50*, 387–391.

Battista, J., & Almond, R. (1973). The development of meaning in life. *Psychiatry, 36*, 409–427.

Bazzi, T., & Fizzotti, E. (1989). *Guía de la logoterapia*. Barcelona: Herder.

Beck, J. (2000). *Terapia cognitiva*. Barcelona: Gedisa.

Beck, J. (2007). *Terapia cognitiva para la superación de retos*. Barcelona: Gedisa.

Bellantoni, D. (2010). E possibile trattare la visione esistenziale e la psicopatología?. Psicopatologia e significato della vita. Il contributo dell Analisi esistenziale alla psicoterapia. En. Pacciolla, A., Mancini, F. *Cognitivismo esistenziale. Dal significato del sintomo al significato della vita*. Milano: FrancoAngeli.

Benware, J. M. (2003). On the compatibility of cognitive therapy and logotherapy. *The International Forum for Logotherapy, 26*, 49–57.

Berti, G., & Schneider-Berti, A. (1994). When an offspring dies: Logotherapy in bereavement groups. *The International Forum for Logotherapy, 17*, 65–68.

Breitbart, W., & Heller, K. S. (2003). Refraining hope: Meaning-centered care for patients near the end of life. *Journal of Palliative Medicine, 6*, 979–988.

Breitbart, W., Poppito, S., Rosenfeld, B., Vickers, A., Li, Y., Abbey, J., et al. (2012). Pilot randomized controlled trial of individual meaning-centered psychotherapy for patients with advanced cancer. *Journal of Clinical Psychology, 30*, 1304–1309.

Brandstätter, M., Baumann, U., Borasio, G. D., & Fegg, M. J. (2012). Systematic review of meaning in life assessment instruments. *Psycho-Oncology, 21*, 1034–1052.

Broomfield, N. M., & Espie, C. A. (2003). Initial insomnia and paradoxical intention: An experimental investigation of putative mechanisms using subjective and actigraphic measurement of sleep. *Behavioural and Cognitive Psychotherapy, 31*, 313–324.

Bruzzone, D. (2003). Il metodo dialogico da Socrate a Frankl. Sulla natura educativa del processo logoterapeutico. En: Ricersa Di Senso. Vol. 1, N. 1, Trento. Edizione Erikson.

Crumbaugh, J. C., Wood, W. M., & Wood, C. W. (1980). *Logotherapy: New help for problem drinkers*. Chicago, IL: Nelson Hall.

Debats, D. L. (1996). Meaning in life: Clinical relevance and predictive power. *Journal of Clinical Psychology, 35*, 503–516.

DeWitz, J. S., Woolsey, L. M., & Walsh, B. W. (2009). College student retention: An exploration of the relationship between self-efficacy beliefs and purpose in life among college students. *Journal of College Student Development, 50*, 19–34.

Díaz del Castillo, J. (2011). *Abordaje logoterapéutico del modo de ser obsesivo-compulsivo*. Trabajo de grado: Universidad los Libertadores.

Drescher, C. F., Baczwaski, B. J., Walters, A. B., Aiena, B. J., Schulenberg, S. E., & Johnson, L. R. (2012). Coping with an ecological disaster: The role of perceived meaning in life and self-efficacy following the Gulf Oil Spill. *Ecopsychology, 4*, 56–63.

Duckworth, A. L., Steen, T. A., & Seligman, M. E. (2005). Positive psychology in clinical practice. *Annual Review of Clinical Psychology, 1*, 629–651.

Duque, T. (1998). Intervención logoterapéutica con drogodependientes en prisión. *Boletín de Logoterapia y Análisis Existencial, 2*, 59–72.

Ellis, A. (1999). *Una terapia breve más profunda y duradera. Enfoque teórico de la Terapia Racional Emotiva Conductual*. Madrid: Paidos Iberica.

Fabry, J. (1981). The frontiers of logotherapy. *The International Forum for Logotherapy, 4*, 3–11.

Fabry, J. B. (1994). *The pursuit of meaning* (New revised ed.). Abilene, TX: Institute of Logotherapy Press.

Fabry, J. (2001). *Señales del camino hacia el sentido*. México: LAG.

Fabry, D., Sheikh, A., & Selman, M. (2007). Logotherapy can enrich cognitive behavioral therapy practice. *The International Forum for Logotherapy, 30*, 100–106.

Fegg, M., Kramer, M., L'hoste, S., & Borasio, G. (2008). The Schedule for Meaning in Life Evaluation (SMILE): Validation of a new instrument for meaning in life research. *Journal of Pain and Symptom Management, 35*, 356–364.
Frankl, V. (1975). Paradoxical intention and dereflection. *Psychotherapy: Theory Research & Practice, 12*, 226–237.
Frankl, V. (1986). *Psicoanálisis y existencialismo. (Ärztliche Seelsorge)*. México D.C. Fondo de Cultura Económica.
Frankl, V. (1988). Logos, paradoja y búsqueda de significado. En M. Mahoney & A. Freeman (Eds.), *Cognición y psicoterapia* (pp. 132–133). Barcelona: Paidos.
Frankl, V. (1992). *Teoría y terapia de las neurosis. Iniciación a la logoterapia y el análisis existencial*. Barcelona: Herder.
Frankl, V. (1994a). *El hombre doliente. Fundamentos antropológicos de la psicoterapia*. Barcelona: Herder.
Frankl, V. (1994b). *Psicoterapia y humanismo. ¿Tiene un sentido la vida?*. México D.C.: Fondo de Cultura Económica.
Frankl, V. (1994c). *La voluntad de sentido*. Barcelona: Herder.
Frankl, V. (1994d). *Logoterapia y análisis existencial*. Barcelona: Herder.
Frankl, V. (1995a). *La psicoterapia en la práctica médica*. Buenos Aires: San Pablo.
Frankl, V. (1995b). *La presencia ignorada de Dios*. Barcelona: Herder.
Frankl, V. (1999). *La idea psicológica del hombre*. Madrid: RIALP.
Frankl, V. (2001). *Psicoterapia y existencialismo. Escritos selectos sobre logoterapia*. Barcelona: Herder.
Freire, J. B. (2002). *El humanismo en la logoterapia de Víktor Frankl*. Navarra: Editorial EUNSA.
Greenstein, M. (2000). The house that's on fire: Meaning-centered psychotherapy pilot group for cancer patients. *American Journal of Psychotherapy, 54*, 501–511.
Guttman, D. (1998). Logoterapia para profesionales. Bilbao. Ed. DDB.
Halama, P. (2003). Meaning and hope: Two factors of positive psychological functioning in late adulthood. *Studia Psychologica, 45*, 103–110.
Henrion, R. (2002). Alcohol use disorders: Alcohol dependence. *The International Forum for Logotherapy, 25*, 30–38.
Henrion, R. (2004). Logoanalysis: For treatment of mood disorder due to medical condition. *The International Forum for Logotherapy, 27*, 3–8.
Hoseinyan, E., Soudani, M., & Mehrabizadeh, M. H. (2009). Efficacy of group logotherapy on cancer patient's life expectation. *Journal of Behavioral Sciences, 3*, 287–292.
Hutchinson, G. T., & Chapman, B. P. (2005). Logotherapy-enhanced REBT: An integration of discovery and reason. *Journal of Contemporary Psychotherapy, 35*, 145–155.
Hutzell, R. R. (1984). Logoanalysis for alcoholics. *The International Forum for Logotherapy, 7*, 40–45.
Julom, A. M., & de Guzmán, R. (2013). The effectiveness of logotherapy program in alleviating the sense of meaninglessness of paralyzed in-patients. *International Journal of Psychology & Psychological Therapy, 13*, 357–371.
Kovacs, G. (1999) A new beginning in application of Frankl's work to emerging issues in psychotherapy. *Psychological Reports, 85*, 945–946.
Leung, D., Fillion, L., Stéphane, D., Brown, J., Rodin, G., & Howell, D. (2012). Meaning in bone marrow transplant nurses' work: Experiences before and after a "meaning-centered" intervention. *Cancer Nursing, 35*, 374–381.
Lukas, E. (1983). *Tu vida tiene sentido*. Madrid: SM.
Lukas, E. (1992). *Asistencia logoterapéutica*. Petropolis: Editorial Voces.
Lukas, E. (1995). *Psicoterapia en dignidad*. Buenos Aires: San Pablo.
Lukas, E. (2000). *También tu sufrimiento tiene sentido*. LAG: México D.C.
Lukas, E. (2003). *Logoterapia. La búsqueda de significado*. Buenos Aires: Paidos.
Lukas, E. (2004). *Equilibrio y curación a través de la Logoterapia*. Barcelona: Paidos Iberica.
Lukas, E. (2006). *También tu sufrimiento tiene sentido. Alivio en la crisis a través de la logoterapia*. México D.C.: Editorial LAS.

Martínez, E. (2002). *Logoterapia. Una alternativa ante la frustración existencial y las adicciones*. Bogotá: Colectivo Aquí y Ahora.
Martínez, E. (2003). Acción y elección. Logoterapia, logoterapia de grupo y abordaje de las drogodependencias. Bogotá: Colectivo Aquí y Ahora.
Martínez, E. (2006). Hacia una prevención con sentido. Bogotá: CAA.
Martínez, E. (2007). *Psicoterapia y sentido de vida. Psicología clínica de orientación logoterapeutica*. Bogotá: Editorial Herder.
Martínez, E. (2009a). La búsqueda de sentido. Bogotá. Ed. Colectivo Aquí y Ahora.
Martínez, E. (2009b). El psicodiagnóstico en logoterapia. En S. Sáenz (Ed.), Logoterapia en acción. Aplicaciones prácticas (pp. 82–108). Buenos Aires: San Pablo.
Martínez, E. (2009c). Modelo Logoterapéutico-ambulatorio en adicciones. En S. Sáenz (Ed.), Logoterapia en acción. Aplicaciones prácticas (pp. 435–450). Buenos Aires: San Pablo.
Martínez, E. (2009d). *El dialogo socrático en la psicoterapia*. Bogotá: SAPS.
Martínez, E. (2011). *Los modos de ser inauténticos. Psicoterapia Centrada en el sentido de los trastornos de la personalidad*. Bogotá: Manual Moderno.
Martínez, E. (2013). Los recursos noológicos en la psicoterapia centrada en el sentido. En E. Martínez (Ed.), Manual de psicoterapia con enfoque logoterapéutico (pp. 107–128). Bogotá: Manual Moderno.
Martínez, E., Díaz del Castillo, J., & Jaimes, J. (2010). Validación de la Prueba "Escala De Recursos Noológicos Aquí Y Ahora" Para Personas Mayores de 15 Años. *Revista Argentina de Clínica Psicológica, 3*, 257–272.
Martínez, E., Schulenberg, S., & Pacciolla, A. (2013). Introducción a la psicoterapia centrada en el sentido. In E. Martínez (Ed.), *Manual de Psicoterapia con enfoque logoterapéutico* (pp. 23–40). Bogotá: Manual Moderno.
Martínez, E., Trujillo, A., Díaz del Castillo, J., & Jaimes, J. (2011). Desarrollo y estructura de la escala dimensional del sentido de vida. *Acta Colombiana de Psicología, 14*, 113–119.
Melton, A. M. A., & Schulenberg, S. E. (2008). On the measurement of meaning: Logotherapy's empirical contributions to humanistic psychology. *The Humanistic Psychologist, 36*, 31–44.
Michelson, L., & Asher, M. (1984). Paradoxical intention: Theory, research and clinical application with anxiety disorders. *Journal of Behavior Therapy and Experimental Psychiatry, 15*, 215–220.
Oscariz, A. (2000). Grupo de madres y padres de drogodependientes. Una experiencia de búsqueda de sentido. *Boletín de Logoterapia y Análisis Existencial, 4*, 33–42.
Overholser, J. (2010). Psychotherapy according to the Socratic method: Integrating ancient philosophy with contemporary cognitive therapy. *Journal of Cognitive Psychotherapy: An International Quarterly, 24*, 354–361.
Park, C. L., & George, L. S. (2013). Assessing meaning and meaning making in the context of stressful life events: Measurement tools and approaches. *Journal of Positive Psychology, 8*, 483–504.
Reker, G. T. (1992). *Manual of the Life Attitude Profile-Revised (LAP-R)*. Peterborough, ON: Student Psychologists Press.
Restrepo, A. (2001). *Viktor Emil Frankl y la teoría logoterapeutica*. Medellín: UPB.
Rodríguez, R. (2004). Borderline personality disturbances and logotherapeutic treatment approach. *The International Forum for Logotherapy, 27*, 21–27.
Rogina, J. (2002). Logotherapeutic mastery of generalized anxiety disorder. *The International Forum for Logotherapy, 25*, 60–67.
Rogina, J. (2004). Treatment and interventions for narcissistic personality disorder. *The International Forum for Logotherapy, 27*, 28–33.
Rogina, J., & Quilitch, H. (2006). Treating dependent personality disorders with logotherapy: A case study. *The International Forum for Logotherapy, 29*, 54–61.
Rogina, J., & Quilitch, H. (2010). Logotherapy treatment of complicated grief syndrome. *The International Forum for Logotherapy, 33*, 30–41.
Rudio, F. (2001). *Dialogo maieutico e psicoterapia existencial*. Sao Paulo: Novos horizontes.

Ryan, R. M., Lynch, M. F., Vansteenkiste, M., & Deci, E. L. (2011). Motivation and autonomy in counseling, psychotherapy, and behavior change: A look at theory and practice. *The Counseling Psychologist, 39*, 193–260.

Schulenberg, S. E., & Florez, I. A. (2013). Advancing logotherapy as a science: A research imperative—Part two. *The International Forum for Logotherapy, 36*, 41–50.

Schulenberg, S. E., Hutzell, R. R., Nassif, C., & Rogina, J. M. (2008). Logotherapy for clinical practice. *Psychotherapy: Theory, Research, Practice, Training, 45*, 447–463.

Scraper, R. (2000). The art and science of maieutic questioning within the Socratic method. *The International Forum for Logotherapy, 23*, 14–16.

Sharp, W., Schulenberg, S. E., Wilson, K. G., & Murrell, A. R. (2004). Logotherapy and Acceptance and Commitment Therapy (ACT): An initial comparison of values-centered approaches. *The International Forum for Logotherapy, 27*, 98–105.

Spring, B. (2007). Evidence based practice in clinical psychology: What it is, why it matters, what you need to know. *Journal of Clinical Psychology, 63*, 611–631.

Steffen, E. (2013). Both 'being with' and 'doing to': Borderline personality disorder and the integration of humanistic values in contemporary therapy practice. *Counselling Psychology Review, 28*, 64–71.

Steger, M., Kashdan, T., & Oishi, S. (2008). Being good by doing good: Eudaimonic activity and daily well-being correlates, mediators, and temporal relations. *Journal of Research in Personality, 42*, 22–42.

Somov, P. G. (2007). Meaning of life group: Group application of logotherapy for substance use treatment. *Journal for Specialists in Group Work, 32*, 316–345.

Southwick, S., Gilmartin, R., McDonough, P., & Morrisey, P. (2006). Logotherapy as an adjunctive treatment for chronic combat-related PTSD: A meaning-based intervention. *American Journal of Psychotherapy, 60*, 161–174.

Ungar, M. (2002). A logotherapy treatment protocol for major depressive disorder. *The International Forum for Logotherapy, 25*, 3–10.

Vos, J., Craig, M., & Cooper, M. (2014). Existential therapies: A meta-analysis of their effects on psychological outcomes. *Journal of Consulting and Clinical Psychology*, Advance online publication.

Winters, M. R., & Schulenberg, S. E. (2006). Diagnosis in logotherapy: Overview and suggestions for appropriate use. *The International Forum for Logotherapy, 29*, 16–24.

Wollburg, E., & Braukhaus, C. (2010). Goal setting in psychotherapy: The relevance of approach and avoidance goals for treatment outcome. *Psychotherapy Research, 20*, 488–494.

Wong, P. T. P. (2011). Positive psychology 2.0: Towards a balanced interactive model of the good life. *Canadian Psychology/Psychologie Canadienne, 52*, 69–81.

Zika, S., & Chamberlain, K. (1992). On the relation between meaning in life and psychological well-being. *British Journal of Psychology, 83*, 133–145.

Experience Processing as an Aspect of Existential Psychotherapy: Life Enhancement Methodology

Dmitry A. Leontiev

Existential psychology still takes a marginal position, though Allport (1955) prescribed the transfusion of existentialism to the veins of the psychology of personality 60 years ago. However, existential ideas are very influential outside the therapist's office. Few psychologists representing other traditions may compete in print runs of their books with Viktor Frankl, Ronald Laing, Rollo May, or Irvin Yalom. This suggests that an existential worldview may be effective not only through therapeutic interventions sensu stricto, but also through some other practices, appealing to the individual's conscious processing of their life experience. Trying to distill the forms of interventions based on clients' conscious processing and self-reflection, I have elaborated a form of group work dealing with existential issues through shared work of understanding rather than emotional dynamics. The chapter describes this form of work both inside and outside the therapist's office.

The Existential Dimension Within Psychotherapy

As early as 1965, James Bugental, in his book *The Search for Authenticity* (rev. ed. Bugental 1981), described two stages of any psychotherapeutic process. He called the first one the analytical stage, when the focus of the therapist's work is the

ORIGINAL PAPER. Published online: 26 August 2014 © Springer Science+Business Media New York 2014.

D.A. Leontiev (✉)
National Research University Higher School of Economics, Moscow, Russia
e-mail: dmleont@gmail.com

D.A. Leontiev
Rybalko str. 7-23, Moscow 123060, Russia

S.E. Schulenberg (ed.), *Clarifying and Furthering Existential Psychotherapy*,
DOI 10.1007/978-3-319-31086-2_7

client's complaints, the inner blocks that psychologically invalidate them, preventing full awareness and hindering living. The therapist must unfold, elaborate, and remove resistances existing in the client. The methodology applied at this stage has no radical divergences from the methodology of psychoanalysis or other in-depth approaches. When this stage is over, it is followed by the second stage, which Bugental called "ontogogy" (from "ontos," being, and "pedagogy"), meaning by this "a leading out into being" (Bugental 1981, p. 318). The therapist's work at this stage is aimed at helping the client to get in touch with his/her life, to discover and fulfill the potential of living. "Ontogogy consists of those understandings and procedures by which a therapist (counselor, consultant) seeks to support the intent of a person (patient, client) to realize more fully the potentials of his being" (ibid.).

Psychotherapy today is a multifaceted enterprise that cannot be reduced to goal-directed elimination of symptoms or underlying psychological disturbances. Existential psychotherapy, however, and not only in Bugental's version of it, has much in common with other schools of psychotherapy in regards to the first stage of working through the complaints and resistances. The second stage is more specific for an existential approach, though in recent decades more than one school of psychotherapy elaborated some forms of work more or less similar to the kind of life guidance Bugental labeled "ontogogy." (Later he spoke of "life coaching," Bugental 1999, hardly having an idea of what an elastic meaning this term would have today). Indeed, existential psychotherapy is professional psychotherapy based on some underlying attitudes, rather than a special school of psychotherapy (May 1967). In this sense it claims to complement, rather than replace, other approaches. Thus ontogogy seems to be the most specific existential component within different forms of psychotherapy.

And not only within them. Bugental himself did not consider ontogogy a therapeutic procedure sensu stricto. Indeed, besides psychotherapy, this guidance is a common component of the work of a good teacher, pastor, or social worker, or any person who is not indifferent to his/her fellows. The issue of the delineation between psychotherapy and non-therapeutic psychological practices, like counseling or coaching, is still disputable and exceeds the scope of this chapter. It makes sense to accept so far a neutral solution proposed by some psychologists: to speak of counseling and psychotherapy interchangeably. "Corsini (2008) points out that the distinctions are becoming less and less meaningful. He argues that 'counseling and psychotherapy are the same qualitatively; they differ only quantitatively,' adding that 'there is nothing that a psychotherapist does that a counselor does not do' (p. 2). Although one might disagree with that view, pressures from health care, organizational, and educational systems for greater efficiency and profitability have resulted in increasingly briefer interventions, resulting in a stronger convergence between the two endeavors.... In addition, the fields of counseling and clinical psychology today are not limited to mental health, and our review draws on counseling within health care and educational situations as well" (Ryan et al. 2011, p. 204).

Existential psychology and psychotherapy (Bugental 1981, 1999; van Deurzen 2002; Frankl 1969; May 1967; Wong 2010, 2012; Yalom 1980, etc.) pays special attention to what has been described by Bugental as the second stage of the therapeutic process for several reasons. The specifics of this stage lie not only in its growth-oriented rather than cure-oriented, and educational rather than therapeutic, natures but also in its highly individualized character that makes it hardly possible to apply well-structured techniques, and its rootedness in one's worldview rather than in mental machinery. There are no objective criteria of "right" or "wrong" except for the client's appraisal of the consequences of this work for one's life and well-being; objectified evidences of outcomes are also more problematic to gather than in other therapeutic methods. This is why the therapist can hardly impose his/her own views on the client's problems and must follow the client's own feelings. "Only the client has a compass" (Bugental 1999, p. 268).

I have been trying to elaborate the ways of working with individual life experiences in their individual frameworks based on the resources of their conscious processing. This chapter summarizes a decade of personal practice and over three decades of learning and discovering both the insights of academic psychology and the personal guidelines for fulfilled living.

Life Enhancement: A Group Ontogogic Practice

In line with the above considerations, the form of existential practice labeled life enhancement has been elaborated upon and successfully applied by the author, mostly in group format, in more than 15 groups that embraced over 300 participants, either as part of educational programs in existential counseling or as separate workshops. Like other existential practices the described approach can hardly be taught and learned in unambiguous scripts and algorithms; the aim of the description below is to reveal some possibilities that therapists may use in their work, rather than to present structured methods for copying.

Professional skills are necessary but not enough for making use of the life enhancement strategy. All work involving the existential dimension presupposes some worldview and the value orientations of the therapist. A skilled professional who does not like CBT methods may still use them effectively in appropriate cases; however, a skilled professional who does not find much sense in existential constructs can hardly be successful in trying to apply them. Indeed, universality never belonged to virtues of existential approaches.

Formal setting. A full-range life enhancement workshop includes one session that takes three full days of work; this is usually enough to elaborate all the problems presented by the participants, if their number is not too big. As experience shows, the optimal size of a group is up to 25–30 participants. 20–25 is better than 10–15, because much use is made of participants sharing problems, which are often strikingly similar, and experiences. I have had, on at least two occasions, groups of up to 50 participants, but this is definitely too many for a single facilitator; however, in the face of excessive demand it makes sense to split the participants into active participants, who are involved in the dialogue, and silent observers. It is worth noting that important changes are often observed also in the latter; not being explicitly involved in group communications, they benefit from inner processing of the topics relevant to them. Sometimes (usually at conferences) the workshops were given in an illustrative 3 h format. It usually suffices to work through two to three problems to give participants an idea of the approach.

Life enhancement groups claim to help participants resolve their long-term life problems through improving their processing of life experience. No specific requirements for the participants are put forward; this practice is, however, not effective in cases with serious clinical problems. True, the possibility of fruitful life enhancement work presupposes a definite level of openness and self-determination on the side of the client (as well as the therapist). A person with a heavily blocked awareness, full of defenses, who cannot take responsibility and initiate changes in his/her life, can hardly make use of life enhancement work. Since life enhancement work is based on the resources of conscious awareness, everything that restricts these resources' availability is counter-indicative to life enhancement work. Some preliminary work in the traditional psychotherapeutic paradigm (the analytic phase, in Bugental's terms) seems to be desirable in such cases, if the problems are not organically rooted.

The introductory part of the workshop sets "the rules of the game," albeit very simple ones, and introduces a few terms.

A. *Needs and problems*. Participants are asked to present major problems with which they have been unable to cope for months or years. The starting point of the work is the single axiom: all people have some needs and strive toward their fulfillment. Problems arise only as a consequence of this striving. It recalls the Buddhist principle, which says that all suffering comes from your wishes. However, whereas Buddhists recommend that you get rid of your wishes in order to stop your suffering, the existential view does not treat both wishes and suffering as ultimately undesirable. An alternative message says only that your problems are the price you have to pay for the fulfillment of your wishes; nothing important can be obtained for free. Even if you are unselfishly loved by someone, in order to unfold and enjoy the full potential of this love you have to invest some inner work in the relationship, otherwise you can make use only of the surface level of this gift. Life is investing efforts to solve the problems arising from your wishes; this is the way you grow up.

B. *Experience*. Not all problems can be solved. There are "eternal" problems that belong to the existential givens of our life, like the one of human finiteness, or of the limited mutual understanding between humans. There are problems produced by some earthly forces beyond people's control, like the threat of terrorist attacks. However, most of the unsolved problems that torment the participants are not irresolvable; their solution resides in the participant's life experience. The point is that the client fails to get access to this experience and to process it in a proper way to draw important implications for the evolution of his/her worldview. Most of the problems emerge from the unsound, erroneous processing of experience.

C. *Investigation*. The access to the experience is provided through making the participant verbalize the problem and then investigating with the whole group whether this problem is logically consistent with reality as the participant construes it. After presenting the problem and explicating its significance, the participant is questioned in a Socratic fashion; the object of the questioning is to establish the way the participant understands the problem. If the problem is significant enough, usually many participants recognize it as a problem residing in their own lives and help to investigate it. It is important that the therapist directs this investigation only within the general framework offered by the participant. He/she may only detect logical inconsistencies in this framework and challenge them; however, unlike in pastoral counseling, no pre-existent values or beliefs are articulated, and unlike in philosophical counseling, no explanatory framework is offered. The therapist may only offer reformulations of the participant's phrasings, or articulate logical inferences from what has been said by a participant, in every case making sure that the participant and the whole group consensually accept this. There is nothing like a "right" view a therapist would possess and teach participants. Only the way the client processes his/her experiences is being explored in a non-evaluative fashion, with the focus on logical contradictions, inconsistencies and indefiniteness in this processing. In particular, the following techniques are applied in the course of the investigation:

1. Location of the problem. It is often the case that a participant articulates a problem that is not theirs; sometimes it is unclear whose problem it is. In the case of a large problem that involves many people, it is important to single out the individual aspect that directly touches the participant.
   Example. *Participant*: My problem is that my son is unable to decide about his vocational preferences. *Therapist*: OK, this seems to be his problem. What and why do you personally feel about this?
2. Deconstruction of words. I try to notice the words the client uses without any awareness of their meaning (like "relations," "the other," "should," "wish," "cause," "can't," "no time," etc.) and to clear out their meaning for the participant. It is often the case that in the course of attempting to define the meaning the problem just dissolves.
   Example. *Participant*: I feel that I fail to be a good enough mother. *Therapist*: What would it mean, in your opinion, to be a good enough mother? And what do you mean by failure?
3. Rephrasing the problem. It is sometimes the case that just rephrasing the initial question in a more logically consistent and clear way provides an important insight and no further work is necessary. More often, however, rephrasing makes a technical step.
   Example. *Participant*: I am overwhelmed with stresses. *Therapist*: Do you mean that you are overwhelmed with situations that make you feel stressed?

4. Questioning implicit assumptions. I try to detect uncritical assumptions beyond clear awareness that have clients at a dead end, and to challenge them, trying to find their sources and reasons.
   Example. *Participant*: I never have time. I am engaged in many really interesting and enriching things but I have no time to stop, to pause... *Therapist*: Do you think that if you are really engaged in your life, free time will somehow appear by itself?
5. Inferring existential laws. Quite often a group comes to the awareness of some law that becomes absolutely self-evident as soon as it is articulated, and the participant sees the cause of his/her problems in having violated the law. At every session the participants come to discover four to five laws, and they are the same for all the groups (by this time the list includes eight of them).
   Example. *Participant*: Why doesn't she change her behavior? *Therapist*: Why does she have to change her behavior? *Participant*: I have been expecting for years that she would change. *Therapist*: What reasons do you have to expect this? *Participant*: She must. *Therapist*: Really? *Participant*: You mean she will not change? *Therapist*: People sometimes change but usually not when we are expecting it. What I mean is that you would do better to expect she will not. Do people tend to behave as they did before? *Participant*: They do, but sometimes... *Therapist*: There are laws, there are exceptions and individual cases. We cannot expect an exception, right? *Participant*: True, we can't. *Therapist*: Can we formulate as a law that people tend to behave every time the way they did before—that does not exclude a chance that it may change one day? *Participant*: It seems so... so I just had false expectations, right? *Therapist*: What does your experience say about this? *Participant*: My experience... people rarely change, it seems to me. So I am neglecting the law? *Therapist*: You seem to neglect your experience, which knows the law.

D. *The outcomes*. There are several possible positive outcomes of working with a problem in the way described above. The first is problem dissolution, as mentioned above: making the participant aware that the words that compose the problem have no references in his/her life experience, making the problem dissolve. "I just don't have this problem anymore." The second is problem reformulation: discovering that the root is a somewhat different problem, the participant is ready to struggle with the new problem, considering it to be more manageable. The third is problem operationalization: finding the algorithm leading to its solution. The problem is thus transformed into a task. The fourth is problem deproblematization: the participant discovers that what has been considered a problem is a logical consequence of, and/or the acceptable price for, something important, e.g., for resolving another problem. Therefore, it cannot be removed without changing the participant's whole way of life or other undesirable consequences. This enables the participant to come to terms with the problem and change his/her attitude towards it.

However, life enhancement strategy is not really focused on the investigation of the specific aspects of the participant's worldview; rather, we are trying to elaborate some basic consensus on the world in which we all live, based only on our own personal experience. The focus of the participant's attention is directed outwards to the world, rather than to his/her experiences and individual obstacles. In life enhancement work the therapist largely neglects all the individual peculiarities and subjective experiences of the participant, his/her psychological "portfolio": individual biography, life history, traits, individual features, experiences, stereotypes, emotions, goals, values, plans, traumas, complexes, introjections, family and career situation, etc. *The work is not about the client—it's about the world.* Two underlying principles of an existential worldview that are discovered and developed in life enhancement work are, first, basing it on one's own experience rather than on a priori assumptions, and second, verifying our experience with the experiences of others. We cannot learn about reality from external sources; we can discover important things about reality in our own experience and check it with other fellow beings, provided that we think correctly and accurately in this process. The task is to make our picture of the world consistent. Inasmuch as it becomes intra-individually consistent, it becomes also inter-individually consistent, consensually shared, and vice versa.

The problem belongs to the realm of the client's experience; it can be solved only by the client himself/herself. Sometimes the client doesn't even describe the problem, he/she feels uneasy and gives some vague statements from which the problem narrative cannot be reconstructed. It is nevertheless enough to start the questioning process. The group learns to think correctly about life issues as the special cases of general laws, the laws not taught by the therapist, but rather deduced or induced by the participants from their own experiences. The common result is that, in the course of group discussion, the group notices that the person who had presented the problem has stopped speaking. Being asked why, he/she answers that the problem does not exist anymore. Often, similar insights are reported by participants who have not directly participated in the discussion, but were just present. I often don't know what a problem was or how it was solved; I only know that the problem existed for months or years, and that it ceased to exist. I have not inspected the personality of the client, nor the ways he/she perceives the world; to put it metaphorically, I have the feeling of having just untied some knots of the client's understanding of the world and himself/herself, or having sensed and massaged a way through some rigid blocks in his/her "experiencing muscles."

The Targets of Life Enhancement Work

Personality changes facilitated through life enhancement work occur at the noetic level of human functioning, the level of meanings. Frankl (1969, 1984; see also Wong 2012), following philosopher Max Scheler, described this level as the superordinate level of human being above the biological one (body) and psychological one (mind); a similar conceptualization was proposed by van Deurzen (2002) in her extended structural model of the human life-world. Meanings and values are more than just our mental constructions, because they exist also beyond individual minds, making what Popper (1979) called "World 3," reducible neither to the "World 1" of material objects and events, nor to the "World 2" of subjective mental constructions of our minds.

Hence, we should not look for the changes in traditionally measured variables that belong to a lower, psychological level. The 10 dimensions listed below can be treated as the targets or tasks of life enhancement work and the changes along these dimensions as its results. This is not a closed list, but rather an inductive generalization of practical experience; most likely this list will be elaborated further.

1. *The curiosity and courage to know and understand.* We take it for granted that any restrictions of the possibilities for gaining new knowledge of the world, as well as new meaning-making contexts and new explanations, are harmful for personality development, even if these restrictions are guided by moral reasons. It is more or less understandable that we impose on children some restrictions on information gathering via the Internet or TV, but doing this for adults means treating them as inferior beings lacking responsibility for themselves. Since life enhancement work helps to use one's consciousness for rational working through one's experiences, it follows from this that the completeness and plurality of experiences do no harm; one is taught not to be afraid of knowledge, nor of lack of knowledge, nor of contradictions, nor of lack of explanations. I can refer to Rollo May's interpretation of the myth of Oedipus: Oedipus' way is the way to the knowledge of the truth despite multiple obstacles. Oedipus strives to find the truth, though he feels it may be painful and even disastrous for him. Sphinx symbolizes the evil we deny in ourselves and project to the outer world, producing the monster behind the town walls and having to sacrifice to this monster. Sphinx destroys herself when Oedipus discovers the evil within himself (killing his father and marrying his mother) and has no more need of the monster out there (May 1972). We also take it for granted that being-in-the-world implies a growing stream of knowledge of this world; what matters is what you do with this knowledge. The strategy of escape from knowledge is hardly beneficial; what can be considered normal is natural curiosity, a non-stop, self-sustaining process of accumulation of knowledge of the world and of oneself. This task is solved when the person is ready to move along the way of knowledge and self-knowledge, no matter what kind of discoveries he/she would have to face.
2. *Coherence of the world*, structural links between its components. Characteristic of those who experience problems in relating to the world, in construing and fulfilling their life projects, and who tend to swim with the stream, is fragmentation of their life-world. There are some research tools that help to reveal the structural links between the elements of one's life-world and through the awareness of this structure they sometimes provide a notable transformational effect. An example is the Ultimate Meanings Technique (Leontiev 2007), which

requires building the meaning chains that explain human activities; the structural properties of the meaning chains and their coherence prove to be important individual variables co-variating with personal growth. The task is solved when the person's picture of the world is coherent rather than fragmented, though absolute coherence is characteristic of paranoia or rigid fanaticism and is thus as unhealthy as complete fragmentation.

3. *Reflective awareness*. This is an important aspect of the anthropological capacity of self-detachment (Frankl 1969). Reflective awareness includes the awareness not only of the surrounding world, but also of us as beings-in-the-world. It helps us to see the borderline between ourselves and the stream of life we are engaged in and thus to relate to this stream, and the forms of activity that proceed according to mental mechanisms ("autopilots") as options that can be accepted, rejected, or transformed, rather than as the "objective" state of events. This is a precondition for any choice, for in order to choose we must see the options and mind the gap between the chooser and the option. In a somewhat different formulation, human freedom is located in the pause we make between the stimulus and response; thus we break a causal chain mechanically guiding our behavior and become capable of choosing its actual direction (May 1981). The task is solved when the persons are able, in critical points of life, to detach deliberately from what they are doing and to consider different possible actions.
4. *Involvement*. Truly authentic being-in-the-world presupposes personal involvement in one's actions. Involvement means contributing some deliberate efforts to one's actions rather than just letting them go. This aspect can be paralleled to self-transcendence as human anthropological capacity (Frankl 1969). The most elaborated psychological theory depicting this aspect of life enhancement is Salvatore Maddi's theory of hardiness (Maddi 1998). Having defined the attitude of hardiness as the variable relevant to the concept of "courage to be" (Tillich 1952), Maddi described three of its components: commitment, control, and challenge. Commitment is the tendency to keep involved in events rather than trying to stay apart from them. As has been shown in numerous experimental studies, commitment, like the other two components, accounts for the capacity to maintain self-regulation and goal-directedness under heavy stress. Another similar concept is engagement; some existentially-oriented authors stress that engagement is a necessary condition for psychotherapeutic (Yalom 1980) or self-developmental (Mamardashvili 1995) transformations. The task is solved when the person is ready to invest himself/herself into the important decisions and enterprises of his/her life.
5. *The scale of the life world*, which distinguishes between the important and unimportant, the central and the peripheral, the necessary and the facultative. A frequent problem to work through in the course of life enhancement work is non-discrimination; the person ascribes too much importance to small things that have little meaning, and gives too little attention to really important things. It is well-known and supported by experimental data that near-death experiences help to re-establish the adequate scale of events in one's life (e.g., Yalom

1980). The task is solved if, despite individual peculiarities of personal meanings, the person does not underestimate really important things at the expense of false values.

6. *Objectivity as the counterpart of narcissism and insult.* Objectivity as one of the basic human capacities has been conceptualized by Fromm (1955), who spoke of the development of this capacity (that can never be complete) in the course of overcoming the narcissistic attitude presuming that everything in the world is being made for one's own pleasure or displeasure. Objectivity, on the other hand, presupposes that events in the world are going on along with their own laws, not necessarily adjusting to our wishes and interests. The feeling of being insulted is a characteristically narcissistic experience. Insult is an extra-punitive response to the violated expectations. It follows from the presumption that other people's behavior must conform to one's own expectations; if it does not, they deserve punishment. This childish presumption is to be overcome. Gratitude as a human phenomenon is becoming possible inasmuch as the person becomes aware that the world at large and all the other people do exist within their own context, rather than the person's own, whether one likes it or not. If someone tries to please me, to fulfill my expectations, it is a special gift to be highly appreciated, because no one owes it to me. The task is thus solved when the person ceases to impose his/her expectations upon other people and to judge their behavior from the viewpoint of these expectations; the alternative is, to use Spinoza's words, not to cry, not to laugh, just to understand.
7. *Time integration and time mastery.* A self-detached position toward one's life provides the possibility of different attitudes to time. The main aspects of the individual attitude to time are: (1) integration versus dissociation of the past, present and future; (2) open (Taoist) versus closed (pragmatic) views on the processes developing in time, the readiness to stay in them as they are versus the striving to control, exploit and accelerate them; (3) perceiving time as a valuable resource to be carefully distributed versus as an empty space to be somehow filled; and (4) culturally-mediated forms of time structuring. The task is solved when the person lives within time, rather than out of time; that is, in the integrated movement from the past, through the present to the future in permanent interaction, with the world moving in the opposite direction, from the future through the present to the past; he/she is able to switch between the open, non-doing and closed, consuming attitude to time resources; he/she perceives time as a valuable resource and never has the problem of "killing time," chronocide.
8. *The essential contact with life.* What is meant here is that the Western philosophical tradition has been conceptualized in terms of ontical versus ontological, and in terms of maja in Oriental thought. The point is that the tangible surface "reality" permanently given to us in our everyday experience contains many illusory experiences not rooted in the in-depth structure of true being-in-the-world; very occasionally we have a chance to get through the superficial, meaningless, illusory experiences to some awareness of the true

being. This cannot be provided by special goal-directed efforts; what is necessary for this is one's readiness to discriminate, to recognize in the experiences we face something true in the stream of otherwise illusory stimuli. The most elaborated view on this discrimination has been proposed in the philosophical anthropology of Mamardashvili (1995), based on the ontology expressed in the prose of Marcel Proust. The task is solved when the person can discriminate between the two layers and is sensitive to the signals from the deeper layer of true life.
9. *Authenticity*. Bugental (1991) has brilliantly expressed it in the metaphorical image of being alive versus being "on tape"—numerous tapes of inborn or acquired nature have been recorded and are waiting in us till something switches them on. The choice we face is either to let one or another tape play in us or to be alive, that is to be able to change, to behave in a different way at every moment of our life (Bugental 1981, 1991; Mamardashvili 1995). Existential psychology at large is conceptualized, in line with this, as the layer of psychology that deals with the person at the level where he/she appears as an auto-determined, rather than a determined being (Leontiev 2004, 2014). The task is solved when the person is able to discriminate his/her authentic "I" from numerous tapes and to stay "alive" till the life is over.
10. The last target is *the provision of mediating mental tools*—mental algorithms, sign systems and orientation frameworks (logic, ideologies, axioms, etc.). Using tools while interacting with nature has long been considered an essential feature characteristic of a human being. However, human beings actively deal with their own nature in the same way. We need some external point of support in order to transform the external reality, according to the well-known Archimedes' demand: give me the point of support, and I will turn the Earth upside down. It is the same with our inner reality: mediation based on self-detachment gives us the possibility of self-determination and self-control. "Impossible to relate directly to oneself. Indirectly it is possible" (Vygotsky 1989, p. 61).

How Does It Work?

In the course of more than 15 life enhancement workshops with over 300 participants I have found multiple confirmations of the hypothesis that *many psychological problems can be successfully treated through improving participants' experience processing*.

Life enhancement work is based on the anthropological capacity of self-transcendence (Frankl 1969), one's intentional directedness at something in the world rather than at oneself. In fact, in life enhancement workshops one never speaks of how to solve the problem, only how did it appear at all. And as soon as all the reasons for the existence of the given problem fail to stand up to critical inquiry, the problem dissolves. Only general ontology is being discussed, with little interest in the individual peculiarities of being-in-the-world or the subjective side of representations. Badly processed and not properly integrated experience is, as we learned, the main source of serious problems burdening and crippling the person. Life enhancement work is philosophical by content and psychological by form; its main objective is to wake up an "inner philosopher" within the person, to stimulate him/her and to help him/her make philosophical sense of the problem in the context of its place and role in the client's individual life. Unlike rational-emotive therapy, reality therapy, or philosophical counseling, life enhancement work takes place totally within the noetic dimension (Frankl 1969, 1987) with the awareness of limitations of rational reasoning upon the background of irrational forces. Refined sensitivity to one's life experience as well as to the world, and the increased capacity to bring previously isolated fragments of the experience together in a coherent but flexible framework, is probably the mechanism producing beneficial effects.

What occurs as a result of life enhancement work cannot be reduced to adaptive cognitive restructuring alone, learning about reality (cf. Glasser 1975). As for the process, life enhancement is not a matter of working with what reality is about, i.e., with the contents, but rather with the process. If a participant expresses an apparently misleading assumption about the reality, what is being done is an exploration of the way he/she has arrived at this assumption and the degree of coherence between this assumption and other elements of his/her experience and worldview, rather than a direct challenge to this assumption by questioning its validity.

As for the outcome, we observe notable personality changes. Participants usually report becoming more quiet and self-assured in facing stresses and uncertainties, even though these stresses and uncertainties stay the same. One participant reported, on the morning after the first day of work, that she had made a critical decision the previous night that she had not been able to make for years. Another participant reported, also after one day of work, that having read in a morning newspaper about a facility for the elderly which was lacking many necessary things, even a TV set, she suddenly suggested to her husband that the following weekend they take an old but perfectly functioning TV set and other items to that facility, even though it was about 300 km away. It was something completely unprecedented and unexpected for her, but she felt it as something authentic, organic. Such outcomes are typical. People get rid of some irrational expectations toward reality and come to a more mature attitude to life.

Sometimes the results exceed any reasonable expectations. Once I worked with a married participant who for many years could not get pregnant, without any medical explanation for this. I was sure that this case was not treatable within the life enhancement framework; what I tried to do in two hours' work with this participant in a group setting was to help her accept this indeterminacy as something that may happen largely independent of our wishes and efforts. Within two months, however, she became pregnant! She stopped making special efforts and simply let it be.

We have recently started empirical investigations aimed at registering changes occurring in the course of life enhancement sessions (Leontiev and Miyuzova 2013). In particular, we analyzed participants' brief self-reports given immediately after session completion during the last four years and retrospective self-reports given by those who participated in groups five to eight years ago. In both cases the participants were asked to write briefly whether they experienced any changes (and if so, what kind of changes). This is an ongoing project and at the moment we have only very preliminary data. Having their self-reports coded by independent experts and the content analyzed, we found that nearly all participants reported changes not only immediately after the session, but also in retrospect, though not all of them can verbalize this feeling. Detailed data will be reported next year.

The key role of tolerance for uncertainty is probably the distinctive feature of the proposed approach as regards some other similar approaches, based both on a rational cognitive-behavioral basis (Ellis 1994; Glasser 1975, a.o.) and on an existential meaning-centered basis (Wong 2010, 2012). If cognitive-behavioral approaches solve the correction task, replacing false beliefs with more rational ones, and a meaning-centered approach offers guidance in finding a meaning, both having elaborated strategies of attaining these goals, the life enhancement approach lacks an a priori working plan and does not offer "truths" to replace misleading beliefs; the participant discovers more plausible constructs himself/herself.

I have an impression that is still to be checked in follow-up studies that in many cases the changes involved deep layers of personality and being-in-the-world. The relationship between progress in understanding the world and progress in personality development seems to be more intimate than has ever been recognized within the psychotherapy context. What does a person feel when an outside observer, armed with multiple tests, says that his/her personality development has been registered? What corresponds to this objective fact in his/her subjective representation?

My hypothesis, based in particular (but not only) on the experience of life enhancement work, is that the progress in world understanding is *the* introspective correlate of personality development, the only form in which our own development is given to us. It can be articulated as a variant of the complementarity principle: *progress in understanding is the subjective side of personality development, and personality development is the objective side of the progress in understanding.* A person changes from the viewpoint of an outside observer, but cannot detect the changes in himself/herself. For this person the picture of the world, or "self-and-world construct system" (Bugental 1999), changes its shape and structure, becoming more differentiated and integrated.

This principle also finds support from experiments. Elena Yatsuta, one of the leading life enhancement practitioners and researchers, has made a series of "developing experiments" with different samples. Having facilitated the understanding of different texts, from classical poetry to classical and modern philosophy, she found significant changes by the end of her work, in terms of such variables as locus of control, meaning in life (the Russian version of the Purpose-in-Life test), anxiety and some others; most interesting is that the key mediating variable largely influencing the effects was the participant's attitude to uncertainty. In the case of the positive attitude personality development effects have been much more pronounced than in the case of negative or neutral attitudes. Yatsuta (2004) called her approach to life enhancement a *content-centered approach,* to distinguish it from the client-centered psychotherapeutic approach, thus stressing its self-transcendent directedness. Her data demonstrate that notable personality changes can be obtained in a direct way through the content-centered self-transcendent work with understanding.

Conclusion

The aim of this chapter was to depict a particular strategy of existential work, eventually becoming an instrument of existential psychotherapy. James Bugental called it ontogogy, though I prefer the term "life enhancement." *Life enhancement is a content-centered practice of the facilitation of self-and-world understanding.*

Life enhancement is not a recent invention; it probably belongs to the oldest forms of human relations. However, it has always been dissolved in more institutionalized practices: in education, art, religion, psychotherapy. Only in some Oriental religious traditions (and in some marginal Western ones) can life enhancement be found in a relatively pure form. Besides special practices, life enhancement comes about in situations of spontaneous communication with other people, with books, with art, with nature, etc. Before becoming the tool of therapists' work, life enhancement manifested itself as a natural process associated with personality development. It is the developmental process of broadening and structuring our subjective picture of the world, its restructuring due to the change of meaning-making contexts (as in the case of religious conversion), movement toward more comprehensive values, toward broadened contexts, approaching "the viewpoint of eternity."

To take in hand one's own development, to choose its pathways, one must be able to elaborate one's life experiences in a complicated and effective way. Life enhancement presupposes self-transcendence toward the world and an understanding of what is going on in the world. Psychological mechanisms of experience processing provide the ongoing understanding, unless some pieces of experience get jammed. This results in incoherence between different fragments of experience and the product of its processing, the worldview. Intervention strategy, sketched in this chapter, removes experience jams and restores the coherence of the worldview.

To feed human beings, one should give them a rod and teach them fishing, rather than just give them some fish. It's not about didactics, but rather about enlightenment. To enlighten human beings, one should help them to understand, rather than just give them some understanding. This is what life enhancement is about.

Acknowledgments The study was supported by the Russian Scientific Foundation, project №14-18-03401.

References

Allport, G. (1955). *Becoming: Basic considerations for the psychology of personality*. New Haven: Yale University Press.

Bugental, J. F. T. (1981). *The search for authenticity: An existential-analytic approach to psychotherapy* (2nd ed. enlarged). New York: Irvingston publs.

Bugental, J. F. T. (1991). Outcomes of an existential-humanistic psychotherapy: A tribute to Rollo May. *The Humanistic Psychologist, 19*, 2–9.

Bugental, J. F. T. (1999). *Psychotherapy isn't what you think*. Phoenix: Zeig, Tucker & Co.

Corsini, R. J. (2008). Introduction. In R. J. Corsini & D. Wedding (Eds.), *Current psychotherapies* (8th ed., pp. 1–14). Belmont, CA: Thomson Brooks/Cole.

Ellis, A. (1994). *Reason and emotion in psychotherapy: Comprehensive method of treating human disturbances* (Revised and updated). New York: Citadel Press.

Frankl, V. E. (1969). *The will to meaning: Foundations and applications of logotherapy*. New York: Plume Press.

Frankl, V. E. (1984). *Der leidende Mensch: Anthropologische Grundlagen der Psychotherapie*. Bern: Huber.

Frankl, V. E. (1987). *Logotherapie und Existenzanalyse*. München, Zürich: Piper.

Fromm, E. (1955). *The sane society*. London: Routledge and Kegan Paul.

Glasser, W. (1975). *Reality therapy*. New York: Harper & Row.

Leontiev, D. A. (2004). Existential psychology as a response to the challenges of the 21st century. *International Journal of Existential Psychology & Psychotherapy, 1*, 103–105.

Leontiev, D. A. (2007). Approaching worldview structure with ultimate meanings technique. *Journal of Humanistic Psychology, 47*, 243–266.

Leontiev, D. (2014). Extending the contexts of existence: Benefits of meaning-guided living. In A. Batthyany & P. Russo-Netzer (Eds.), *Meaning in positive and existential psychology* (pp. 97–114). New York: Springer.

Leontiev, D., & Miyuzova, A. (2013). Metodicheskii podkhod k fiksatsii izmenenii lichnosti v rezultate ekzistentsialnoi raboty (A methodological approach to registering personality changes in the course of existential work). In D. Leontiev (Ed.), *5 Vserossiiskaya nauchno-prakticheskaya konferentsiya po ekzistentsialnoi psikhologii: Materialy soobschenii (5th Russian National Scientific and Practical Conference in Existential Psychology: Proceedings)* (pp. 138–141). Moscow: Smysl.

Maddi, S. R. (1998). Creating meaning through making decisions. In P. T. P. Wong & P. S. Fry (Eds.), *The human search for meaning* (pp. 1–25). Mahwah: Lawrence Erlbaum Associates.

Mamardashvili, M. K. (1995). *Lektsii o Prouste (Lectures on Proust)*. Moscow: Ad Marginem.

May, R. (1967). *Psychology and the human dilemma*. Princeton: Van Nostrand.

May, R. (1972). *Power and innocence*. New York: Norton.

May, R. (1981). *Freedom and destiny*. New York: Norton.

Popper, K. (1979). *Objective knowledge: An evolutionary approach*. Oxford: Clarendon Press.

Ryan, R. M., Lynch, M. F., Vansteenkiste, M., & Deci, E. L. (2011). Motivation and autonomy in counseling, psychotherapy, and behavior change: A look at theory and practice. *The Counseling Psychologist, 39*, 193–260.

Tillich, P. (1952/1977). *The courage to be*. Glasgow: Collins.

van Deurzen, E. (2002). *Existential counseling and psychotherapy in practice*. London: Sage.

Vygotsky, L. S. (1989). Concrete human psychology. *Soviet Psychology, 27*, 53–77.

Wong, P. T. P. (2010). Meaning therapy: An integrative and positive existential psychotherapy. *Journal of Contemporary Psychotherapy, 40*(2), 85–99.

Wong, P. T. P. (2012). From logotherapy to meaning-centered counseling and therapy. In P. T. P. Wong (Ed.), *The human quest for meaning* (2nd ed., pp. 619–647). New York: Routledge.

Yalom, I. (1980). *Existential psychotherapy*. New York: Basic Books.

Yatsuta, E. I. (2004). Ot klient-tsentrirovannogo podkhoda v psikhoterapii k kontent-tsentrirovannomu vzaimodeistviyu v obrazovatelnom protsesse (From the client-centered approach in psychotherapy to the content-centered interaction in the educational process). In D. Leontiev (Ed.), *2 Vserossiiskaya nauchno-prakticheskaya konferentsiya po ekzistentsialnoi psikhologii: Materialy soobschenii (2nd Russian National Scientific and Practical Conference in Existential Psychology: Proceedings)* (pp. 180–189). Moscow: Smysl.

Structural Existential Analysis (SEA): A Phenomenological Method for Therapeutic Work

Emmy van Deurzen

Introduction

My work as an existential psychotherapist has always rested firmly on the basis of the phenomenological method. This method has guided my work, both in terms of formulating and understanding a client's position in the world and in terms of doing research in the field (van Deurzen 2010, 2012). This chapter will demonstrate the phenomenological principles as applied to the practice of therapy.

When speaking about phenomenology I refer back to the original formulations of Edmund Husserl. Husserl's work (Husserl 1900, 1913, 1925, 1929) needs to be read and studied before we can fully appreciate how much his methodology contributes to psychotherapy research. His books, from *Formal and Transcendental Logic,* through his *Ideas*, to his *Phenomenological Psychology* are essential reading for those who want to do phenomenological psychology or therapy. But if you are a beginner in phenomenology I would recommend Husserl's *Cartesian Meditations* (1929) which is the text of an introductory lecture he gave. Otherwise try an introductory text like that of Moran (2000). Phenomenology is not just the foundation of qualitative research, a technique to rival with statistical analysis. It is a new way of looking at the world, which you cannot practice unless you are prepared to immerse yourself in the spirit and philosophy of phenomenology. Practising phenomenology teaches you the capacity for observation and self-observation. It demands that you challenge yourself in your affective and experiential life and that you are prepared to become aware of your usual

ORIGINAL PAPER. Published online: 26 August 2014 © Springer Science+Business Media New York 2014.

E. van Deurzen (✉)
New School of Psychotherapy and Counselling, Existential Academy,
61-63 Fortune Green Road, London NW6 1DR, UK
e-mail: emmyvandeurzen@gmail.com

S.E. Schulenberg (ed.), *Clarifying and Furthering Existential Psychotherapy*,
DOI 10.1007/978-3-319-31086-2_8

assumptions, values and biases. In other words, it requires you to see how you make sense of the world and how you situate yourself in it. This is an essential prerequisite for doing phenomenological therapy. We cannot understand other people's worldviews unless we have learnt to consider our own.

What Is Phenomenology?

Many people have at least heard of phenomenology these days, but they often have misconceptions about it. Phenomenology is the study of phenomena as we experience them. It is not, as many people imagine, the study of subjectivity. It is the study of all conscious phenomena. It is a systematic study of the process of human awareness and the experiences we have. Brentano's concept of intentionality is its starting point. Brentano was both Husserl's and Freud's teacher. Husserl carefully elaborated Brentano's original idea, that human consciousness is always related and directed towards something outside of itself. To refine intentionality is the objective of phenomenology. As a mathematician Husserl aimed to provide a better method for dealing with human consciousness than mathematics or logic, since he considered these methods to be inadequate in capturing the essence of human reality and because of this also the essence of anything human consciousness tries to make sense of.

Husserl observed that any statement we make or any experience we have includes three elements: a subject, a predicate and an object. The below Fig. 1 reminds us of this basic arc of consciousness and provides us with a guide towards phenomenology.

Each act of consciousness has a subject, a predicate (which is our intentionality in action) and an object.

As Husserl put it:

> in perception something is perceived, in imagination something is imagined, in a statement something is stated, in love something is loved, in hate something is hated, in desire something is desired etc. (Husserl 1900/1970, p. 554)

Phenomenology proceeds by systematically considering each aspect of consciousness and by setting aside any prejudice and bias, methodically, through a process known as the '*Epoche*,' or suspension, which is sometimes better known as the act of 'bracketing' our assumptions. Phenomenology is about focusing on our consciousness, purifying our intentionality and clearing our minds of any obstacles that come from previous knowledge.

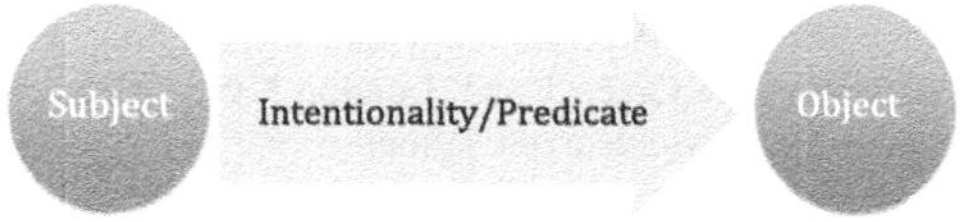

Fig. 1 The intentional arc of consciousness

In this search for truth, we remain aware that truth is complex and can be approached from many directions. Phenomenological observation can never make any claims to absolute truth. As Sandberg (2005) puts it:

> as the researcher is intentionally related to the research object, the truth claim does not refer to an objective reality as such but to the specific meaning of the research object as it appears to the researcher. Within the interpretive research tradition, therefore, truth can only be defined, as Lyotard claimed, "as lived experience of truth—this is evidence" (p. 61). (Sandberg 2005, p. 56)

What we aim to grasp in phenomenological work is the complex reality of what another person experiences and how this person makes sense of the world. There is an ongoing loop of verification, to remind us to check our observations against reality. Ultimately the closest we get to the truth of anything related to consciousness is arrived at through dialogue. In dialogue we refine our understanding of something until it fits the experience of several people rather than just the experience or opinions of one person. Gadamer (1960/1994), Buber (1923, 1929), Scheler (1921, 1926), and Bohm (1996) all considered dialogue to be the best way of achieving or at least approximating truth in human matters. In phenomenological work dialogue is central. This means that our exchange with clients is equally divided. We are not silent observers like analysts and we are not prescriptive, didactic teachers, as in cognitive-behavioural work. We are fully present and engage with the client's consciousness.

All our observations about our clients should be based in constant verification of our own and our clients' statements about their reality, until a more and more true picture emerges. In doing so we aim for coherence and simplicity of our interpretation of the facts. Such interpretation is always done from a hermeneutic stance, which ensures that meanings arrived at correspond to the meaning that was actually intended by the subject in the situation. Interpretations do not come from a theoretical outlook that we impose on the client. It is the client who is the judge and jury. We look for the essence of their experience and know this has been found when they feel a sense of intuitive rightness that feels whole, simple, consistent and congenial. We keep returning to the process of verification until this is achieved.

In entering into this dialogue we aim for transparency and seek to view each phenomenon from many different perspectives. We constantly keep clearing and polishing the lenses of our perception. We throw light where darkness is, allowing the client to get a sense of clarity, overview and perspective. The method requires us to become aware of and become reflective about at least three levels of consciousness that we normally take for granted, thus leading us to a fourth, ultimate level of consciousness, which is that of the *Wesenschau*, or the direct observation of essences, where our observations become one with what is universally true. Husserl described a number of reductions that needed to be applied to achieve phenomenological clarity. We shall look at three of these: the phenomenological, eidetic and transcendental reductions and consider how these apply to therapy. We will then take a brief look at the four worlds model, the timeline model and the emotional compass model, which can all help in making clear phenomenological formulations of a client's reality.

In order to bring the method to life, we shall apply each of these elements to the experience of a fictitious client, Jane.

The Reductions

Figure 2 summarizes three of the essential reductions that Husserl described to clarify our minds. They are:

1. The phenomenological reduction, to clarify the process of consciousness
2. The eidetic reduction, to clarify the object of consciousness
3. The transcendental reduction, to clarify the subject of consciousness.

In therapy practice this means that we filter out (a) our prejudice about the client, (b) our prejudice about the process of our interaction with the client, and (c) our own response to the client and the impact this is having on us as a therapist. The principle of the double hermeneutic requires us to apply the same to the client as well. So, when I meet Jane, I engage with her as fully as possible, being as real as I can manage, observing my impact on her, whilst constantly checking in myself how I am relating and how this is different to other relationships I have been in therapeutically. I will also observe how Jane is relating and how she is with me and I will furthermore consider how our joint relationship is progressing and how she responds to things I say or do. I will ask myself continuously what sense Jane is making of all these elements and will enquire about this.

Some people consider the three layers of phenomenological reductions to translate to the process of analytic or psychodynamic therapy, in terms of transference (the bias of the object, i.e., the patient), the countertransference (the bias of

Fig. 2 The essential reductions

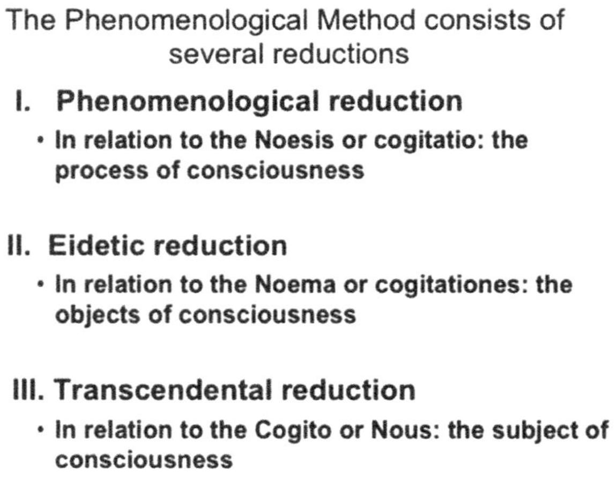

the subject, the analyst) and the therapeutic process (the bias of the particular interaction between therapist and client). However, phenomenology takes us beyond these reductions into the realm of seeing essences (Wesenschau), using our intuition after the lens has been cleared and the bias has been located and isolated. Phenomenology does not speculate about a person's reasons and motivations. It merely locates and deals with the how of his or her experience. Let's look at how this works in practice.

Firstly the Phenomenological Reduction

I have described the process of phenomenological reduction in several of my books (van Deurzen 2010, 2012; van Deurzen and Adams 2011). This reduction focuses on the process of our conscious mind. It helps us sharpen our awareness of our different ways of perceiving, thinking and knowing. It calls us to be more clear about the way in which we are conscious. The Greek word *noesis* refers to the process of thought, which in Latin is known as the *cogitatio* or the thinking process. For Husserl this process is always about intentionality and therefore to apply the phenomenological reduction is to apply a double take in relation to the very intentionality that we normally take for granted. This is often referred to as the *Epoche,* as we have seen above. This asks us to suspend the lazy way of observing we normally take for granted. We pay attention to our actual process of observation and experience. We do a double take. We stop ourselves. This does not mean we can get rid of our previous presumptions or that we un-think them or are able to un-know anything we already know. It only means that we put ourselves through the discipline of thinking about it anew and again and again until we begin to see a lot more than we saw before. We take the trouble to watch ourselves doing the thinking, or in this case, we watch our own process of engagement with our client. When I meet Jane and say hello to her, I mentally watch myself falling into a particular mode of relationship, for instance I catch myself either admiring her or pitying her. Perhaps I catch myself trying to be a really great neutral therapist, which can be an equal hindrance (Fig. 3).

Fig. 3 The phenomenological reduction

I. Phenomenological reduction

1. Noesis, cogitatio or process of intentionality.
2. Epoche: suspend your assumptions about what is happening.
3. Description: invite narrative instead of explanation or interpretation.
4. Horizontalization: be aware of the limit and context of your observations.
5. Equalization: initially accord equal importance to everything in sight.
6. Verification: don't jump to conclusions but check again and again that you are processing things correctly.

As we slow our mind down and pay attention to the process, we stop ourselves merely automatically doing what we are inclined to do, though we may continue to do it. Now we can begin to start describing carefully what is actually going on. We describe rather than explaining or interpreting. We embark upon a painstaking and repeated process of observation and description of these observations. This applies to the narrative of the client as much as to the narrative of the therapist about the client or in this case specifically about the therapeutic process. Jane's story about herself will change as I interact with it and she recounts it in different sessions. My views about Jane will similarly change dynamically as her being unfolds in front of me. Our joint narrative will evolve week after week as we keep correcting things we had not understood previously. This is slow work which creates a new way of being. It has to be learnt.

There are some rules of thumb to help us do this.

1. Stick with **description** instead of analysing or explaining. Observe, note, watch, describe and withhold yourself from jumping to conclusions. Repeat the same process patiently until what we see starts to shift shape and we realize we are beginning to see through the surface, to the essence. I will keep encouraging Jane to talk to me more about the things that matter to her, until they begin to be polished and find their right place. I will suddenly hear her repeated complaint that other people treat her badly and understand that this is her reality, even though it may not be the truth. She may eventually hear the bias in her own words as she is invited to observe it, over and over again.
2. Use the process of **horizontalization**, i.e., set your awareness so that it seeks out the limit of your vision at the horizon. Be aware of the limit of what you can see. Be aware of the particular perspective you hold and account for it. As Jane tells me of her sadness and loneliness, I see only as far as previous experiences of sadness and loneliness can take me. I need to keep describing to Jane what I understand her words to mean, so that she can correct me and take me beyond that horizon. She will, in this process also take herself beyond her own horizon of understanding. In dialogical exploration we both expand our understanding of what it means to be sad and lonely.
3. Value the process of **equalization**, bringing each element into view with equal emphasis, noting that this is hard to do and that all that is closest or loudest tends to initially seem more important. Rather than imposing my ideas of what is important in Jane's narrative, I will invite more details on many different aspects of it. In this way we establish a broad view of the situation rather than immediately falling into one particular narrow valley of understanding. The more I can keep a broad beam of light shining on Jane's experience the more she will realize that there is much more that she knows about her own reality than I do. She will become amazed at her own understanding and begin to expand her capacity for roaming around her world, instead of feeling trapped in it. Jane will remember many occasions when people treated her badly, freely, and eventually will contradict herself, or find memories that show her other sides to her experience.

4. Last but not least be disciplined about **verification.** Everything you observe is bound to hold some error and very often it is not clean of interpretation. So, check and check over and over again that your observations fit reality. Keep correcting the picture that is emerging. As I speak with Jane I say things like: 'It seems to me that you are looking at this from a perspective of passivity, rather than a perspective of possibility.' Jane may correct me by saying for instance 'The opposite is true, I am just constantly afraid of all these possibilities. They all involve other people getting ahead of me.' We can then explore some of the possibilities that frighten her. We can think about the ideas of 'getting ahead' or 'falling behind.' This may lead us to looking at destinations and directions to be taken, or pace of progress. In following up all these implied but unspoken avenues we discover new seams that need exploring. Some of these investigations will amaze and delight Jane, as she will get a feeling of life being an adventure, that she need not be quite so afraid of as she has been.

The Eidetic Reduction

When we come to the eidetic reduction, we are dealing with the actual objects of our observations. The *noema* of our intentionality, or the *cogitationes* of our thoughts, are the objects of our consciousness that we are trying to explore. This is of course the bit that the sciences are most thorough about. They have learnt to carefully subject the objects of our investigations to various procedures that allow us to make calibrated observations. In phenomenology we deal with it differently as we are looking at the objects of consciousness, rather than at the objects per se. We are for instance looking at the ideas that Jane is bringing to the therapy. We do not want to know about the actual measurements of her house, we want to hear what each part of her house means to her personally. To apply the eidetic reduction to her observations about the world is to try to see it in the most accurate and genuine manner. We want to grasp what Jane truly believes to be the case, without trying to immediately correct her or judge her. We draw out her authentic, intimate existence, rather than its outward appearances and objective qualities or quantities. We do not tear the client's views apart to see what they are composed of. We patiently collect them and wait until we are in a position to grasp the whole phenomenon. We aim to get a grasp of what we observe, in order to comprehend and understand it in a deep way, rather than to merely handle it and pull it to pieces. The eidetic reduction inspired the whole field of Gestalt psychology. The German word *Gestalt*, or form or shape, is a good rendering of the Greek word *eidos*, which means essential shape. Of course, the word has led to other words and concepts such as the word 'idea' or the word 'ideal.' The eidetic reduction helps us appreciate a person's ideology, by collecting the essential connotations of things that represent the elemental qualities of his or her life. The eidetic reduction is after the very spirit or soul of what a person observes and experiences. Getting familiar with this is to appreciate what it is that makes things important or valuable to a person. Of course, getting a hold of

Fig. 4 The eidetic reduction

II. Eidetic reduction

1. Noema, cogitationes: this is about the object of our observation.
2. Abschattungen: each object comes to us in various profiles, various adumbrations, facets or aspects. We need to check we are not eliminating or ignoring some.
3. Wesenschau: we look for essences directly; aiming to grasp what is really the case, rather than how it seems.
4. Genetic constitution (vs. static): bear in mind everything is in movement and changes dynamically; we only really know something when we see it changing.
5. Universals beyond the properties; ultimately we seek to unite all aspects to come together in an infinite manner.

the *eidos* of something is to grasp it as a whole. This is usually the opposite of what scientific investigations achieve as they aim to analyse things by pulling them apart. Science looks for components, treating things (or people) as objects, which have to be analysed and divided into their smallest parts or characteristics. The usual eidetic reduction of scientific enterprise is executed in an I-It manner rather than in the holistic manner of a phenomenological eidetic reduction, which seeks to capture the sense or meaning of the object under inspection in an I-Thou respectful manner. We do this as follows (Fig. 4):

1. **Profiling** requires us to bear in mind that each thing has many different mani-festations and comes to us under different guises, or different adumbrations or tonalities. In working with Jane I need to invite her to give me many instances of the same thing. I need to be able to resonate with, or taste, Jane's experience. This means drawing her out about many different circumstances or situations. We cannot claim to have knowledge of anything that we have not experienced any length of time and from different angles and in various settings. In doing this we will inevitably come to realize that experience shifts over time. Jane may tell me of her fear in relation to authority figures, only to differentiate quite clearly between the teacher at her son's school or the headmistress at her daughter's school and again showing a very different attitude towards a neighbour she is in awe of or the meter reader who inspired her with terror. Only slowly, in profiling many different examples of what is apparently the same thing, does it become clear how this is dynamically different in each case and what makes this so.
2. Husserl describes the **Wesenschau**, or the seeing of essences as looking directly for the core of something, for the heart of the matter. Instead of being waylaid and distracted by the outward appearances in their differing manifestations we look to what is the steady internal coherence and core of the being of something. What is the real nub of the matter here? What is the secret? What is the thing without which this would not be what it was? That is what we are asking ourselves. We try to resonate and get direct intuition of what it is we are trying

to understand. We get into the spirit of it. We do not alienate ourselves from what we behold. On the contrary, we make ourselves akin to it, so that we can do justice to it, apprehending it in all its inward truth. This is a crucial quality to have as an existential therapist. To be able to see through a person towards the inner concern and the preoccupation and yearning or regret that particularly drive her is to be able to communicate and make a difference. With Jane, the very sharpness of my attention to what it is we are witnessing together begins to loosen her own sense of constriction in relation to other people. No, it is not just a fear of authority. No, it is not just a habit of thinking that men are superior. No, it is not a leftover of being treated badly by her father. It is much more intense and infinitely more specific and interesting. She is trying to find out where to place herself in relation to all these people. She is fearful of all of them, but only until she recognizes what they want from her. She discovers that she is fine as soon as she has a role to play in relation to another person, a distinct role, that leads somewhere. Now we uncover a new reality, which tells us that Jane is lost in life. She is searching for a path and has felt that someone needed to show her the road to take. But now she begins to play with the idea that perhaps she can find a path of her own, in all these different situations.

3. In this process it helps to remember that things are **genetic** rather than static. The essence or the *eidos* of something or someone is never fully manifest in one second, in one moment, but always needs to reveal itself slowly over time and changes, as it comes into its own. Each being is dynamic, or as Husserl preferred to put it, is genetically constituted, which means that the full potential of a person or an event or an object is only slowly realized and revealed in all its capacities and abilities. Essences are not fixed, they are merely the core of something that is in progress and that is eminently variable and usually to a large degree unstable and often unpredictable in the way it will be altered. Life is in movement and phenomenology addresses life rather than matter. Perhaps the most predictable constant about human existence is our observation that life is always in flux, and that human beings are situational and respond differently in different circumstances. We need to get to know what they are about by observing and being with them in different contexts and see them evolve and dynamically adapt. Jane quickly discovers that she feels more at ease when she gets a sense of her previous lostness, juxtaposing this with her current exploration of a path to take. She can now differentiate the different challenges different people pose for her. She can also learn about her capacity to respond in many different ways. She is not statically anxious or phobic. These were temporary, transitional states. She can experiment with approaching, joining or avoiding others. She can learn to be many different things. As soon as she is finding out about the world, she is no longer just passive, not just caught in it. She is active. She is on the move. As soon as she re-establishes a more dynamic experimental way of life, her previous symptoms of distress shift dramatically into the background. She regains confidence in her ability to be alive and change. We have de-pathologized her view of herself. She is human again. She has possibilities.

4. **Universals** can now also be observed. By collecting several sketches of the same situation or the same experience over time it becomes possible to eliminate aspects that were momentary and fleeting. A picture begins to emerge of the universal qualities we observe in action. Husserl was very keen on universals to counterbalance the idea of genetic constitution. There is something compelling about beginning to grasp what the essential universals behind the phenomena under observation are. Husserl was more interested in such long-term findings than in anything else. With Jane this search for her universal values is very satisfying. She begins to accumulate a knowledge about things that matter to her as well as an understanding of the things that she is good at. She is good at being playful, for instance, and terrified when she tells herself that everything is so important that it has to happen in one set way. She learns about her own priorities, for instance she learns that it matters enormously to be with people who enjoy being with her and who appreciate her capacity for playfulness, creativity and care. She starts to feel stronger as she formulates these ideas and stops thinking other people define all the rules.

The Transcendental Reduction

As we progress with the phenomenological and eidetic reductions we come to see how our bias as therapist can be both obstructive and facilitative in the therapeutic process. We now have the challenge of working more with our personal bias. This was something invaluable in Husserl's approach and is an important part of the phenomenological process. It requires self-reflection. To turn to the transcendental reduction is to turn to the *cogito* or thinking subject itself. In Greek we may term this the *nous*, or the mind, the thinking subject of our intentionality. This subject is as biased and distorted as everything else under observation, so here too we need some practical rules in our dealings with that bias (Fig. 5).

1. We seek to uncover the **transcendental ego**, which is that aspect of consciousness that is beyond our ego experience. This applies to Jane as much as it applies to the therapist. Both learn to see that their initial views have been

Fig. 5 The transcendental reduction

III. Transcendental reduction

- 1. Cogito or nous: this is the thinking self, the subject of intentionality.
- 2. Transcendental ego: we seek to go beyond the personal ego towards a pure observing ego.
- 3. Solipsism overcome: this unites us as we go beyond ourselves and connect in intersubjectivity.
- 4. Horizon of intentionality: but there is still a limit to what we can see from where we stand; know this limit.
- 5. Self as point zero: be aware your vision always comes from the centre of your own world.
- 6. Transcendental inter-subjectivity: seek to connect your perceptions with those of others; interactive checking of truth.

corrected. Jane is no longer that rather pathetic, frightened, incompetent person she thought she might be, nor is she the passive and discontented, protesting client the therapist feared she was. Each learns to respect the other's capacity for interacting in a truth-finding manner and in that process new people emerge. Jane becomes more self-assured and the therapist becomes more respectful. It is hard to say which of these happens first, though initially they may each feel humiliated by the mistakes they have made in the process of dialoguing together and be inclined to pin this on the other's failings. It is important to transcend such pettiness and not hold it against oneself or the other but go beyond it. Instead of being concerned about our personal motivations or critical observations, we aim to note them so we can set them aside, allowing us to reach towards the inner self that makes observations, experiences the world and reflects about all that to create a point of view. Jane and I soon achieve such transcendence where we can laugh about misunderstandings. I can say: 'I did you an injustice there, remembering how you would have dealt with this last year, when you have gone so far beyond that already,' and we can laugh about it. She can say: 'You have no idea how suspicious I used to be of you as a therapist. I imagined you wanted to control me and be superior to me, now I know we are exploring my way of living, together, side by side. It is such a freeing feeling.'

2. While some have criticised Husserl for going into **solipsism** at this point, making it sound as if consciousness needs to be studied as a very separate and personal experience, this was not his objective. He wanted to precisely go beyond personality, character and psychology and he believed that when we get a hold of our actual consciousness in doing so we access consciousness as a general entity and in this moment connect with consciousness worldwide, or the principle of consciousness itself, of which we are only a small manifestation or example. This is often demonstrated in therapy, where I count it as a sign of progress when I feel genuinely as if I am learning new things from working with my client. Jane and each other client, willing to explore their difficulties with human reality, help me to open windows and doors on existence I could never have discovered without them. They of course feel likewise. The net effect is one of global liberation.
3. It is in this respect that Husserl began to speak of **inter-subjectivity**, by which he meant the bond he perceived between people, the bond that makes each of us like an element, or beam of awareness. Our personal consciousness only comes into its full reality when it joins with the broader bundle of light that is consciousness in general. It is our connectivity that sheds most light on reality. We are tied together and can never experience anything in a solipsistic manner, as we are essentially just one aspect of multifaceted being that connects and does not exist in solitude or separation. Because this is the case for Husserl, Heidegger's early work was so centrally based around the idea of *Mitsein*, being-with, rather than just about *Dasein*, being-in-the-world. Of course, from the outset Heidegger perceived this *Mitsein* as problematic as he saw it as a handicap for human beings to be so fallen in with the opinions of others. Husserl

did not think this was a problem, as long as each of us claimed our capacity for self-reflection. Husserl's phenomenology, as opposed to Heidegger's philosophy, leads us away from individuality. The objective is to unite and rise above separateness as we aim to apprehend a greater truth than we can achieve alone. When I work with Jane, or any other client, it is in order to discover truth, a truth just as valid for me as for her or any other person. That is the standard by which the work is measured. As long as I fall into superiority or my clients into dependency or counter-dependence, I know we have not gotten to the core of it. We are not yet collaborating.

4. For Husserl it remained important to account for our own centre of consciousness and not lose this in the movement of transcendence. For the centre is not only a limitation, it is also a focal point. It is, what he called the **point zero** of our experience and it matters to keep checking that all of our observations come centrally from that focal point of experience in ourselves. If we feel that we get pushed out of shape by other people we engage with, it is time to gather ourselves around that centre again. If we feel we are bending over too much to remain true to our method we may become alienated from our own reality and lose our foothold in reality. It is crucial that our vision is clear and it can only remain so if we hold on to our point zero, and remain aware of our point of view and perspective. We need to keep checking with our own sense of reality and rightness. Of course, this is true for our clients as well as for us as therapists. When Jane feels able to relate to herself in this centering manner, she no longer worries about fitting in with my perspective, or anyone else's for that matter. Finding the point zero goes with finding a settled kind of peace in oneself. As long as I feel keen to please, or frightened to offend I have not found the safety of my own centre.
5. On the one hand we keep checking that things make internal sense to ourselves. On the other hand we keep getting feedback about how it feels and seems to the other. The therapeutic project is existential and explorative. It leads to people feeling at ease with their own life philosophy and purpose. This is more easily done when there is dialogue. This is particularly true in couple work (van Deurzen and Iacovou 2013) or in work with groups. It is in the tension between different foci of ideas and reality that we are likely to find the truth of the matter. This is how transcendental inter-subjectivity is achieved, with ongoing creative tension and with a sense that human consciousness is clearest when it hangs together.

Working with Space in the Four Worlds

While we have viewed the main parameters of the phenomenological framework, it is worth mentioning that there are a number of other tools we can use in this process. One is that of working with a person's use of space on four dimensions, especially by paying attention to the way they deal with the inevitable existential tensions on each of those dimensions. Another method is to tune into feelings or affectedness. Finally, there is the phenomenological process of working with time. We shall now consider each of these briefly. For fuller descriptions please refer to *Everyday Mysteries* (van Deurzen 2010) or *Existential Counselling and Psychotherapy in Practice* (van Deurzen 2012). Structural existential analysis has many aspects and many layers, and we do not necessarily apply all of its capacities in each session. What we always do is to be clear and systematic in our observations.

Working with space in a structured manner is one way of seeing to it that we cover all bases of a person's actual existence. Human space is multidimensional. Human beings move and act in relation to a physical world, in which they move forwards towards things, or backwards away from things, where they interact with the material world in specific ways, creating a particular kind of intertwinement and interaction. They also move in an interpersonal, inter-subjective way, where they engage with others or disengage from them. Where they open to some people and close off to others, where they try to connect with some and disconnect from others at the same time as being welcomed as kind by some and rejected with hostility by others. They also have the experience of an inner world, where they can retreat into a sense of personal privacy and intimacy and they can be more or less open or closed to that and in which they can move in time, by recollecting the past, focusing on the present or imagining and anticipating the future. They also have a world of ideas, or a spiritual world, where they create meanings and organize their understanding of and purpose in the world. To pay attention to these different dimensions will provide a first framework of organization of the data we collect. We need to learn to observe carefully and systematically at which level the studied phenomena take place and what movement the protagonist makes in relation to this. Are they located in the physical dimension, the social dimension, the personal dimension or the spiritual dimension? And if so, in what way are they experiencing this and acting on it? And how do all these layers affect each other and weave together?

The four relational layers can be represented in many different ways. If we consider them in terms of the depth of experience of the person and their points of contact with the world around them from their centre, the circular representation is helpful, but if we prefer a hierarchical organization the pyramidal representation is more illustrative, showing how each layer builds on the previous one in a Maslovian manner. I tend to think of the circular version as a cross section of the spherical experience of existence, and the triangular, pyramidal one as a slice out of that same sphere (Fig. 6).

Of course, the four worlds model is only one possible representation or map of how human existence is experienced and organized. It is a structural heuristic device to facilitate our observations and understanding, but we should not mistake the map for the territory. In order to keep the dynamic element of our phenomenological observation alive, it is important to keep an eye on the tensions, dilemmas, conflicts and polarities that divide each of these dimensions. We face challenges on every level and of course challenges often spread across several

Fig. 6 Relational layers

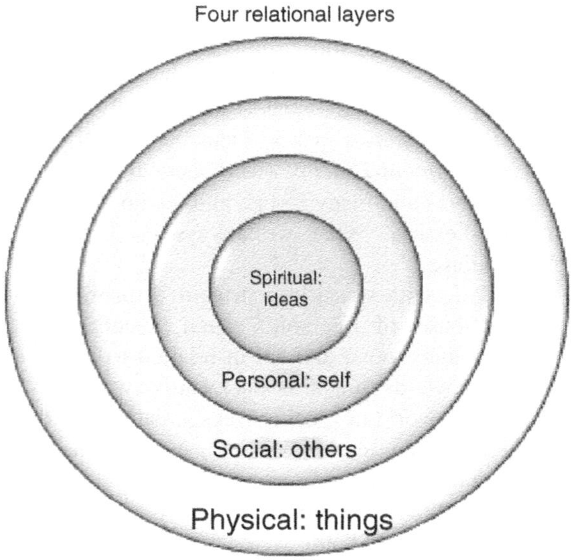

layers or dimensions. Things are not neatly separated into four quarters in the real world (Fig. 7).

The tensions on each dimension are multiple and manifold, but we can sketch out a blueprint of some of the major predictable tensions all human beings are inevitably exposed to. This gives us a framework to help us find our way in formulating where the client is. Predictable tensions are experienced as conflicts but they can be learnt to be experienced as polarities instead. Resolving the paradoxes

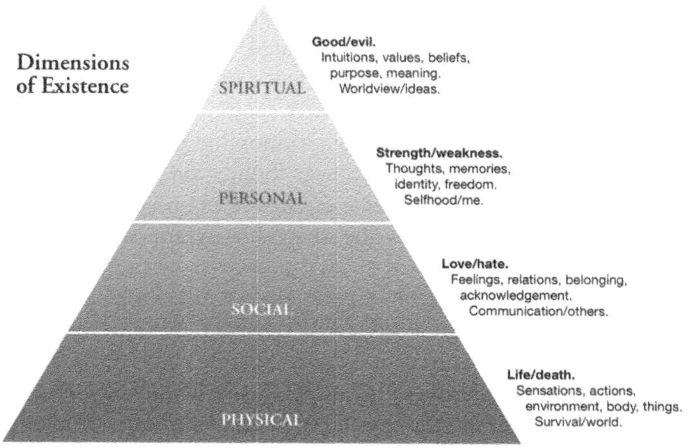

Fig. 7 Dimensions of existence

of human existence is best done by understanding that none of us can avoid either side of these tensions for long and that most of our troubles come from trying to pretend it can be done. The paradoxical nature of existence is that only to the extent that we are willing and able to deal with one side of the equation can we manage the other side as well.

Many people wish for the positive side of these tensions to grow and last forever, while wishing away the negatives. For some other people life seems but a sequence of negatives and they find it impossible to allow the possibility of the positives to ever be part of their lives. As far as Jane was concerned, initially, life had singled her out for bad treatment, and she desperately tried to get away from the negativity of her fate by hiding away and hoping for improvement. She was desperately seeking pleasure and comforts for herself and her children, but as a single parent came to fear all the threats that might oppose that objective. She was also desperately seeking love, but not expecting to find it. She despaired of her children's love when they misbehaved and expected all men to treat her badly. This was one of the reasons she was so fearful of other people: because she was terrified that they would reject and hate her, so that she would become yet further isolated. Jane also desperately aimed to establish her identity by various means, such as dressing provocatively in short, tight clothes, only to feel bad about herself when other people criticized or ridiculed her. She wanted to be good, but often felt that her children knew her better than that as they called her names or scorned her. She was caught in the contradictions of existence by trying to avoid the challenges and opt for what was 'best.' Getting to know a more complete map of living helped her find courage to face her fears (Table 1).

It helped Jane to go into more detail on each of the aspects of life she was struggling with. She became expert at making daily observations and then looking for the ways she had tried to get away with not facing her challenges.

In the more complex representation of 16 possible ways of being on four dimensions of existence the paradoxes of life become more obvious. This helps us think about the more ordinary dynamics of day-to-day living that makes so many demands, we often get confused about it. Nevertheless, we may also find that we overlook some aspects of life, where we are quite able to hold our own already (Table 2).

Table 1 Dimensions of human existence with their inevitable paradoxes, tensions and dilemmas

	Desires	Fears
Physical	Life	Death
	Pleasure	Pain
Social	Love	Hate
	Belonging	Isolation
Personal	Identity	Freedom
	Integrity	Disintegration
Spiritual	Good	Evil
	Purpose	Futility

Table 2 Overview of conflicts, challenges and paradoxes on four dimensions

World	Umwelt	Mitwelt	Eigenwelt	Uberwelt
Physical	**Nature**: Life/ death	**Things**: Pleasure/pain	**Body**: Health/illness	**Cosmos**: Harmony/chaos
Social	**Society**: Love/hate	**Others**: Dominance/ submission	**Ego**: Acceptance/rejection	**Culture**: Belonging/isolation
Personal	**Person**: Identity/freedom	**Me**: Perfection/imperfection	**Self**: Integrity/disintegration	**Consciousness**: Confidence/confusion
Spiritual	**Infinite**: Good/evil	**Ideas**: Truth/untruth	**Soul**: Meaning/futility	**Conscience**: Right/wrong

Jane's issues were in almost each of these categories, as she systematically approached life from the perspective that she had to try to avoid any problems, making things as good and ideal as she could do for herself and her children. She soon began to see that the extent to which she disallowed any negatives was the extent to which she became paralysed and frightened of existence. When she could see the world as a place to enjoy rather than endure challenges in order to get better at living, her mood lifted.

Working with Time and Noting the Direction of the Life-World

The next layer of phenomenological structural work is to consider the element of time, which is another dimension that runs through all human lives and needs to be plotted in any therapy.

The timeline of a person's experience is eminently important and dictates the direction in which a person's thinking is proceeding. Phenomenologists have made many observations about time and the most well known of these is Heidegger in his magnum opus *Being and Time*. His idea was that human beings as they are born are in some kind of way time in motion. They are themselves pockets of time in progress and are always in the throw of having been born and being as such always on the way towards their inevitable demise. Heidegger's notion of temporality is closely wound in with the notion of historicality: that movement of time in which we can look back and create a different narrative depending on how closely to the actuality of the experience we can bring ourselves to be. The same can be said for the future, which we can contemplate with more accuracy and resoluteness as we are more capable of anticipating our end. Heidegger's term is that of the Ec-stasies of time, where we literally stand out of ourselves in past remembering or recollecting, stand out of ourselves in re-presenting ourselves in the given time of the moment, engaged or disengaged, and where we reach out more or less energetically towards a future, anticipating possibility as well as the end of possibility. Famously

Heidegger spoke of the moment of vision, the Augenblick, in which we somehow bring past, present and future vision into one, and rise above our being in time, in the blink of an eye, temporarily overseeing life in an experience of authentic presence in the situation.

Working with the Movement of Emotion, Mood, Attunement, Values and Actions

The same can be said for focusing on the issue of affections, which are essential, as all human life happens in a mood. Heidegger had a lot to say about affectedness, or *Befindlichkeit,* the way in which I find myself in relation to the world. Husserl himself spoke of our connectivity to our world. This attunement is elemental and happens in a preverbal manner. Emotions are always already there when we become aware of a connection or a relation to anything in the world. Sartre spoke of values as partridges springing up in the world as soon as we act in it. Indeed, we cannot live or exist without setting off these partridges of our values and we cannot stop feeling the emotions they evoke in us. Because of this the lens of emotions is a particularly important one for us to consider and find a systematic way of working with. The model of the compass of emotions can help us understand how emotion and value are connected and in which direction a person is moving in relation to his or her value. The model is simple, but needs some practice for full understanding. The basic compass of emotions, below, shows the top of the compass, indicating the magnetic north of happiness, which occurs when a person is united with his or her value. The bottom of the compass indicates the point of greatest loss, when the value is forsaken or out of reach. The movement around the compass is clockwise, with the mid-points between ownership of value and loss of value leading to anger, and the regaining of hope of achieving value leading to desire and love (Fig. 8).

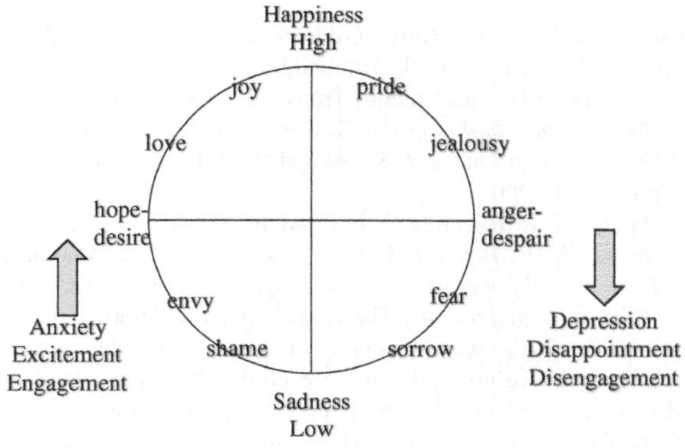

Fig. 8 Compass of emotions

This diagram shows only a few, easily recognised emotions, but it is possible to create diagrams that can illustrate a more phenomenological descriptive of the particular 'feel' of our place in relation to our value, lost or found. Jane had lived most of her life dreaming of eternal happiness, but finding herself, in reality at a position somewhere at the bottom, where she experienced much sorrow about what she had lost and much shame about what she felt incapable of achieving in the world. It was hard for her to start believing she could slowly build a more realistic life for herself, but this became possible as she felt able to create a more clear ideology of dedicating herself to being a more loving person. Jane became much more joyful as she allowed her talents to develop. Her creativity flourished, and she also began to value her own courage in moving forwards, in spite of challenges, and often because of them. She found that as she became stronger, her faith in life was also more firm and it was easier to withstand inevitable pressures and tensions.

Final Remarks

Existential therapy is so the stronger as it bases itself on a firm foundation of phenomenological work and in particular on the systematic approach of structural existential analysis. There are many therapists of different orientations who have taken the trouble to learn these methods. There are analysts, cognitive-behavioral therapists, humanistic and positive psychotherapists, person-centred therapists and logotherapists, whose work has become more efficient in integrating these methods into their usual ways of working. You do not have to opt for being an existential-phenomenologist to gain the benefits of this potent philosophy in your therapeutic work.

References

Alvesson, M., & Sköldberg, K. (1999). *Toward reflexive methodology*. London: Sage Publications.
Bohm, D. (1996). *On dialogue*. New York: Routledge.
Buber, M. (1923). *I and Thou* (W. Kaufmann, Trans.). Edinburgh: T and T Clark (1970).
Buber, M. (1929). *Between man and man* (R. G. Smith, Trans.). London: Kegan Paul (1947).
Gadamer, H.-G. (1994). *Truth and method* (Sheed and Ward Ltd., Trans.). New York: Continuum (Original work published 1960).
Husserl, E. (1900). *Logical investigations* (J. N. Findlay, Trans.). London: Routledge (1970).
Husserl, E. (1913). *Ideas* (W. R. Boyce Gibson, Trans.). New York: Macmillan (1931).
Husserl, E. (1925). *Phenomenological psychology* (J. Scanlon, Trans.). The Hague: Nijhoff (1977).
Husserl, E. (1929). *Cartesian meditations*. The Hague: Nijhoff (1960).
Moran, D. (2000). *Introduction to phenomenology*. London: Routledge.
Sandberg, J. (2005). How do we justify knowledge produced within interpretive approaches? In *Organizational research methods* (Vol. 8, 1, pp. 41–68). London: Sage Publications.
Scheler, M. F. (1921). *On the eternal in man* (B. Noble, Trans.). London: SCM Press (1960).

Scheler, M. F. (1926). *The nature of sympathy* (P. Heath, Trans.). New Haven: Yale University Press (1954).

van Deurzen, E. (2010). *Everyday mysteries: A handbook of existential psychotherapy* (2nd ed.). London: Routledge.

van Deurzen, E. (2012). *Existential counselling and psychotherapy in practice* (3rd ed.). London: Sage Publications.

van Deurzen, E., & Adams, M. (2011). *Skills in existential counselling and psychotherapy*. London: Sage Publications.

van Deurzen, E., & Iacovou, S. (2013). *Existential perspectives on relationship therapy*. London: Palgrave Macmillan.

Existential Psychotherapy—The Genetic-Phenomenological Approach: Beyond a Dichotomy Between Relating and Skills

Daniel Sousa

Models, Techniques and Research

A model in psychotherapy can be defined as a unified theory, or a set of theoretical assumptions about what is needed to promote change, and includes insight into personality and individual development (Anderson et al. 2009). The therapeutic technique is a well-defined procedure implemented to achieve a specific task or objective, and skill is defined as the competence or ability to do something (Cooper 2008). The techniques can be operationalized according to their type and content (interpretation, paradoxical intervention), by the way they are implemented (level of empathy, congruence), and quality (application moment, suitability to the client's need) (Hill 1995). The rationale of psychotherapy is that the therapist, based on a theoretical model, applies specific techniques informed by the model, in order to promote therapeutic change. In 1936 something changed. Rosenzweig suggested there are common factors—which he called unrecognized factors—that are present in all therapies, and could have more impact than the specific techniques (Rosenzweig 1936). An example of a common factor is the therapeutic relationship, which has been regarded as one of the most important common factors for a successful outcome (Asay and Lambert 1999). A specific technique is a particular

ORIGINAL PAPER. Published online: 26 August 2014

D. Sousa (✉)
Health and Clinical Psychology Department, ISPA—University Institute,
Rua Jardim Tabaco, 34, 1149-041 Lisbon, Portugal
e-mail: daniel.sousa@ispa.pt

S.E. Schulenberg (ed.), *Clarifying and Furthering Existential Psychotherapy*,
DOI 10.1007/978-3-319-31086-2_9

intervention of a given model, for example, interpretation in psychoanalytic transference. Since the publication of Rosenzweig's article, the field began to experience a dichotomy between common and specific factors. The American Psychological Association's (APA) "Empirically Supported Treatments" and "Empirically Supported Relationships" are an expression of that contrast. The first highlights the techniques and the model and are based on more objective research, such as randomized clinical trials (RCT); while the latter emphasizes the role of interpersonal processes and subjective experience, and are based on correlational studies of change (Castonguay and Beutler 2006). The first aims at defining particular treatments for specific problems, based on the same procedures of the medical model, assuming various advantages including cost-benefit (Chambless and Hollon 1998). However, it has been asserted, "the existence of specific psychological treatments for specific disorders is a myth" (Hubble et al. 2009, p. 28). In this way it is important to consider the interdependence and complexity of factors such as: the personal characteristics of the client and the therapist; the client as an active participant and his/her personal characteristics beyond the diagnosis; and, the importance of the therapeutic relationship (Norcross and Wampold 2011). There is a lack of empirical evidence supporting the assumption that specific treatments for particular disorders have better results than general therapeutic approaches (Wampold 2001).

The literature has emphasized the need to go beyond the narrow and simplistic view that divides the field into "techniques" and "relationship" (Castonguay and Beutler 2006), and that the common factors vs. specific factors debate is not adequate to conceptualize the complexity inherent in the therapeutic process (Samstag 2002). Research has suggested a mutual dynamic and interdependence between common and specific factors (Asay and Lambert 1999; Hubble et al. 2009) and that there is an intersection between the therapeutic relationship and therapeutic change techniques (Goldfried and Davila 2005). A recent study highlights that insight by the client was more evident in sessions where therapists used more directive interventions, and was less evident in sessions in which therapists used more exploratory interventions. However, insight arises more often in sessions during which the directive interventions are strongly associated with high levels of common factors. Again, to abandon an either/or approach with respect to common and specific factors is highly suggested (McAleavey and Castonguay 2013). Research has produced evidence that: both the relationship and the techniques contribute to change; the therapeutic relationship contributes to the efficiency of the techniques; the relationship can be applied as a technique or a technique can be applied in the therapeutic relationship; both the relationship and the techniques are dependent on the client's engagement; the relationship, the techniques and the client's engagement vary during the therapeutic process (Geller 2005; Goldfried and Davila 2005; Hill 1995). Therefore, the field defends tailoring psychotherapy to the individual client, and it is possible to balance and adapt the psychotherapy to the peculiarities of the individual through generalities identified through research (Norcross and Wampold 2011).

Existential Psychotherapy and Techniques

Existential psychotherapy (EP) has traditionally focused on issues of being over doing, promoting understanding above explaining and enhancing description over interpretation (May 2004; Spinelli 2007). The essence of existential therapy is found in the notion of presence, which is to say that presence can emerge and be experienced in the human encounter between the client and the therapist (van Kaam 1966). More than putting forward a set of new therapeutic techniques, EP aimed since its foundation to present an analysis of human existence. The therapist who would read existential handbooks as texts of therapeutic techniques would be disappointed (May 2004). Several reasons may have contributed to this situation. Historical reasons: EP was characterized at one point of the twentieth century as a critical alternative to psychodynamic and behavioural models. Theoretical reasons: EP does not advocate the application of the medical model of psychotherapy. Practical reasons: the therapist's main goal is not to apply a set of techniques that would entail the remission of symptoms or diseases. Scientific reasons: the existential-phenomenological tradition criticized the scientific context that attributed the epistemological decision-making process, regarding the definition of what is valid scientific knowledge, to the monopoly of the natural sciences. Cultural reasons: existential phenomenology criticized the danger inherent in the excessive technologisation of human beings. In sum, explaining the techniques of EP could mean adherence to a medical model, the manualization of the existential approach, the loss of its most important specificity—the human dimension. Thus, some authors argue that EP is philosophical, not a psychological method, and that it is an anti-technical approach (van Deurzen and Adams 2011). The techniques and skills are an obstacle to a true understanding of the human being, thus EP is based solely on a set of "attitudes" (van Deurzen 1995). However, this position may result in a methodological eclecticism (Walsh and McElwain 2002), leading to a lack of specificity about the know-how of the approach, or in adopting interventions that are inconsistent with the theoretical principles of EP (Spinelli 2007). Other authors argue that, maintaining the primacy of being over doing, EP does not reject a systematization of the know-how and of the therapeutic practices. The "being qualities," not excluding specific therapeutic postures, maintain the latter in perspective, not granting them primacy in the conduction of the therapeutic process (May 2004; Schneider and May 1995; Spinelli 2007). This chapter will be in support of this position and will refute the idea that EP is anti-technical or a philosophical method.

The arguments of the chapter are: (a) every psychotherapist needs a theoretical model to understand the phenomena and to inform his/her clinical practice; (b) EP is based on an existential-phenomenological epistemology, but is not distinguished from other therapeutic models for being philosophical—all models have philosophical roots—since its theoretical principles are rooted in psychology and psychotherapy; (c) EP has a set of theoretical principles that inform the practice based on inter-relational dimensions of a human encounter between the client and therapist; (d) the practice of EP includes both stances and therapeutic techniques that are directly related to the theoretical principles of the model; (e) at the practical level, there isn't a dichotomy between "being qualities" and techniques, as both are present and influence each other; (f) the practices of EP fall under the common factors essential to the therapeutic process; and (g) since its founding EP defends theoretical and practical principles that are in line with the latest research results in psychotherapy. The chapter aims to present a brief summary of the theoretical underpinnings of EP and of the genetic-phenomenological perspective, and specify the practices and techniques of the approach.

Existential Psychotherapy: Theoretical Underpinnings and the Genetic-Phenomenological Approach

Existential psychotherapy can be defined by five key concepts.

(1) Intentionality implies an intrinsic relationship between consciousness and the world. Because we are in the world, we are condemned to give meaning to our existence (Merleau-Ponty 2002). EP will then have meaning in life as a main focus of the therapeutic process (Frankl 1992).
(2) Inter-Relatedness—Everything that is constructed about us, about others, or the world, is grounded in relatedness (Spinelli 2007).
(3) The givens of existence—EP assumes that human existence is characterized by several general dimensions (ontological) lived by every human being, as for example, embodiment, time, space, etc. However, these general dimensions are lived in a unique and specific way by each person, which is considered to be the ontic way of living the ontological dimensions.
(4) Existential angst—Human beings construct meaning in their lives and therefore face a constant openness to the uncertainty of the very meanings they establish in the existential dimensions (Heidegger 1962; Kierkegaard 1980).
(5) Worldview—Existential angst is a natural result of the conflict that can occur between the worldview structure (in which personal meanings are constructed as part of the existential project), and the specific ways a person deals with the givens of existence and the uncertainty present in all relational contexts (Spinelli 2007).

The theoretical underpinnings of the genetic-phenomenological approach, as proposed by the author, were made explicit in another context (Sousa 2014) and include the five theoretical assumptions of EP outlined above. However, it adds three concepts: inner time-consciousness theory, the experiential self, and the theory of passive geneses. The passive geneses are the beliefs a human being creates along his/her life. These concepts are methodologically framed by Edmund Husserl's static and genetic methods.

The 'Static' and the 'Genetic' Methods

When existential therapists refer to the phenomenological method, they are actually referring to the first phenomenological method (static) developed by Husserl. However, the author developed it, not with the intention of studying the experience of an individual, but to serve as a methodological basis for establishing phenomenology as a theory of knowledge. When Husserl focused on the individual, on the facticity of a person's life and history, he developed the genetic method. This method is not considered by existential therapy yet. The central point for this methodological change came from the development of inner time-consciousness theory. The static method is characterised by its attempt to describe the way in which objects are manifested to consciousness. The descriptive method is the gateway to phenomenological research. However, according to Husserl, we can have "a new task" (Husserl 2001a, p. 639) when this is applied to personal individuality. Thus, another function of the phenomenological project is to consider the specificity of the person and his/her personal history, which is constantly in the process of becoming. Genetic investigation aims to explore the rational and affective, conscious and pre-reflective dimensions of a historical temporal awareness, influenced by past sedimented meanings and by future expectations and desires. When Husserl comes up against the depth of personal existence, he modifies the aim of phenomenology. The central question is: each lived experience (noema) has a deep temporally constituted dimension, which only the genetic method can explore (Donohoe 2004). While the static method is centred on the description of lived experiences, the genetic method investigates the genesis of the meaning of those experiences of life. The process of genetic-phenomenological analysis will be, in part, an analysis of the sedimented layers of meaning that intersubjectively constitute the client's personality and his/her experiential horizons. From that interrelational context from which human existence derives, conflicts, existential tensions and traumatic processes may emerge, for their part sedimented in dissociative processes that operate at the pre-reflective level. Husserl maintained a constant interrelationship between the two methods through the notion of the "leading clue" (Husserl 2001a), to describe the constant dynamic and connection between the static and genetic methods. The two methods are mutually integrative and do not function exclusively in separation.

> These are fundamental questions concerning the distinction, but also the ordering of necessary phenomenological investigations. Where they are concerned, I will always speak of *static* and *genetic* phenomenology (Husserl 2001a, p. 643).

Inner Time-Consciousness Theory

Husserl considered inner time-consciousness theory to be the cornerstone of phenomenology. The author considered that consciousness perceives temporal objects in a three-part dynamic temporal structure in which the temporal phases (past, present and future) are lived in a concentrated way in "inner consciousness"

(Zahavi 1999). Husserl used three technical terms for this structure: primordial impression to express the moment now of objective time, retention for the past and protention for the future to come (Husserl 1994). But in consciousness the three times are given together and the process happens in a pre-reflected way. Inner time-consciousness theory is a basic permanent dimension of human consciousness and is a theory about a pre-reflected consciousness (Husserl 1989; Zahavi 1999). There is unity, a flow of consciousness, a self, a personality (Husserl 1989). Inner time-consciousness makes explicit how identity is established in time, and how a person lives, prior to a self-consciousness way, the experiences of the past, of the present and of the future, at the "same time."

Experiential Self

Zahavi, basing himself on classical names from phenomenology, suggests that there is an 'experiential dimension of selfhood' (Zahavi 2005). This is a basic form of selfhood, a core self (the 'experiential self') which precedes and underpins the narrative self. The main point is: in an experiential dimension, all and any experience in a first-person perspective immediately implies a basic awareness of self (Heidegger 1988; Husserl 1994; Merleau-Ponty 2002; Sartre 1994b). To be self-aware is to have first-person experiences that are characterised by the quality of being "mine" (Sartre 1943). The basic dimension of human existence and the constitution of self do not take place in opposition to the stream of consciousness or separately from it; on the contrary, the core self is submerged in the experiential world, i.e., in the experiential flow of temporal awareness. The experiential self is the conceptual articulation of the being-in-the-world (Zahavi 2005). Self-consciousness is not tangible only when it reflects about itself, but it is already present, though in non-thematic form, in lived experience. However, at this level, it is not a matter of the person's transparency to himself/herself, or of a reflective process of construction of self-knowledge (Zahavi 2003a). The crucial aspect is the direct connection between the phenomena experienced and the first-person perspective, in which a primordial pre-reflective dimension of self already exists.

Passive Geneses

For Husserl, there are also intrinsic motivations belonging to each person, which are veiled, hidden, and not immediately accessible. These are what were considered to be a backdrop of experiences that the self does not immediately understand, but which nevertheless, continue to "knock on the door of consciousness" (Husserl 1989, p. 105). These are geneses of meaning that have been established passively, without the participation of the active self, and which have gradually formed sedimentations and habits that become part of the person's history and influence experience (Husserl 1989). Research using the genetic method acquires pertinence when the aim is to understand not only the active self but to deal with the depth of passive experience that involves the development of the person and present and future expectations. The genetic method, thus, makes vertical connections between the experiential self and a personal identity. There is a dimension that is totally passive, in which associative networks of meaning creation occur without the active participation of the self. These are the experiences that gradually lose their salience and are relegated to the space of "affective zero-consciousness," what Husserl denominated "the so-called unconscious" although with a different meaning from Freud's unconscious (Husserl 2001a; Steinbock 1995).

Existential Psychotherapy: Aims, Practices and Techniques

In sum, the inner time-consciousness, the experiential self and passive geneses form a theoretical triad that is fundamental for psychological and psychotherapeutic practice, elaborating a theory of change and personal development (Sousa 2014) of the genetic-phenomenological approach. The main goals of EP are:

- Facilitating a more accurate and authentic attitude to make choices towards one's experience of being;
- Facilitating the processes of meaning making towards one's life;
- Promoting self-strength and self-knowledge;
- Increasing the ability to confront the dimensions of existence;
- Identifying and engaging with existential angst;
- Improving reflective self-awareness with respect to worldview (beliefs, emotions, thoughts, experiences);
- Increasing consciousness as to interpersonal processes;
- Increasing personal responsibility for the existential project (accepting freedom, limits and personal autonomy);
- Exploring the essence (what I am) of existence (how I am) and personal identity (who I am) (Spinelli 2007).

EP is defined in contrasting versions, taken as descriptive, or more interpretive, as having a phenomenological nature, or conversely focusing on the analysis of existence (Cooper 2003). This chapter advocates the application of static phenomenological (descriptive) and genetic (hermeneutic) methods together to go beyond those oppositions. The methods are articulated to each other dialectically, fit specific aims, practices and techniques. The notion of leading clue (see below) is the bridge that gives clues for the psychotherapist to position in a more descriptive (phenomenological) or more genetic (hermeneutic) manner, at a given time of a session or during the therapeutic process. The static phenomenology addresses the intentional experience and informs therapeutic stances (*epoché*, phenomenological reduction, description, active listening, experiential immediacy, dialogical attitude, empathic exploration, clarifications and eidetic analysis). Genetic phenomenology focuses on the genesis of meaning and frames the intervention techniques (interpretation, oneself as another dialogue, reflexive reactivation, existential challenge, analysis of dreams and embodiment focus) (Fig. 1). There is no assumption that the stances and techniques are unique to the approach. For example, different models use interpretations. What is specific is how the postures and techniques are framed in the theory and practice of EP. On the other hand, the practices here proposed are not new, some have already been addressed by the authors of EP or even by other psychological approaches. Some specific techniques are proposed in a new way by the author arising from the genetic-phenomenological approach (e.g., experiential validation, oneself as another dialogue, reflective reactivation). The genetic-phenomenological approach analyzes both the experiential self and personal identity. Between both, the existence of a person is constituted and the analysis of the meaning of life, of existence, occurs.

The beginning of the therapeutic process focuses on three essential dimensions.

(1) The use of the descriptive phenomenological method, implying the *epoché* (the therapist attempts to suspend all theoretical, personal and cultural assumptions, and identifies and avoids a judgmental attitude towards the client); the phenomenological reduction (to focus exclusively on the intentional experience of the client, and the meanings associated with subjective experience) and description (to describe the client's experience and worldview, the meanings constructed, and sedimented issues, that is, beliefs incorporated during one's life; to understand the inter-relational contexts and to recognize existential conflicts and paradoxes).
(2) The definition of the therapeutic contract (where the therapist and model have to adapt to the client's aims and expectancies).

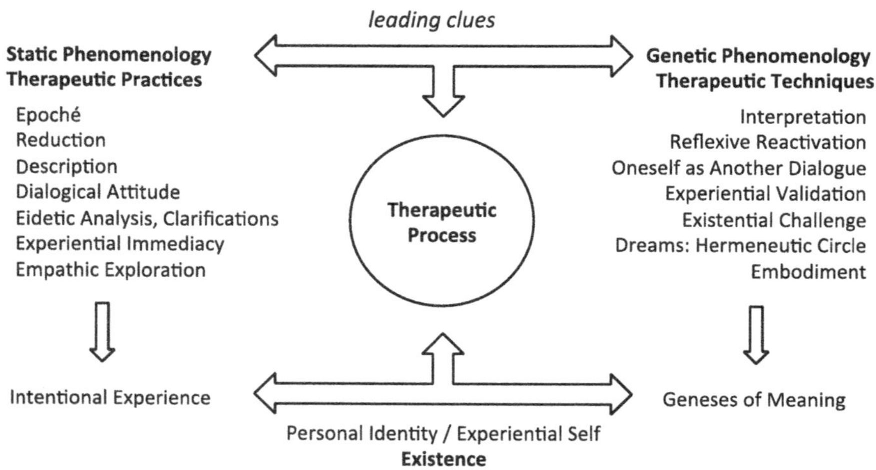

Fig. 1 Existential psychotherapy: The genetic-phenomenological approach

(3) The establishment of a humanized relationship based on mutual trust with a humanized setting.

The other therapeutic stances are not specific techniques but general principles that are tailored to each particular situation, the moment of psychotherapy, and what the client brings to therapy. The practices are dependent on the clinical judgment of the therapist and are based on their validation or non-validation, the context and relational network of meanings that is established between the client and the therapist. The therapeutic practices have a holistic nature, influence each other, intertwine and form connections with each other, and must not be construed as specific and isolated application techniques. The other stances applied with the static phenomenological method are: experiential immediacy (the therapeutic relationship and experiential immediacy are fundamental dimensions to access the client's inter-relational contexts and to the client-as-is-relationally-present) (Spinelli 2007); active listening (the therapist tries genuinely to listen to the subjective, personal experience of the client without trying to change or propose alterations to the client's worldview or behaviour. The feeling of being genuinely heard is identified by clients as being the first experience of acceptance and of personal change); dialogical attitude (the dialectic of question and answer focused exclusively on the life and experience of the client, promotes an opening of horizons. The question in this context takes the lead, fosters a growing questioning of the self of the client, which is perceived as both challenging but also as a self-knowledge and discovery process) (Gadamer 2003); reformulations, clarifications, eidetic analysis (the therapist will intervene using clarification and rephrasing aiming to clarify and simplify significant issues found in the client's narrative and the eidetic analysis allows the client to become aware of what is essential of lived experience instead of aspects that blur or simply bring "noise" to the communication and self-awareness); empathic exploration (having a particular resonance to the client's emotions and affects. The therapist can put into words the emotional content that isn't specifically identified by the client but is present implicitly and permits the client's contact with his/her whole being, his/her feelings and emotions, even those felt as hard to deal with).

The static phenomenological method with these therapeutic postures promotes: a trust in which the client feels understood, heard and secured; a space perceived as empathic, safe and supportive; and the acceptance of the client as is presented. With these therapeutic postures, EP is fully in line with the common factors mentioned in the literature (Norcross and Wampold 2011). Not least important, since the beginning of the process, EP promotes an active involvement of the client, considered an essential common factor (Tallman and Bohart 1999). Since its origin EP has advocated something that research has consistently emphasized: clients are not dependent variables where the independent variables are applied, they are not diagnoses where techniques are applied (Tallman and Bohart 1999). However, the phenomenological method (static), although based on descriptive research, is a challenge to the client (Spinelli 2007). The description promotes issues and challenges the beliefs and assumptions (thoughts, emotions, behaviours) partly immersed in a pre-reflective level in the experiential self. The phenomenological method promotes what I call relational *epoché*. Together, client and therapist form an experiential space framed in time and space where one can create a single, unique and different world from the outside world, and that allows the client to be in an emotional and reflective dome, distinct from the one he/she usually has in the natural attitude. Empathy plays an important role, a double phenomenological reduction (Husserl 2006) is imported to the intersubjective space and applied in the face-to-face encounter with the other. However, the therapist doesn't have access to the same thoughts, emotions and experiences of the other (Husserl 2006). The crucial question is that the empathic experience may become fundamental precisely because there is no total connection or fusion between two people, otherwise alterity (the difference between me and the other) would be compromised (Zahavi 2005). An asymmetry in the face-to-face encounter is present although this does not mean one person is more certain than the other is, but rather that they have different access to the experiences.

The use of the genetic method enables a therapist the application of therapeutic techniques. These are not applied in manualized form but in conjunction with the therapeutic stances of the static method. The use of an interpretation can be preceded by an empathic holding or by the descriptive phenomenological method. The therapeutic stances are a constant background of the process; the techniques are embedded with more specific objectives. For example, after performing over the sessions a descriptive investigation of the sedimentations of the client's worldview (beliefs elaborated during a lifetime), the therapist can introduce existential challenges to those beliefs, aiming at improving the client's awareness. The techniques of the genetic method are: reflexive reactivation (which aims to uncover deep sedimented meaning of the client's experiential self, enhancing insight, self-understanding and self-knowledge); experiential validation (the client feels validated, emotionally and cognitively reaffirmed, and this promotes the creation of a stronger foundation for personal identity encouraging self-acceptance of hidden issues that are typically unrecognized, guilt-ridden or seen as being worthy of criticism); oneself as another dialogue (where the goal is to create a distance between different parts of self, to encourage their acknowledgment, and promote a dialogue between these different dimensions of self that are often only present in a pre-reflected way); interpretation (which is always preceded by a structure of comprehension of the client's lived experience and is above all else an openness to possibilities. It promotes articulation between the client's experience and exposes new meanings) (Heidegger 1962); existential challenge (the therapists challenges and confronts, sometimes quite directly, the client's assumptions, beliefs and sedimentations regarding his/her worldview. The goal is not to offer alternatives or solutions but to increase the client's responsibility in order to undertake a greater awareness of his/her beliefs and emotional experiences, which in turn, may lead towards occasional behavioral changes, deeper change of sedimentations or even some general change in the worldview); embodiment focus (where therapists invite clients to describe their body experience and to consider where it is located in a felt sense. The aim is to assist clients in developing a more connected, or "owned," relationship to their experience via their embodied investigations); analysis of dreams (dreams are valued and are generally treated as analogies of the relational dimensions of the client's existence, but also as an analogy of the therapeutic process); self-disclosure (sporadically, the therapist may employ self-disclosure. It is to be used exclusively to help unveil client worldview sedimentations, personal experience or emotions).

As stated above, what seems important is also how the therapeutic interventions, for example, reflexive reactivation and experiential validation, are linked with the theoretical underpinnings of the approach. Reflexive reactivation is linked with inner time-consciousness and the passive geneses theories. For Husserl reflection impels a modification, a transmutation, an alteration of lived experiences (Husserl 2001b). Reflection does not therefore have a merely reproductive action; it actually alters the primitive state of experiences of the pre-reflective consciousness and gives rise to new cognitive acts and transforms experience. Reflective self-awareness introduces difference and alterity in the self (Zahavi 2005). According to Husserl, there is an experience of mirroring, which in the sphere of the therapeutic encounter can be termed as experiential validation. It is not only a cognitive or merely emotional process but also a profound empathic experience between two people where the client integrates parts of the experience that sometimes are detached or dissociated.

The application of the static and genetic method means to go beyond the dichotomy between relationship and techniques. There are several advantages and EP should be able to express the skills that therapists use, why and how, and by which theoretical rationale. Moreover, there is now well-documented evidence as to the effectiveness of the humanistic-existential tradition (Elkins 2012), but the area still needs to make a real choice on going with evidence-based research and the policies of mental health care systems (Hayes 2012).

Finally, a small excerpt from two sessions is presented with the aim of exemplifying the concept of leading clue and the connection between the two methods. The therapist can use clues from the client's speech to change his/her position, for example, move from a more descriptive mode to a hermeneutic one. The therapist may be more focused on exploratory interventions, or conversely, challenge or interpret sedimentation of the experiential self. A leading clue can be a word, an expression, a memory; essentially aspects that arise in the client's narrative that the therapist retains for himself/herself and that can lead to a change of therapeutic positioning. Sometimes this change occurs in other moments of the process. In the example presented below, the therapist makes a more interpretative intervention, based on a leading clue, which had appeared in the previous session. In the first excerpt, the client refers to the feeling of being inferior and this is synonymous with not being able to define herself as a person. The client also speaks of the criticism she felt and that lead her to refrain from showing others a thesis she was writing. This situation is repeated in other circumstances of her life. For the therapist, the connection "feeling inferior—define oneself as a person—show oneself," served as a leading clue to an intervention of a genetic nature. For the leading clue to arise and later, for a hermeneutic intervention to take place, there was prior experiential validation and use of descriptive phenomenology, demonstrating the interdependence between both phenomenological methods.

C = Client, T = Therapist

C—I feel worse for not being able to move on with things... And I shouldn't even be here...in Lisbon...
T—How so? (descriptive phenomenologic question)
C—I am sharing a rented place with my brother, he says many times that I shouldn't be here, that I don't need to be here to write my thesis... that I am spending my parent's inheritance money... deep down that I am spending his money...(silence)...
T—...
C—But if I were in my parent's house it would be very hard... I would feel like I was suffocating... the relationship with my father is very difficult... he has a very particular character; we basically don't have a relationship.
T—It is like you are not able to be well there nor here... (experiential validation)
C—Yes. And I can't move on with my thesis, I always think it's all wrong... But maybe it was always this way...
T—How was it always this way? (descriptive phenomenologic question)
C—I always felt I was worse than others, that I wasn't able to do things well.
T—What do you mean with "I always felt this way"? (empathic exploration)
C—I think my brother wasn't doing it on purpose but he was always saying I didn't know how to do things, he criticized me... I, I went on living things this way, it seemed like I was always making an effort to do things... then I became close to my cousin and she was very critical... but even before... when I went to university I was already like that... I always felt inferior (leading clue)... it seemed everyone told me how I should be... even to define myself... as if I couldn't define myself (leading clue)... now it has been harder... it is always hard to go home over the weekends, it only gets worse...

The Following Session

C—I'm still doing badly with my thesis...
T—How's work?
C—I have been trying to show the thesis to some people, but still can't. I tried but then I think people are criticizing me or I get irritated...then I give up... and then I think it's better to stay still...
T—How come?
C—I don't know, it's hard for me... I always think others are going to see things... That they'll criticize...
T—Showing the thesis is showing yourself, it is like if you defined yourself from showing yourself to others... (hermeneutic intervention based on the leading clue from the previous session).

The stances and techniques of the therapist are defined and presented separately for conceptual reasons with the aim of clarifying their roles and objectives.

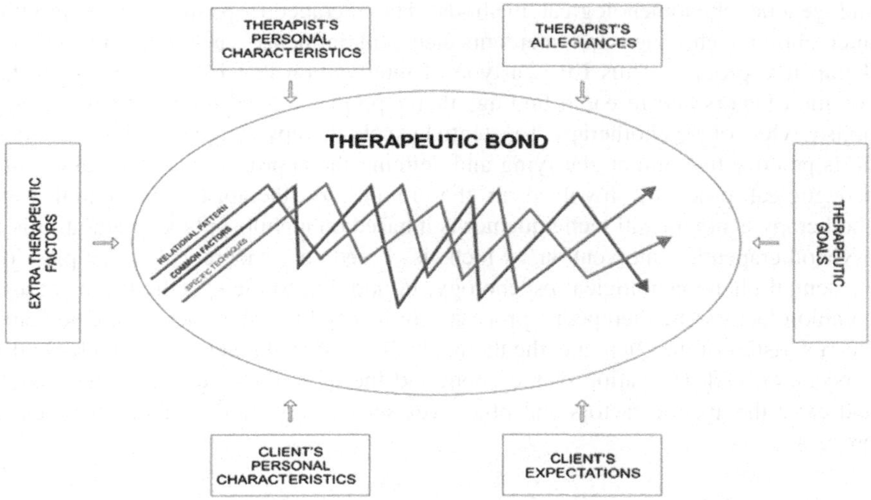

Fig. 2 The therapist's and client's personal characteristics and therapeutic goals

However, the relational interaction of the therapeutic process, the postures and techniques, are not added to each other, on the contrary they are interconnected, and influence each other (Hubble et al. 2009). Other factors contribute to the complexity of therapy: the client's expectations, the therapist's allegiances, extra therapeutic factors, the therapist's and client's personal characteristics and therapeutic goals (Fig. 2). The importance of two key factors that need to be combined for psychotherapy to be successful has been stressed as two sides of the same coin: the therapist's fidelity to his/her model and the client's expectations (Hubble et al. 2009). This does not mean that in psychotherapy anything goes (Frank and Frank 1993) but essentially that psychotherapy is an act in which the therapist follows a model (a myth) that includes a set of techniques (rituals) which both the therapist and the client believe to be efficient (Frank and Frank 1993). Although this chapter emphasized more the practical aspects of EP interventions through the static and genetic methods, it seems crucial those postures and techniques be in complete congruence with EP theory, since as was clearly expressed (Wampold 2012), the skilled therapist will provide, more than a scientific explanation, a sound rationalization that is adaptive for the client's complaints.

Conclusion

The genetic-phenomenological approach allows for a theoretical and practical framework of existential psychotherapy. It allows a non-dichotomous view of the existential therapeutic intervention since there is a constant dialectic between static and genetic phenomenological methods. The therapeutic positions and specific intervention techniques are interconnected and influence each other during the therapeutic process. Thus EP is a type of intervention that is consistent with the common factors and research findings that support the need for an integrated and holistic view of psychotherapy. Existential psychotherapy can present interventions in its practice that aim at clarifying and defining the approach, also facilitating the pedagogical processes involved in the training of therapists. Existential psychotherapy is not an anti-technique nor is it based on a philosophical method. It is a psychotherapeutic intervention, which is based on theoretical principles of existential-phenomenological psychology. In addition to the specific technical and common factors, the therapeutic process is influenced by other factors: the personal characteristics of the client and the therapist; the relational pattern between both; the expectation and motivation of the client and the therapist's fidelity to the model; and extra-therapeutic factors and objectives set by both parties of the therapeutic process.

References

Anderson, T., Lunnen, K. M., & Ogles, B. M. (2009). Putting models and techniques in context. In B. L. Duncan, S. D. Miller, B. E. Wampold, & M. A. Hubble (Eds.), *The heart and soul of change: Delivering what works in therapy* (pp. 143–166). Washington: American Psychological Association.

Asay, T. P., & Lambert, M. J. (1999). The empirical case for the common factors in therapy: Quantitative findings. In M. A. Hubble, B. L. Duncan, & S. D. Miller (Eds.), *The heart and soul of change: What works in therapy* (pp. 33–55). Washington: American Psychological Association.

Cain, J. D., & Seeman, J. (2001). *Humanistic psychotherapies: Handbook of research and practice*. Washington: American Psychological Association.

Castonguay, L. G., & Beutler, L. E. (Eds.). (2006). *Principles of therapeutic change that work*. Oxford: Oxford University Press.

Chambless, D. L., & Hollon, S. D. (1998). Defining empirically supported therapies. *Journal of Consulting and Clinical Psychology, 66*(1), 7–18.

Cooper, M. (2003). *Existential therapies*. London: Sage.

Cooper, M. (2008). *Essential research findings in counselling and psychotherapy*. London: Sage.

Donohoe, J. (2004). *Husserl on ethics and intersubjectivity: From static to genetic phenomenology*. New York: Humanity Books.

Elkins, D. N. (2012). The humanistic and behavioral traditions: Areas of agreement and disagreement. *Psychotherapy, 49*(4), 465–468.

Frank, J., & Frank, J. (1993). *Persuasion and healing*. Baltimore: The Johns Hopkins University Press.

Frankl, V. (1992). *Man's search for meaning*. London: Rider Books.

Gadamer, H. G. (2003). *Truth and method*. New York: The Continuumm International Publishing Group, Inc.

Geller, J. D. (2005). Style and its contribution to a patient-specific model of therapeutic technique. *Psychotherapy: Theory, Research, Practice, Training, 42*(4), 469–482.

Goldfried, M. R., & Davila, J. (2005). The role of the relationship and technique in therapeutic change. *Psychotherapy: Theory, Research, Practice, Training, 42*(4), 421–430.

Hayes, S. C. (2012). The choice humanistic psychology faces. *Psychotherapy, 49*(4), 461–464.

Heidegger, M. (1962). *Being and time*. Oxford: Basil Blackwell.
Heidegger, M. (1988). *The basic problems of phenomenology*. Indianapolis: Indiana University Press.
Hill, C. (1995). Therapist techniques, client involvement, and the therapeutic relationship: Inextricably intertwined in the therapy process. *Psychotherapy: Theory, Research, Practice, Training, 42*(4), 431–442.
Hubble, M. A., Duncan, B. L., Miller, S. C., & Wampold, B. E. (2009). Introduction. In B. L. Duncan, S. C. Miller, B. E. Wampold, & M. A. Hubble (Eds.), *The heart and soul of change: Delivering what works in therapy* (2nd ed., pp. 23–46). Washington: American Psychological Association.
Husserl, E. (1989). *Ideas II pertaining to a pure phenomenology and to a phenomenological philosophy*. Dordrecht: Kluwer.
Husserl, E. (1994). *Lições para uma fenomenologia da consciência interna do tempo*. Lisboa: Imprensa Nacional - Casa da Moeda.
Husserl, E. (2001a). *Analyses concerning passive and active synthesis: Lectures on transcendental logic*. Dordrecht: Kluwer Academic Publishers.
Husserl, E. (2001b). *Meditações cartesianas*. Porto: Rés.
Husserl, E. (2001c). *Logical investigations*. London: Routledge.
Husserl, E. (2006). *The basic problems of phenomenology*. Dordrecht: Springer.
Kierkegaard, S. (1980). *The concept of anxiety*. Chichester: Princeton University Press.
Lambert, M. J., & Ogles, B. M. (2004). The efficacy and effectiveness of psychotherapy. In M. J. Lambert (Ed.), *Bergin and Garfield's handbook of psychotherapy and behavior change* (5th ed., pp. 139–193). New York: Wiley.
May, R. (2004). Contributions of existential psychotherapy. In R. May, E. Angel, & H. Ellenberger (Eds.), *Existence* (pp. 37–91). Lanham: Aronson.
McAleavey, A. A., & Castonguay, L. G. (2013). Insight as a common and specific impact of psychotherapy: Therapist-reported exploratory, directive, and common factor interventions. *Psychotherapy, 51*(2), 283–294.
Merleau-Ponty, M. (2002). *Phenomenology of perception*. London: Routledge & Kegan Paul.
Mohanty, J. N. (2008). *The philosophy of Edmund Husserl*. New Haven: Yale University Press.
Montavont, A. (1999). *De la passivité dans la phenomenology de Husserl*. Paris: Presses Universitaires de France.
Norcross, J. C., & Wampold, B. E. (2011). Evidence-based therapy relationships: Research conclusions and clinical practices. *Psychotherapy, 48*(1), 98–102.
Orlinsky, D. E., Ronnestad, M. H., & Willutzki, U. (2004). Fifty years of psychotherapy process-outcome research: Continuity and change. In M. J. Lambert (Ed.), *Bergin and Garfield's handbook of psychotherapy and behavior change* (5th ed., pp. 307–389). New York: Wiley.
Rosenzweig, S. (1936). Some implicit common factors in diverse methods of psycho-therapy. *American Journal of Orthopsychiatry, 6*, 412–415.
Samstag, L. W. (2002). The common versus unique factors hypothesis in psychotherapy research: Did we misinterpret Rosenzweig? *Journal of Psychotherapy Integration, 12*(1), 58–66.
Sartre, J. P. (1943). *L'être et le néant*. Paris: Gallimard.
Sartre, J. P. (1994a). *A transcedência do ego*. Lisboa: Edições Colibri.
Sartre, J. P. (1994b). *A consciência de si e conhecimento de si*. Lisboa: Edições Colibri.
Schneider, K., & May, R. (1995). *The psychology of existence: An integrative, clinical perspective*. New York: McGraw-Hill.
Sousa, D. (2014). Phenomenological psychology: Husserl's static and genetic methods. *Journal of Phenomenological Psychology, 45*, 27–60.
Spinelli, E. (2007). *Practising existential psychotherapy: The relational world*. London: Sage.
Steinbock, A. J. (1995). *Home and beyond: Generative phenomenology after Husserl*. Evanston: Northwest University Press.

Tallman, K., & Bohart, A. (1999). The client as a common factor: Clients as self-healers. In M. A. Hubble, B. L. Duncan, & S. D. Miller (Eds.), *The heart and soul of change: What works in therapy* (pp. 91–131). Washington: American Psychological Association.
van Deurzen, E. (1995). *Existential therapy*. London: Society for Existential Analysis.
van Deurzen, E., & Adams, M. (2011). *Skills in existential counselling and psychotherapy*. London: Sage.
van Kaam, A. (1966). *The art of existential counselling*. Pennsylvania: Dimensions Books.
Walsh, R., & McElwain, B. (2002). Existential psychotherapies. In D. J. Cain & J. Seeman (Eds.), *Humanistic psychotherapies: Handbook of research and practice* (pp. 253–278). Washington: American Psychological Association.
Wampold, B. E. (2001). *The great psychotherapy debate: Models, methods, and findings*. Mahwah, NJ: Lawrence Erlbaum Associates.
Wampold, B. E. (2012). Humanism as a common factor in psychotherapy. *Psychotherapy, 49*(4), 445–449.
Yalom, I. (1980). *Existential psychotherapy*. New York: Basic Books.
Zahavi, D. (1998). Self-awareness and affection. In N. Depraz & D. Zahavi (Eds.), *Alterity and facticity* (pp. 205–228). Dordrecht: Kluwer Academic Publishers.
Zahavi, D. (1999). *Self-awareness and alterity: A phenomenological investigation*. Evanston: Northwest University Press.
Zahavi, D. (2000). Self and consciousness. In D. Zahavi (Ed.), *Exploring the self: Advances in counsciouness research* (pp. 55–74). Amsterdam: John Benjamins Publishing Company.
Zahavi, D. (2003a). Inner time-consciousness and pre-reflective self-awareness. In D. Welton (Ed.), *The new Husserl: A critical reader* (pp. 157–180). Bloomington: Indiana University Press.
Zahavi, D. (2003b). Phenomenology of self. In T. Kircher & A. David (Eds.), *The self in neuroscience and psychiatry* (pp. 56–75). Cambridge: Cambridge University Press.
Zahavi, D. (2005). *Subjectivity and selfhood: Investigating the first-person perspective*. Cambridge: The MIT Press.
Zahavi, D. (2007). Self and other: The limits of narrative understanding. In D. Hutto (Ed.), *Narrative and understanding persons* (pp. 179–202). Cambridge: Cambridge University Press.

Experiencing Change: An Existential Perspective

Ernesto Spinelli

Preamble

It would be difficult to imagine any approach or model in psychotherapy that did not assume the importance of change in some significant way. Indeed, for many, change is the *sine qua non* of psychotherapy. Change is what clients expect to get out of their therapeutic experience. And change is what psychotherapists seek to provide, either directly (and directively) or indirectly. Nonetheless, as central as this assumption is within psychotherapy, it remains to be asked to what extent psychotherapists have addressed key issues and questions surrounding change.

Experiencing Change: The Constancy Paradox

As has been noted numerous times, and usually ascribed to the Greek philosopher, Heraclitus, change is an unvarying constant (Khan 2008). One thing that we can be sure about is that change occurs. Continuously. Regardless of whether it is deemed to be expected or unexpected, desirable or unwanted, or whose impact opens up or closes down possibilities.

With this, psychotherapists are confronted with not only the foundational paradox of change but also with a major challenge. If there can be nothing but change, what then are we offering to clients when we offer the possibility of change through therapy? Clearly, it cannot be change in any general sense as that would be all too akin to the offering of an atmosphere wherein a client can breathe ordinary air. If the constancy of change is a given, then the psychotherapeutic concerns about

E. Spinelli (✉)
ES Associates, London, UK
e-mail: esa@plexworld.com

S.E. Schulenberg (ed.), *Clarifying and Furthering Existential Psychotherapy*,
DOI 10.1007/978-3-319-31086-2_10

change require some clarification. On reflection, it becomes apparent that psychotherapy is not so much focused change in and of itself, but, rather, that its concerns lie with persons' reflective experience of change.

Even then, the vast majority of change experiences do not generate the sorts of concerns that might lead someone to undertake psychotherapy. Rather, such concerns only arise with particular instances or conditions of experienced change. What is it about these that distinguishes them from more general instances such that, through them, the experience of change can become so threatening that all manner of evasive strategies to off-set its impact are enacted?

Experiencing Change: Variant Change Experiences

As a first step towards addressing the above question, three primary variants related to the experience of change can be identified:

(a) *Non-Reflective Change*: This variant includes the great majority of change events that occur throughout our lives. Non-reflective change events are multiple and constant throughout every moment of our lives. They elicit responses that 'meet' the change event such that its presence and impact upon us is incorporated without reflective awareness, hesitation or attempted deviation or obstruction.

(b) *Reflectively Accepted Change*: This variant is comprised of those change experiences that enter our awareness and which might enthuse, excite, shake, move and/or surprise us whether positively or negatively. Reflectively accepted change experiences may dominate our thoughts, feelings and behaviors for substantial periods of time. They may be experienced as illuminating, enlightening and/or overwhelming. Like non-reflective change events, our response to reflectively accepted change experiences remains that of a willingness to 'meet' and accept their impact upon us. Unlike non-reflective change events, however, we are reflectively attuned to their presence and assess their impact as having anything from minor to 'life-altering' consequences.

(c) *Reflectively Troubling Or Rejected Change*: This variant contains those change experiences that are designated as being unwanted, unfair, unacceptable and/or intolerable such that our focus rests upon attempts to reject, prevent, reduce or deny their occurrence. It also subsumes those experiences linked to the perceived incapacity to bring about desired change since these rely upon instances of change that have occurred at an imaginary level but which fail to be enacted at the lived level. Like reflectively accepted change, reflectively troubling change experiences may dominate our thoughts, feelings and behaviors for substantial periods of time and are seen to have a notable impact upon us. Unlike our responses to both non-reflective change events and reflectively accepted change however, reflectively troubling or rejected change experiences generate levels of unease and disturbance which can range from irritating to life-shattering and which arouse defensive reactions whose intent is to minimize, deflect or refute either the existence of the change experience or its impact upon us, or both.

It is important to note the potential experiential plasticity inherent between instances of reflectively accepted change and reflectively troubling or rejected change. Through reflective reconstructions and re-evaluations of change events, reflectively accepted change experiences may be re-construed as instances of reflectively troubling or rejected change, and vice versa.

What is being proposed here is that 'the problem with change' is not with our experience of change in a general sense, but with specific instances of change experiences which predominantly (if not exclusively) fall into the parameters set by the third variant—reflectively troubling or rejected change—as described above. Change experiences identified with this variant stand out for us as being disturbing and unacceptable such that we seek to fend off, diminish or deny their occurrence and impact in any number of ways—including psychotherapy.

If we consider psychotherapy's interest in the experience of change, it becomes evident that psychotherapy in general concerns itself with the undesired, unexpected and unwanted disruptive consequences arising either from clients' experiences of change or their inability to bring it about. Again, it is this third variant of change experience that is of primary concern to psychotherapy in general, including existential therapy.

What is it about this third variant that makes it so 'problematic' for clients? What are the conditions that lead people to identify certain experiences of change as reflectively troubling or demanding rejection? And what is it that existential therapy (perhaps psychotherapy in general) offers, stimulates, removes or provides such that clients' experiences of disturbance, denial and rejection are opened to the possibility of being reconfigured in ways whose direction shifts towards that of reflectively accepted change?

Various existential therapists have argued that what fuels those change events that have been deemed to be so troubling or so intolerable that their denial or rejection is demanded is that they provoke significant challenges and disruptions to the person's very sense of being (Cooper 2003, 2015; van Deurzen and Adams 2011; Langdridge 2013; Spinelli 2005, 2015). More specifically, I have proposed that these challenges provoke existential insecurities in the person's worldview in that they address embodied concerns focused on some aspect or aspects of the self, an other or others, or on the world in general. Broadly, these challenges serve to de-stabilize the worldview in that they are experienced as perceived threats to some aspect of its temporal permanence (e.g., matters of health, unemployment, the ending of a relationship), its dispositional stances (e.g., the values, beliefs, assumptions, meanings, it seeks to maintain) and/or its identity (e.g., identificatory claims as to who I am and am not, who an other/others is/are or is/are not, what the world is or is not) (Spinelli 2015).

Experiencing Change: Sedimentations and the Experience of Change

In common with many other approaches, existential therapy proposes that human beings perceive an object-world (Langdridge 2007; Spinelli 2005). It argues that it is a 'given' of being human to substantiate our reflective experience of being. This reflective ability to 'thing-ify' our lived reality permits us to construe relatively fixed meanings and identities and, in general, provides much of the basis for our felt sense of existential continuity, security, and constancy. In general, all human beings generate reflective sedimentations—fixed, often deeply rigidified, thoughts (including assumptions, biases, beliefs, etc.), feelings and behaviours regarding self, others and the world—that persist over time and which continue to be maintained regardless of their limitations or experiential validity (Langdridge 2007, 2013; Spinelli 2005, 2015). Examples of such sedimentations would include statements such as 'I am Ernesto,' 'All people should always tell the truth' or 'Citizen Kane is the greatest film ever made.' If problems and issues surrounding sedimentations arise, such problems are not so much *that* sedimentations exist (since it is apparent that sedimentations are a necessary condition for structure-based reflective experiencing), but, rather the extent to which the maintained sedimentation is congruent with our actual experience of being.

If, for example, I insist that I am committed to a healthy lifestyle, but avoid any form of exercise and eat only 'junk' food, the sedimentation—I am committed to a healthy lifestyle—is substantially challenged by my lived experience of indolence and unhealthy diet. This challenge might provoke unwanted or unexpected change events such as my becoming dangerously obese or experiencing a heart attack. In order to deal effectively with the unwanted change event, I must face up to the existing incongruence between my sedimentation and my actual experience. In doing so, I might alter the sedimentation (e.g., I would like to commit myself to a healthier lifestyle) or, alternatively, change my lifestyle to one that is healthier and closer in line with the maintained sedimentation. In principle, either strategy is straightforward. However, in cases of reflectively troubling or rejected change it is clearly not. What might it be in such instances that prevents persons from facing up to the experience-based challenges to their sedimentations?

Experiencing Change: A Challenge to Security, Constancy and Continuity

The experienced tension generated by challenges to our sedimentations points us toward the second great paradox of experiencing change: the reflective experience of change also requires the experience of continuity.

If our experience of being held no quality of reflectively sedimented continuity, then we would still be ever-changing, but have no reflective experience of change.

Without continuity, we could never make statements like: 'I have changed' or 'You are different' or 'The world is no longer as interesting as it used to be.' We would just be constantly changing beings with no reflective awareness at any point of who we/others/the world had been or who we/others/the world might become. We would only be experiencing an 'ever-changing now' that might well substantially restrict and impair any sort of reflective experiences and, indeed, might erase all possibility of our reflecting upon any 'thing' or any 'one,' much less upon the experience of change.

If I say 'I have changed,' I am implicitly invoking a connection between 'who I was' and 'who I am now being or becoming.' But I can only make such a connection if I recognise that the experience of change always expresses an interaction between disruption and continuity. The reflective experience of change disrupts the current trajectory of my life experience in that not only does it generate questions as to the person I was (or, perhaps more accurately, the person I claimed to be), it also threatens the person I want to become in that it challenges assumptions, expectations, hopes, and aspirations that form the future-oriented aspects of being. The temporal aspects contained within all experiences of change clarify the continuity that must be part of the experience.

All three variants of change discussed above highlight that the experience of change is always an interaction between disruption and continuity. This interaction and its impact may be 'met' non-reflectively as in those instances expressed via the first variant. Alternatively, with regard to the second and third variants, change is reflectively experienced as a disruption to some sedimented aspect or aspects of our currently-maintained worldview. The major difference between these two reflectively-attuned variants is that the former values those disruptions as 'opening' possibilities through which the worldview is willing to de-stabilize or re-structure the challenged sedimentation and thereby 'meet' the change event and embrace its unknown possibilities and consequences, whereas the latter seeks to protect and maintain the threatened sedimentation by deflecting, rejecting or denying the impact of the change event upon it.

Experiencing Change: A Movement-Towards-Death

From an existential perspective, experiences of either the second or third variant of change enkindle a felt sense of a movement-towards-death. This movement-towards-death is much more extensive than the 'death' of that which is the immediate content or focus point of change—be it the end, loss, closing down or re-direction of a relationship, a hope, a dream or a set of possibilities and options. Much more all-encompassing, this movement-towards-death expresses the disruption to the continuity of one or more sedimentations that serve to stabilize, define and identify the currently maintained worldview.

As an existential therapist, I have come to the conclusion (along with many others) that, because every aspect and facet of our worldview is relationally and inseparably entwined and inter-connected with every other facet, a change in any particular facet will impact upon, and, therefore, in some way change *the whole* of the worldview (Spinelli 2015). As such, the reflective acceptance of a change event signals the 'death' of the currently maintained worldview.

This idea of change as a movement-towards-death provides the means with which to reconsider and broaden the existential notion of death anxiety. In my view, when it is discussed conceptually, death anxiety is typically presented from an unnecessarily all-too-literal perspective. Of course, an existential understanding of death anxiety addresses both the person's awareness of the inevitability of death (be it personal, or that of others or of the world) as well as the unpredictability of his or her moment of ceasing to be (Cooper 2015; van Deurzen and Adams 2011; Langdridge 2007, 2013). But this tension between the certain and the uncertain upon which death anxiety hinges can also be seen to be apparent in the interplay between continuity and disruption in all variants of change experience. As with death anxiety, change is experienced as provoking a disruption whose impact upon our worldview continuity remains both certain (in its inevitability) and uncertain (in its experiential consequences). Considered in this way, every moment of change connects us to our death anxiety. Like (or, perhaps, through) change in general, death anxiety permeates our every moment of being (Spinelli 2015).

Of course, each potential change-generated 'death' also provides the possibility of a 'resurrection'—the emergence of a new worldview. But what sedimentations will this novel worldview retain? And what sedimentations will have become untenable? How will it identify itself and be identified by others and the world? What will it feel like to embody this novel worldview? Will it be experienced as owned or alien? Will the person connect to the embodied thoughts, feelings, affects and behaviors it provokes or will he or she experience a sense of disconnection from them? No one of these questions can be answered in advance. They require an openness to an uncertainty which, if embraced, must also embrace its irreversible, and as yet unknown, consequences.

In those instances of reflectively accepted change, we embrace the existential possibilities that change brings forth, even if we cannot know what they will be or who we will become or how we—or others, or the world in general—will experience them.

However, in those instances of reflectively troubling change we seek to reject or deny the existential death that the change event has already provoked so that we can claim to have withstood the wider, unpredictable and de-stabilising impact of change upon us. In short, in our attempts to reject change, we seek to elude death—the death of the worldview that has existed up until the moment of reflectively troubling change.

Experiencing Change: In-Between (New) Life and Death

It is not uncommon for those persons who seek to reject or deny the impact of change events to express their experience as a felt sense of being 'pulled and torn apart'. In this way, they give expression to their lived experience of the persistent tension between two opposing demands—one that insists that they resist the challenge of change and the other that dares them to embrace that self-same challenge.

But why willingly choose such an option? What possible value is there in adopting such a divisive stance? An existential proposal would argue that in remaining with this tension, persons permit an 'in-between' experience of being wherein they are no longer the being who existed prior to the reflectively troubling change event *and* they are also not yet that unknown being who emerges from the unpredictable consequence of the change event. It is an 'in-between' strategy that, on the one hand, acknowledges the 'death' of the maintained worldview while at the same time insists upon that same worldview's continuing existence. In the same way, this strategy protects and maintains those sedimentations that the change experience is challenging via displacement, denial or dis-ownership. However, such strategies, even at their most successful, place the person in an 'in-between' mode of existing, a sort of zombified or vampiric form of 'living death' or 'deathly living.'

For example, Victor is suffering because his relationship with Joanne has ended. He experiences the event as being unwanted, painful and terrifying and speaks of his feeling of being torn apart. He comes to therapy because he wants to end this pain by coming to terms with what has happened and get on with his life but, somehow, finds himself unable to achieve this. Victor accepts that change has occurred. What he does not accept are the consequences of that change which threaten any number of sedimentations he continues to maintain. So, for example, he tells me that when he goes out food shopping, he knows that he is now shopping only for himself but buys enough food to feed two; or he continues to buy food which he personally does not like but which he knows that Joanne does. When he realizes what he does, Victor feels miserable, wretched, overwhelmed by the pain of memory and loss. If he partially accepts, equally he partially rejects the change event. As a consequence, he is being 'ripped in two' by the experience. He and I explore descriptively just how it is for him to experience this felt sense of being pulled apart. In doing so, Victor realizes that the maintenance of this painful experience has its pay-off: As long as he remains 'in-between' disruption and continuity he can claim to be both 'Victor who is no longer in a relationship with Joanne' *and* 'Victor who is still the same as he was when he was in a relationship with Joanne.' In this way, incongruences appear to vanish, everything is different and yet exactly the same. The problem with this solution is that its price is the incessant experience of that unpleasant, at times overwhelming and unbearable, pressure and tension required to maintain his dissonance. Under such conditions,

Victor's experience of being is that of 'not-quite-being' and 'not-quite-not-being,' a lifeless sort of life, a perpetual verging-on-death.

But why turn to this solution when, seemingly, it would be so much the better or simpler—or possibly even more rational—to shift towards reflectively accepted change? While most other psychotherapeutic models and approaches tend to view the question from the perspective of exclusively negative, destructively-tinged tendencies such as, for example, 'irrational beliefs,' 'unconsciously-derived eradicative instincts' or 'manifestations of false self deviations in living,' existential therapy reminds us that as limiting, debilitating and divisive as it may be as a solution, the 'in-between' strategy is, nonetheless, still a solution. And what does it solve? Nothing less than the problem of maintaining those sedimentations that are challenged by the change experience and, by doing so, maintaining the known worldview as a whole.

How? By offering a means with which to neutralise the impact and effects of change such that it prevents the necessity to embrace the unknown and unknowable consequences that any fully-committed reflective acceptance of change would impose. By remaining 'in-between' disruption and continuity the most troubling consequences of experienced change can be denied, diluted, or dissociated.

It works. At a price. Nonetheless, it is a price that many conclude is still worth paying. What convinces them of that?

Experiencing Change: Evading the Polarities of Change and Continuity

For years, in a semi-jokey fashion, I have been suggesting to trainees that the definition of a client is that of someone who both wants to change and to remain the same and who, as a result, continues to experience all manner of instances of dividedness in his or her relations with self, others and the world.

As with clients in general, Victor would be far more willing to embrace change were it the case that its consequences were predictable and guaranteed sufficient worldview stability, security and continuity. Again, like clients in general, Victor wants to know beforehand that the option before him will lead to something positive, perhaps make him a better or happier or more fulfilled person. More to the point, like clients in general, Victor wants to be reassured beforehand that any experiential embrace of change will be limited in that its impact will *only be* upon that sedimentation that is under challenge and that it will leave the rest of his worldview pretty much unaffected and, hence, still sufficiently secure and recognizable despite disruption. Unfortunately, he can be given no such guarantee. Existentially speaking, the worldview's inter-relational make-up is such that any change to the particular will alter the whole.

If this were not provocative of unease in itself, it is also the case that, at present, no one, and certainly no model of psychotherapy, has the ability to predict with any degree of accuracy how and to what extent any particular experience of change will affect the person as a whole. Regardless of how seemingly insignificant or minor is the 'tweaking' of one facet of our experience of being, the change to the whole being can be subtle or hardly noticeable or can be dramatic and wide-ranging. In similar, if opposite fashion, major alterations to a single facet may have either enormous or barely notable effects. Currently, we have no way of predicting the impact, focus or direction of any instance of experienced change. Our openness to the experience of change reflects an openness to the unknown and uncertain. It risks 'the death' of all that we currently hold as being meaningful, stable, continuous and secure about our experience of being. Indeed, seen from this perspective, it would seem that if there is anything truly surprising about our responses to the experience of change, it is the extent and frequency to which we seem to be so open to it rather than seek to avoid it.

In contrast to our broader stance toward change and its consequences, evasive, rejecting 'in-between' responses to change dominate the issues and concerns brought to psychotherapy by clients. As far as our clients are concerned, those instances of change which they present in psychotherapy are deemed to be so threatening to their worldview stability, constancy and continuity that they are experienced as being unwanted, dangerous and/or intolerable. Understanding that, it becomes somewhat obvious to realize that clients are likely to make attempts to off-set, reject or deny those disruptions, even if those attempts manifest themselves as experiences of a perpetual, lingering tension which threatens to erupt into something far more painful and debilitating. Nonetheless, as awful as this 'in-between' existence can be, viewed from the standpoint of the attempt to off-set the unknown consequences of uncontainable disruption and to maintain stability, security and continuity, it makes a good deal of sense. Just as the therapeutic encouragement to 'go with' change and, hence, risk whatever stability, security and continuity one has and desires might well make very little, if any, sense at all—at least initially.

But what might provoke clients to be courageous enough to willingly take that step into unknown possibilities and consequences?

Experiencing Change: Embracing the Polarities of Change and Continuity

In an attempt to respond to the above question, let me return to my example of my client, Victor.

Eventually, in some manner or other, Victor decides that the pain and misery required to maintain his in-between position is to some degree worse than that of embracing the uncertain and unknown consequences of change. What could have possibly convinced him to take such a step? Perhaps a moment of illuminating therapeutically-informed insight. Perhaps exhaustion. Perhaps his own—or others'—growing irritation or boredom with the stance being maintained. Perhaps something that he experienced or gleaned from his encounters with me. Perhaps something I said, or that he heard me say. So many 'perhapses' that we, as psychotherapists, might prefer to label as 'factors' both shared (or common) across all models of psychotherapy and specific to any particular model and which, while deemed to be the basis to the effectiveness of psychotherapy, currently remain a mystery as to *why* they are so (Cooper 2008; Duncan et al. 2010; Norcross and Wampold 2011). So many uncertain possibilities that became Victor's means to take the step. What seems clear, however, is that whichever 'perhaps,' or combination thereof, served as catalyst, what was required of him was an attitude or stance of acceptance.

Yes, but acceptance of what?

I would suggest that it is the acceptance of both polarities inherent in change, namely disruption and continuity. Further, it is necessary for this acceptance to occur in a manner that simultaneously bequeaths each polarity with equal value and co-presence. This reflective embracing of polarity from a 'both/and' rather than 'either/or' stance and, through it, the attempt to balance contradictory demands as being equal in value and sharing a co-presence in relation to one another, allows a shift away from the reflective rejection of change and towards that of reflective acceptance.

In Victor's case, this acceptance requires him to acknowledge himself as a 'new' Victor who exists reflectively through his acceptance that he is 'the Victor who once lived with Joanne but now no longer does so.' In accepting this, Victor embraces both disruption and continuity and opens his experience to the potential discovery of novel possibilities, meanings, interactions with self and others, and so forth.

This turn towards reflective acceptance reveals yet another paradox: Rather than seek to 'erase,' resolve or impose hierarchies of validity, meaning and import upon the contradictory demands being expressed through existential polarities such as continuity/disruption, security/uncertainty and identity/alterity our openness to change emerges through the willingness to hold the polarities in such a way so that the tension created between them attempts the achievement of an 'owned balance.' Of course, any such attempt will ultimately succumb to subsequent change events and, hence, ultimately fail. But, as Samuel Beckett's refrain reminds and entreats us, our enterprise is not one that leads to success but rather to the on-going experience of 'failing better' (Beckett 1983).

But by what mechanism, or through what step-by-step manualized set of interventions do we, and our clients, find the means to attempt this paradoxical balance? Here, like everyone else, I have no single, satisfactory all-inclusive answer. However, there do exist some 'hints' as to what might some day become an answer.

When, as psychotherapists, we are curious—or foolhardy—enough to ask our clients: What allowed you to take that change-accepting step? Often, they will answer: you, the therapist, did. Or: the effect of your presence upon my presence did. Or: the relationship we co-created did. Or, if Lesley Farber is correct, the step was taken because clients take pity on their therapist who keeps trying so hard to understand/meet/be-with/be-for them, and continually fails in this endeavor (Farber 2000).

Or, if I and numerous other existential therapists are correct, the client notes and becomes encouraged enough to try out for him or her self that which we, as therapists, are seen to be willing to attempt.

Which is what, exactly?

One term might be that of 'un-knowing'—which is to say: that as existential therapists (perhaps even psychotherapists in general), we attempt to remain as open as possible to that which presents itself, in the way it presents itself, in the current and on-going encounter; that we attempt to treat the seemingly familiar, assumed to be understood or understandable, as novel, unfixed in meaning, and, hence, accessible to previously un-examined lived possibilities; that we attempt to demonstrate our willingness to explore the world of the client in a fashion that not only seeks to remain respectful of the client's unique experience of being, but also by attempting to remain receptive to the challenges that this unique way of being elicits upon our own beliefs, biases and assumptions—be they personal or professional or both (Spinelli 1997).

Or put it another way: that, as existential therapists, we commit ourselves to an enterprise that urges us to express and embody that person who attempts to embrace, work-with and work-through the experience of reflectively accepted change in all its relationally-attuned, uncertain and anxiety-provoking ever-presence. And that we are willing to attempt this in the presence of another, the client, in an open-minded and open-hearted manner which both meets and is receptive to the 'I,' the 'you,' and the 'we' experiences that make up our encounter. This requires a cock-eyed sort of courage, which is in equal measure arrogance and humility, and which asks nothing more—or less—of the therapist than is being asked of the client.

Experiencing Change: A Summary

Paradoxically, change is a constant of lived experience. Also paradoxically, the reflective experience of change requires reflective continuity. Our lived experiences of change reveal a polarity of disruption and continuity. The reflective acceptance or attempted rejection of our experiences of change rest upon the degree to which we are willing to embrace both polarities as co-present and equally valid.

The majority of change experiences rest upon either a pre-reflective or reflective existential 'openness' through which we are willing 'to meet' the event and embrace its unknown possibilities and consequences. The dilemma of change is not with such instances of change, but rather with a particular variant of change experience. Namely, those reflective change experiences whose impact is deemed to be too threatening or too dangerous or too undesirable to the maintenance of existing sedimentations and to the worldview as a whole. Alternatively, this same dilemma is encountered when a desired change cannot be enacted. In this latter instance, the focus rests upon preferred and desirable, yet still imaginary, change experiences that alter, amend or remove a particular sedimentation in isolation and, hence, do not impact upon the whole of the worldview in unforeseen and unpredictable ways.

Rather than the change events in themselves, the dilemmas faced by change focus upon issues regarding their consequences upon the experienced worldview that remain both certain (in their inevitability) and uncertain (in their experiential impact, focus and magnitude).

Experiences of reflective change can be understood existentially as movements-towards-death that accompany the disruption to the stability, identifiability and continuity of the worldview that existed prior to the change event. Viewed in this way, one can note significant parallels and points of convergence between the reflective experience of change and the key existential notion of death anxiety.

Accepting change in any particular aspect of a person's worldview will affect the whole of that worldview in ways that, at least currently, cannot be predicted beforehand. In those instances of reflectively accepted change, our focus rests upon the novel potential of the event and we look forward to the possibilities of the newly-emerging, if still unknown and unpredictable, possibilities of being. In instances of reflectively troubling change, however, we acknowledge the presence of change but seek to reject or deny its unpredictable and destabilising impact upon the whole worldview. This 'in-between' strategy has its value: it goes a long way toward maintaining the person's worldview experience of stability and continuity—but at a price which is typically experienced as disturbing, dissociative and debilitating.

The courage to embrace threatening and undesired change demands a fundamental willingness to risk everything that we claim to be, know and value about and expect from our selves, others and the world. It is precisely that courage which permits us to leap into and accept the uncertain and unknown possibility which is a constant throughout our lives.

References

Beckett, S. (1983). *Worstward ho!*. London: John Calder.

Cooper, M. (2003). *Existential therapies*. London: Sage.

Cooper, M. (2008). *Essential research findings in counselling and psychotherapy: The facts are friendly*. London: Sage.

Cooper, M. (2015). *Existential psychotherapy and counselling: Contributions to a pluralistic practice*. London: Sage.

Duncan, B. L., Miller, D. S., Wampold, B. E., & Hubble, M. A. (Eds.). (2010). *The heart and soul of change: What works in therapy*. Washington DC: APA Books.

Farber, L. (2000). *The ways of the will: Selected essays*. New York: Basic Books.

Khan, C. H. (2008). *Art and thought of Heraclitus: A new arrangement and translation of the fragments with literary and philosophical commentary*. Cambridge: Cambridge University Press.

Langdridge, D. (2007). *Phenomenological psychology: Theory, research and method*. Harlow, Essex: Pearson Education.

Langdridge, D. (2013). *Existential counselling & psychotherapy*. London: Sage.

Norcross, J. C., & Wampold, B. E. (2011). Evidence-based therapy relationships: Research conclusions and clinical practices. *Psychotherapy, 48*(1), 98–102.

Spinelli, E. (1997). *Tales of un-knowing: Therapeutic encounters from an existential perspective*. London: Duckworth.

Spinelli, E. (2005). *The interpreted world: An introduction to phenomenological psychology* (2nd ed.). London: Sage.

Spinelli, E. (2015). *Practising existential therapy: The relational world* (2nd ed.). London: Sage.

van Deurzen, E., & Adams, M. (2011). *Skills in existential counselling & psychotherapy*. London: Sage.

Creating the World Congress for Existential Therapy

Emmy van Deurzen and Digby Tantam

Introduction

The first World Congress for Existential Therapy took place in London, from 14 to 17 May 2015, attracting over 650 existential therapists from around the world, to come and debate what existential therapy is and dialoguing about the different ways in which existential therapists work on different continents. It was hosted by the Existential Academy and sponsored by the Society for Existential Analysis.

The event took place in Westminster, at a stone's throw from Big Ben and the Houses of Parliament, at the Church House conference centre, which has a unique and historic location in Dean's Yard, next to Westminster Abbey. This was the building where the British government met during the blitz in the Second World War and also the building where the synod of the Church of England recently voted to have female bishops.

The large round meeting room was one of the particular features that made the building attractive for a Congress of this nature, as it allowed us to create a circular space where people could debate and dialogue more easily and where a sense of collegial equality could be created.

E. van Deurzen (✉) · D. Tantam
New School of Psychotherapy and Counselling, Existential Academy,
61-63 Fortune Green Road, London, NW6 1DR, UK
e-mail: emmyvandeurzen@gmail.com

D. Tantam
e-mail: d.tantam@sheffield.ac.uk

S.E. Schulenberg (ed.), *Clarifying and Furthering Existential Psychotherapy*,
DOI 10.1007/978-3-319-31086-2_11

What Is Existential Therapy?

Creating such a Congress presented an immediate difficulty of definition and boundaries. We asked ourselves: What is existential therapy? Who should we invite? Who would be our speakers? One solution to this problem might have been for us to provide a definition in the call for papers, but we decided to postpone the task of arriving at a definition till the Congress. There was a lively debate and a challenge to integrate many different perspectives. A group of colleagues, representative of different existential approaches, have been stimulated by the Congress to keep working on this joint definition and this group, originally of about 40 people, has exchanged over one hundred emails, often of considerable length. A consensus definition, to be placed on the website www.existentialpsychotherapy.net is close to being agreed upon.

Existential therapy is a broad church, and unites therapists from many different schools. There are colleagues who consider themselves to be existential-Gestalt, existential-psychoanalytic, existential-humanist, existential-phenomenological, existential-positive, existential-body work, and so on.

We wanted to create a forum for colleagues who felt committed to the existential approach, knowing that there were likely to be many of them who were working in isolation. So we stuck to the main groupings which have widely been recognized as composing the field of existential psychotherapy (Cooper 2003; van Deurzen and Adams 2010). These are:

1. Daseinsanalysis, following Binswanger and Boss
2. Humanistic-existential, following Bugental and May
3. Existential-phenomenological, following Laing and van Deurzen
4. Logotherapy, following Frankl and Längle.

Correia et al. (2016), confirmed our intuitions in a systematic sample. The best way forward, we felt, was to implement a snowballing method of recruitment using the opportunities provided by social media, specifically LinkedIn. Our scientific group—the core reference group for the Congress—grew out of a small group of avowed existential therapists that we recognized as existential who each identified other colleagues, who recommended others to be considered by the existing group, and so on. Eventually our scientific group numbered over 84, which was too unwieldy for planning but ideal as the nucleus for the speakers, seminar leaders, chairs, and workshop participants who eventually contributed to the Congress. As we were aiming for inclusiveness, the number of participants was itself unusually large, and did increase our administrative and other costs. But it led to many of our attenders saying that they felt that they had 'come home,' which was a benefit that outweighed all of the costs.

Objective of the Congress

Although existential therapy has been practised for over a century, existential therapists had remained fairly isolated and idiosyncratic and had never come together as a profession in this way. This historic and unique event brought together existential therapists from as far away as Russia, even Siberia, China, Nigeria, Ghana, Israel, Australia, Canada, the United States, Mexico, Argentina, Peru, Brazil, Colombia, and from most countries in Europe, including many Eastern European countries. Common ground amongst the therapists who attended was that they shared a way of working that is directly rooted in understanding human existence from a philosophical rather than just a psychological perspective.

The exploration of what existential therapy meant for each of these delegates was a very important part of the four-day encounter and revealed as many differences as similarities. The outcome of this meeting of minds was the tangible sense that existential therapy had not just become visible, where previously it has remained hidden, arcane and isolated, but that it now had a worldwide base and a critical international mass to become noted, recognized and adopted by many more professional psychotherapists internationally.

Outcomes of the Congress

The co-presence of so many existential theorists and practitioners allowed for regional groupings to meet as well. European attenders chose this opportunity to found a Federation of Existential Therapists in Europe (FETE) and an interim executive was voted in. This group is now working with the European Association for Psychotherapy (EAP) to become the representative group for existential methods in the EAP.

There was also a general interest in planning a second Congress at a general meeting of interested Congress attenders, and it was agreed that a World Confederation of Existential Therapists (WCET) should be created to take this project on. The Confederation would also ensure that communication between like-minded existentially-orientated therapists could continue before the planned date of the next World Congress (in 2019). An interim executive, research committee, and publications committee were voted in; it was agreed that the location of the next World Congress would be Buenos Aires (and that the one after that would take place in Beijing); and that the organization would be carried out by the Latin American Association for Existential Psychotherapy (ALPE), which has already organized seven conferences in Latin America.

These organizations now have the task of creating existential organizations that remain true to the spirit of existential freedom, open to change and diversity without imposing too dogmatic and formulaic a view of how to work as an existential therapist. This has created interesting tensions and discussions in the online groups and is leading to a productive collaboration worldwide to strengthen the existential voices.

Choice of Title and Other Preparations for the Congress

These tensions were already evident in the run up to the first Congress. They were particularly noteworthy in the debates around the choice of title for the Congress. We settled eventually on: 'Freedom, Responsibility and the Meaning of Being,' which was felt to be the best formulation of some of the essential themes in existential therapy. This title had been arrived at by the group of honorary scientific committee members in an on-going dialogue in the LinkedIn group.

This dialogue made it obvious that one of the qualities of existential therapy is to enable people to hold the existential tension between responsibility and freedom. It soon became evident that the dialectic in overcoming that tension whilst holding on to its paradoxes is also very much part of existential therapists' everyday work and that this presents very different challenges in different cultural contexts.

Existential therapists have always been pioneers in addressing such philosophical and existential issues, holding their finger on the pulse of what is wrong in the world today and how it affects people everywhere. Existential therapists do not dismiss people's discomforts and disease as medical illness, but aim to address the social, cultural and political context that can give rise to people's problems in living. Existential therapists have always thought in terms of emotional and existential health rather than in terms of mental illness. Today, such issues remain controversial, even though existential therapy has a history of a century of development in its present form and even though existential therapists pride themselves in being philosophical therapists, tracing their history as far back as the Athenian philosophers, who made it their business to dialogue with people in order to help them to work out how they could live better lives.

Existential therapists continue to be pioneers in addressing crisis situations and in reminding other psychotherapists that philosophical understanding is crucial when people face difficult and transformative human situations (van Deurzen 2010). Existential therapy is therefore the method of choice in political, cultural or social crises. It is also particularly relevant where people are facing loss (Stolorow 2007) and trauma (Neimeyer et al. 2002) and therefore the existential approach, though still a minority method, is prized in countries like the Ukraine, Israel, Greece, China, Korea, Nigeria, Latin America and other places around the globe, when catastrophes or war zones make it necessary to use a method that is non sectarian and open to the special needs and worldviews of those who find themselves in deep states of distress and under much social and political pressure.

Existential therapy is therefore used in very different ways in different situations. What it always provides is an opportunity for a person to become aware of their situation, in its context and in terms of the person's own worldview. Existential therapists help people make sense of their difficulties rather than to eliminate symptoms of their discomfort and anxiety. Existential therapists value the suffering that people experience and which they believe will be not only the start of their strength and courage, but the condition of it (Schneider 2008).

Existential therapists are a bit different to other sorts of therapists in other ways as well. They prize anxiety as a form of energy. They believe that the human condition presents continual problems and difficulties as well as with amazing and wondrous possibilities and realities. They enable a person to put his or her own life into perspective and get that fabulous feeling of being fully alive. They therefore invite people to come out of hiding and face the music, no matter what that music may be. Creativity comes forth from deep emotions (van Deurzen 2014) and from existential freedom in facing up to troubles (Corbett and Martin 2009).

Impulse for the Congress

The Congress was long in the planning. One of the co-authors of this paper, Emmy van Deurzen, had founded the Society for Existential Analysis in 1988, bringing together those working from an existential perspective in the UK and reaching out to other European countries to become part of this new movement. This had had a deeply settling effect on existential therapy in the UK, which became accepted as a form of psychotherapy by the United Kingdom Council for Psychotherapy in 1993. Important training organizations, such as the Philadelphia Association, the Arbours Association, The School of Psychotherapy and Psychology at Regent's University and the New School of Psychotherapy and Counselling at the Existential Academy were represented by the Society for Existential Analysis (SEA) and over the years this group, sometimes referred to as the British School, has influenced many other groups around Europe and in other parts of the world. It is now generally referred to as the School of Existential Phenomenological Therapy.

Emmy van Deurzen and Digby Tantam, who co-founded both the New School and the Existential Academy were also the authors of a forerunner of the World Congress: ICECAP, the International Collaborative of Existential Counsellors and Psychotherapists, founded in 2006 in London. It was these worldwide contacts and the fact that we have travelled to many countries over the decades to speak at conferences and offer lectures and training workshops that allowed us to gather the enthusiasm around the project of the World Congress. Two conferences in 2012, one in Canada, organized by the International Network on Personal Meaning and another in Lima, Peru, organized by the Asociación Peruana de Análisis Existencial y Logoterapia made it clear to us that there was an international appetite for a World Congress. Ongoing collaborations across Europe, since the late nineties, to establish online training in existential therapy, with the help of European funding, had enabled us to establish a strong European network, which included some notable strengths in Sweden, Greece, Austria, Belgium and Portugal.

Without these preceding efforts the Congress would not have been possible, but it also benefited from other networks that had been created previously, for instance by the East European Association for Existential Therapy which has gathered countries like Lithuania, Latvia, Estonia, Belarus, Ukraine, Russia and Siberia for several decades in ongoing training in existential therapy. Also the Latin American

Association had gathered countries like Argentina, Peru, Colombia, Brazil and also Mexico, often around the logotherapy denomination of existential therapy. And of course there is also the long-standing and well organized movement of Daseinsanalysis, which has had its international federation for many years. We should also mention the amazing initiative of Saybrook University in having had several years of joint existential conferences with colleagues in China. We are probably forgetting to mention others who have pre prepared the ground for this coming together. But it was obvious that there was a worldwide swell of interest in meeting up.

Creating a Worldwide Group Online

It was largely through the benefit of social media and electronic means of international communication that the atmosphere and mood were being prepared for the massive effort that was going to be necessary to coordinate this geographically dispersed group of people who identified as working existentially to find a place and a time to meet. It was clear from the start that this would need a long lead in time as people needed to save up and plan for the huge journey this was going to involve and that diaries needed to be coordinated several years ahead of time.

We opened a conversation about these matters by simply stating that we were going to host a World Congress for Existential Therapy and sent this statement to colleagues around the world whose addresses we had gathered. The list of addresses had been brought together by Edgar Correia as part of his doctoral research and he helpfully let us use these data to reach out far and wide.

We were able to invite strategically placed colleagues in these groups and countries and invited 85 people to be part of our 'honorary scientific committee' which would help us to ensure that the right people would be chosen as keynote and invited speakers and that those who had important contributions to make would be able to offer talks or workshops as well. The honorary scientific committee started communicating daily in a private LinkedIn group set up for this purpose. At the same time a wider conversation was opened in a public LinkedIn group, which had already gathered several thousands of existential therapists. This allowed us to test ideas both with the leaders in the field and the wider existential community. Out of these conversations decisions were made, as democratically and collaboratively as possible.

Choosing the Topics and Speakers

It was agreed early on that Irvin Yalom should be invited to give a special speech at the opening ceremony, where we would also be able to honour him for the lifelong contributions he has made to the field. Irvin Yalom accepted our invitation, but was unable to attend in person. Fortunately, we were able to not only have a live interview with him via satellite link, but also show the film '*Yalom's Cure*' for the first time in the UK at the Congress. In addition, we arranged to launch his most recent book '*Creatures of a Day*' at the Congress.

It was soon agreed that the three keynote speakers would be the most well known representatives of the different strands of existential therapy worldwide. We invited Alfried Längle (Austria) to represent logotherapy, Kirk Schneider to represent existential-integrative therapy (USA) and one of us (Emmy van Deurzen) to represent existential-phenomenological therapy (UK). Daseinsanalysis was represented through Alice Holzey Kunz (Switzerland) and Erik Craig (USA), who were both invited speakers. The other invited speakers were: Mick Cooper (UK), Susana Signorelli (Argentina, chair of the Latin American Association), Xuefu Wang (China, co-organizer of the Chinese conferences), Louis Hoffman (USA, the other co-organizer of the Chinese conferences), Paul Wong (Canada, meaning therapy and positive psychology), Betty Cannon (USA, specialist on Sartre), Dmitry Leontiev (Russia), Evgenia Georganda (Greece), Bob Stolorow (USA, representing the intersection between existential therapy and psychoanalysis), and Digby Tantam (UK, intersection between existential therapy and group analysis). Drs. Stolorow and Cannon, though due to come, had to pull out at the last minute. Erik Craig represented Dr. Stolorow's views, and Dr. Cannon attended by video link and also curated relevant YouTube videos for the participants who attended video demonstrations that ran parallel to other events.

The Congress coincided with tensions between Russia and Ukraine over the sovereignty of Eastern Ukraine, and a number of the presenters from the Ukraine had their visa applications denied by the UK authorities. This was particularly disappointing for the presenters of a planned seminar on 'Forced migration,' but we were able to set up a video conference in which they participated.

The Congress provided an opportunity for new voices to be heard. There was a valuable seminar organized by contributors from Nigeria, Ghana, and other West African countries, for example. Several of these new voices—or new to many of the Europeans and Americans attending the Congress—emanated from Eastern Europe. There was, for example, a memorable demonstration of the use of dramatized role play with life-size dolls by Dr. Gnezdilov. This method of approaching psychotherapy was a novelty for many of the attenders, and the seminar was packed with an enthusiastic audience almost spilling out of the room.

As soon as these speakers were agreed an announcement and website were prepared and our contacts worldwide were notified of the forthcoming Congress. Enthusiasm was immediately immense and while there were some grumbles about the price of the Congress, people realized that a four-day Congress in central London was the right way to go in order to finally put existential therapy on the international map.

Each of our keynote and invited speakers attracted interest in the Congress, in their own right and so it proved fairly straightforward to start selling tickets. We had however made life rather complicated for ourselves in terms of the organization of a four-day event with over 80 speakers in total.

Preparations for the Congress

We were fortunate in being able to draw on staff at the Existential Academy to help us with the administration of the long process of organizing the Congress. We started preparing for the Congress in 2013 and were just about ready a week before the Congress when we began to train the enthusiastic student volunteers that we had recruited. Even then there was a tremendous amount of work to do during the four days, registering and guiding people around the Congress, and dealing with the complexities of parallel presentations. The volunteers and our own office staff were invaluable throughout as were the expert technicians and conference organizers at the venue.

The Congress was in English but inevitably this was a hurdle for some participants. We were able to make last minute arrangements for some simultaneous translations. Rather than hiring in headphones, we relied on attenders having smart phones or tablets, and broadcast the translations to them using 'BeOnAir,' an app for both iOS and Android devices. This worked remarkably well.

Opening Ceremony World Congress for Existential Therapy May 2015

The opening of the Congress was very moving. It was obvious that everyone there had been very committed in making it to London. We ourselves were exhilarated and relieved that after so many years of hoping, wishing, planning and organizing, we were finally together. We were ready to create a new unity in order to find the strength to recognize and address our differences, talking with each other, listening to each other, meeting each other and letting the world know what we are about.

For so many decades existential therapists had been silent, isolated, withdrawn, secretive. Existential therapy had long been one of the more arcane and less well known therapies. We had always hidden our light under a bushel, even been secretive about our practices. Even though our tradition reaches as far back as the pre-Socratic philosophers in Europe and the great philosophers of East and West, who searched for wisdom and greater understanding of the human condition, through study and dialogue, this kind of therapy remained the province of insiders only.

For so many years we had ploughed our own furrows, each within our home culture and each of us thinking deeply about human existence, whilst working with people to help them go through existential crises, tackling the existential despair and angst of life. We had separately established particular ways of working, though reading some of the same philosophers to inspire us.

Now we were bringing these different ways of working together, like never before. We were going to be able to challenge each other and we were going to validate each other. We expected that there would be much mutuality, reciprocity and resonance, but none of us were prepared for the amazing sense of comfort in each other's company, that was captured best by the sense of having come home that we felt during those four days. It was just astonishing to be with so many people from so many different countries who thought similarly and had worked with people along similar lines though in very different contexts and with slightly different methods. The reverberations of this will have long consequences and change the future of our profession.

Our long, deep roots in philosophy will enable us to grow steadily from here and to affect the fields of psychology and psychotherapy more than we have been able to affect them in the past. We were able to claim our pedigree in having applied philosophy to real life and not just to any kind of life, but to the life of those who suffer most and are confused. That is an amazing test of any ideology and especially of the philosophy of life that is existential therapy. Is our knowledge and wisdom actually of help to suffering human beings? That was the question that informed our work throughout. It became clear that we shared a practical knowledge and pragmatic understanding of human existence that we had kept to ourselves.

We became aware that philosophers on every continent and, probably, in every culture throughout human history have searched to understand the human condition better and have tried to formulate the principles and ideas that would help people to live more fruitful lives and create a fairer world. Their words often help us and inspire our interventions. We also have an outstanding history of contributing to the overall profession of psychotherapy throughout the 20th century, from Binswanger and Jaspers, through Boss and Frankl, to Tillich and May and Laing. We have influenced other therapies, and therapists, like Perls, and Rogers, and more recently psychoanalysts and third-wave cognitive-behavioural therapists, whose re-discovery of the Buddhist practice of mindfulness (van Deurzen and Tantam 2016) is also a rediscovery of the philosophical practice of 'reduction' described by Husserl (van Deurzen 2014).

And yet, it also became obvious how contemporary existential therapists of different orientations and nationalities stand outside of these other traditions, as we keep returning to philosophy as it currently is and discipline ourselves to improve the clarity and depth of our thinking, as we challenge our thoughts to be useful and helpful to breathing human beings who suffer and need our help. The objective obviously was to combine critical awareness and logical thinking with our therapeutic abilities to enable us to remain silent and hold tension, to understand human development and evolution, alongside human ingenuity and creativity. The Congress showed how this strength was thriving around the globe.

The other thing that became really obvious was that one of the most important and defining aspects of existential therapy is actually its breadth, variety and diversity, its multiplicity of models and ideas, such that we are very adaptable to different cultures and different settings. This breadth has allowed existential therapy to be practised differently in accordance with the different cultural backgrounds and philosophies of people on every continent. Instead of existential practice having been imposed as a set practice with prescriptive modes of operating, it has organically grown into different ways of practicing the art of understanding human existence in different parts of the world.

We became more aware of the way in which existential therapists have quietly made a difference in the real world and this was the theme of the opening speech by one of us (Emmy van Deurzen) who said: "I get emails from colleagues all over the world on a regular basis. A few weeks ago I was gathering information from colleagues to send to an existential therapist in the Ukraine, who could not be here today because she is working at the front of a sad and intractable conflict, with acute trauma and she had no access to information on how to do so existentially. Trauma is one of the recurring themes in this Congress, even though our official title is 'Freedom, Responsibility and the Meaning of Being.' Perhaps we never learn as much about these three as when we suffer or are deprived of some of these aspects of human living. There is no doubt that most of us have come to choose existential therapy as our profession or vocation, because we have found ourselves in deep crisis at the edge of existence at some stage. Working existentially means to stand in the midst of turmoil and to find the best way to enable people to find their strength and courage in tackling such problems. I cannot wait to hear from all of the amazing speakers and workshop leaders we have lined up for the coming days and get inspired by your ideas about life and your practice."

It was very moving to discover our mutual respect in that process, it was very heartening to discover that we were part of a worldwide tribe. A new tribe, but really an ancient tribe of practising applied philosophers wanting to heal the mind and emotions of those who suffer most. It was tangible that many had prepared for years to be able to come to this gathering and had made considerable sacrifices to be there. The sense of community was all pervasive. One of us called it a long honeymoon. And indeed after the Congress was over we went back to email exchanges that were much more challenging and critical than anything experienced at the Congress itself, though this was more often voiced by colleagues who had not attended and so did not share the warm atmosphere generated at the Congress itself. At the Congress we were focused on the best ways in which we could learn from each other and contribute something new to the world, something of value to the whole of mankind, especially to those who are in mental, emotional and existential pain and who need us to help them articulate this without us pushing them into the abyss of mental illness, labelling them and entrapping them in chemical alienation.

It was a deep and utter joy to be briefly united with so many other people who shared the same commitment to finding philosophical understanding of the human predicament, not just in theory, but in action, in practice, in working with the people who need to make sense of it all and find meaning and purpose.

We struggled hard with our definitions of 'Freedom, Responsibility and the Meaning of Being,' and it was the value of staying in that struggle that we took away with us. That we fell into conflict with those who had not come to the Congress about the definition of existential therapy immediately afterwards was actually very healthy. It created new tensions in which we had to try ever harder to speak a common language. It is clear that existential therapists will always generate this kind of controversy and intense mutual dialogue. It is one of the strengths of this school of psychotherapy, to accommodate and welcome that instead of deploring it and trying to impose a party line.

Post Congress Products

Apart from the founding of the FETE and WCET organizations another product from the Congress has been that of articles and films. There were special existential editions of the *International Journal of Psychotherapy (19:1, March, 2015)* and the *Journal of Contemporary Psychotherapy (45:1 March, 2015)* for the occasion. Another important book project, the *Wiley World Handbook of Existential Therapy*, was commissioned by Wiley and this major volume is currently being edited by Emmy van Deurzen, Alfried Längle, Kirk Schneider, Erik Craig, Simon Du Plock, and Digby Tantam with the help of many other participants at the Congress. The book is the first of its kind, bringing together the major authors in existential therapy in one tome. It will show the variety of forms of existential therapy that are being practised and taught around the world and provide an invaluable source for those who want to know more.

Professional quality recordings of the opening ceremony and each of the keynote and invited talks are available for sale via the website of the Congress hosts, the Existential Academy (www.existential.academy).

Conclusions

Inaugurating a World Congress turned out to be an exhausting and expensive process without the backing of an established group or society, but it may have been the only way to bring together the developments of existential therapy that have been developing since the initiatives of Binswanger, Boss, Frankl, and their successors. We were unsure what to expect and were therefore surprised and pleased not just with the number of attenders but with the common ground and goodwill that was established between them. It seems to us that existential therapy is a growing modality, and is well-suited to support each of us in answering the questions that Frankl (1963) found were posed to him and others *in extremis*: "It did not really matter what we expected from life, but rather what life expected from us. We needed to stop asking about the meaning of life, and instead to think of ourselves as those who were being questioned by life—daily and hourly" (ibid, p. 122).

References

Cooper, M. (2003). *Existential therapies*. London: Sage.

Corbett, L., & Martin, M. (2009). Existential therapy: A useful approach to trauma. http://epubs.surrey.ac.uk/27627/2/Existential%20Trauma%20revised%20v1.0.pdf. Retrieved from http://epubs.surrey.ac.uk/27627/2/Existential%20Trauma%20revised%20v1.0.pdf

Correia, E. A., Cooper, M., Berdondini, L., & Correia, K. (2016). Existential psychotherapies: Similarities and differences among the main branches. *Journal of Humanistic Psychology*.

Frankl, V. E. (1963). *Man's search for meaning: An introduction to logotherapy*. New York: Washington Square Press.

Neimeyer, R. A., Prigerson, H. G., & Davies, B. (2002). Mourning and meaning. *American Behavioral Scientist, 46*(2), 235–251. Retrieved from ISI:000178080800004.

Schneider, K. (Ed.). (2008). *Existential-integrative psychotherapy: Guideposts to the core of practice*. New York: Routledge.

Stolorow, R. D. (2007). *Trauma and human existence: Autobiographical, psychoanalytic, and philosophical reflections*. New York: Analytic Press.

van Deurzen, E. (2010). *Everyday mysteries: Existential dimensions of psychotherapy* (2nd ed.). London: Routledge.

van Deurzen, E. (2014). Structural existential analysis (SEA): A phenomenological research method for counselling psychology. *Counselling Psychology Review, 29*, 70–83.

van Deurzen, E., & Adams, M. (2010). *Skills in existential counselling & psychotherapy*. London: Sage.

van Deurzen, E., & Tantam, D. (2016). Phenomenology of mindfulness. *International Journal of Psychotherapy*.

Index

S.E. Schulenberg (ed.), *Clarifying and Furthering Existential Psychotherapy*,
DOI 10.1007/978-3-319-31086-2

The manufacturer's authorised representative in the EU is Springer Nature Customer Service Centre GmbH, Europaplatz 3, 69115 Heidelberg, Germany. If you have any concerns regarding our products, please contact ProductSafety@springernature.com

Printed and bound by CPI Group (UK) Ltd, Croydon, CR0 4YY

30/09/2026

02225264-0015